PRAISE FOR THEIR WORDS

For the first time, in Guard, the reader will learn what prison is really like and not what television and movies portray. For the first time and in spellbinding fashion, the readers will learn of the tremendous courage, professionalism, and heroism of the unheralded and under appreciated keepers of the key.

Bill Cunningham, Retired Kentucky Supreme Court Justice
Author of numerous books including *Castle: The Story of a Kentucky Prison*

Warden Philip Parker is a highly respected, legendary old school guard and Warden that will go down in the history books. Read his book. You will understand.

Ronnie Davis, Retired Lieutenant, Kentucky State Penitentiary

---

I was a Deputy Warden under Warden Parker's leadership in Ohio and Kentucky. His book is a great tribute to the men and women who serve not only in Kentucky, but in prisons throughout the country.

Ernie Williams, Retired Deputy Warden

No one is more qualified than retired Warden Phil Parker to take the reader into the culture of a maximum security prison and into the hearts and psyches of its inmates, including thieves, fraudsters, and some of the most violent murderers on the planet. And, no one knows more than Mr. Parker about the dangers faced daily by the men and women who have charge over those inmates.

Bobbie Foust, freelance journalist with 54 years experience as a reporter and editor at seven weekly and daily newspapers in West Kentucky

---

Warden Phil Parker has written the best book I've ever read about what a maximum security is really like, not like what you see in movies. A must read.

Dale "Snake" Woolum, inmate who spent 44 years in prison, much of it with Phil Parker as warden.

GUARD

A TRUE STORY OF DUTY, SACRIFICE, AND LEADERSHIP IN KENTUCKY'S MAXIMUM SECURITY PENITENTIARY

PHILIP W. PARKER

Genius
Book Publishing

Guard: A True Story of Duty, Sacrifice, and Leadership in Kentucky's Maximum Security Penitentiary

This book is a memoir. It reflects the author's present recollections of experiences over time. Some names and characteristics have been changed, some events have been compressed, and some dialogue has been recreated.

Published by Genius Book Publishing, PO Box 250380 Milwaukee Wisconsin 53225 USA

https://GeniusBookPublishing.com

Contact the author at keeperksp@gmail.com

First edition, 2024

Hardcover ISBN: 978-1-958727-44-7

Paperback ISBN: 978-1-958727-41-6

240811 Trade

Dedicated to the courageous men and women who work tirelessly behind the scenes of the Kentucky State Penitentiary.

"Never humiliate a person when they are helpless."

—Justice Bill Cunningham
Kentucky Supreme Court

PREFACE

Without warning, in the dim lights on Thirteen Left Walk in Three Cell House, I saw William "Snake" Woolum throw down the gun and run down the walkway to an empty cell. I was standing at the control panel, so with the flip of a switch, I shut the cell door. The hostage situation was over.

I quickly opened the crash gate, and a small army of heavily armed E-Squad and State Police SRT (SWAT team) members stormed the unit and took up positions. My task as hostage negotiator had ended as suddenly as it began. I lit another cigarette and waited for the hostage, Officer Paul Jasper, to walk out. He was visibly shaken. Neither of us knew what to say, so nothing was said. He wanted out of there, and so did I. We walked together through Two Cell House then One Cell House. As we entered the administration building, I could see a gauntlet of state police officers and prison administrative staff waiting for us. Everyone started cheering, clapping, and shaking our hands. Officer Jasper was led to an office and debriefed. I walked to the warden's office and lit another cigarette. Warden Al Parke and Deputy Warden Mike Samburg both congratulated me on a job well done. I just sat there for a while, replaying the events of the day in my mind. I was all used up, totally exhausted. It was the longest eight hours of my life.

I had never been involved in a life-or-death event before. There was no one there to debrief me. No counseling. No follow-up. I simply went home and came back the next day ready for whatever happened next.

I always maintain that those eight hours took ten years off my life. This was the toughest thing I had ever experienced, but there would be much worse things in store for me in the years to come. I was just getting started on my journey.

ONE

FINDING MY FOOTING

I grew up about two miles from Possum Trot, a rural community in Western Kentucky. I was a shy, awkward kid who was not particularly good at sports, nor was I a good student. I was average at best. I didn't have a lot of friends in school. I just tried to blend in. It was 1970 when I graduated from North Marshall High School. Most of us were just hanging out waiting to see if we would be drafted. My first job out of high school was as a riverboat deckhand. It was good money, but it wasn't for me. In fact, the job was not the adventure I thought it would be. It wasn't long before I decided I needed to do something else with my life just in case I wasn't drafted. I enrolled in a community college where I had to really study and apply myself just to make average grades. I guess this was because I had not learned much in high school.

After two years in community college, I enrolled in Murray State University, where I earned a bachelor's degree in psychology. I attended one year of graduate school, but I was burned out. I was tired of being so poor and living on student loans. When I finally got my draft notice, I went for my physical and was turned down because I had flat feet.

Probably the biggest influence in my life was my practice of Karate while I was in college. I had a knack for it. I would practice every day for hours. I became obsessed. When I earned my black belt in Wado Ryu–style Karate, I started entering tournaments. One of my instructors was Sensei Vic Milner. I became an instructor and taught Karate at the university. I also taught in several local Dojos. I had won tournaments in the black belt division in Kentucky, Tennessee, and Arkansas. I only lost two times, once in a full-contact event in Alabama and once in a "Battle of Champions." Some of my students were guards and supervisors from KSP. I had a standing offer as a guard if I ever needed a job.

I graduated from college in the Jimmy Carter years while the economy was stalled. There were no jobs. Finally, I decided to give the prison a try. What did I have to lose? I didn't have any other prospects for a job unless I wanted to go back on a riverboat or go back to graduate school. So I applied for the job and was hired as a correctional officer. I never looked back.

THE BELLY OF THE BEAST

My first day at KSP (Kentucky State Prison) was July 3, 1978. And I was nervous. As I rounded the curve and drove down the road from Pea Ridge, there it was, looming like a medieval fortress on the banks of Lake Barkley. The Castle on the Cumberland River. What had I gotten myself into? I could only imagine what convicted inmates might think when they see the Castle for the first time. The prison itself resembles something out of the Middle Ages, with its soaring walls, stone parapets, and heavily guarded watchtowers. An imposing place, with a reputation to match.

As I started up the crumbling steps to the main entrance, I heard a grumpy voice say, "HALT! State your business." I stopped dead in my tracks. The command to halt sounded threatening—as if I might be shot if I didn't obey.

I looked up and saw a middle-aged man peering down at me from the gun tower. I responded, "I am Philip Parker, and I am reporting to work."

"Go ahead," was all he said. I didn't know what to think about this first encounter, but I knew I was about to enter a strange, new world.

As I approached the front gate, I stepped aside as several uniformed men with shotguns came running from the armory located at just off the top of the steps. Startled, I stepped aside and froze as they passed. I thought to myself, *What in the hell is this about?*

I learned later that there had been a mass escape from Four Cell House. My very first day. Three inmates, Joe Craig, James Hatfield, and Charles Murphy, had cut through their cell bars and made their way down the short distance from the opening to the ground using bedsheets fashioned into a braided rope. As with every prison escape, their luck was fleeting; the men were apprehended a few days later. As first impressions go, this was a lot to take in for a new corrections officer.

I stood at the entrance, waiting to be ushered in. There was no control center at the time to automatically open prison doors. After the front gate officer keyed the lock, I crossed the threshold and entered the belly of the beast. One of the things I never quite became accustomed to after all my years in the Castle was the smell. The Castle has an odor unlike anything I have ever experienced: an ungodly combination of cigarette smoke, body odor, sewer gas, death, and history. It still smells that way to me. Some five decades later, I still notice that odor as I walk up to the prison gates. Half-jokingly, I always say it is the smell of the Castle Beast, the one that trolls the front entrance, taunting all those who sense its presence.

After filling out employment paperwork with two other new hires, we were told to go to the receiver's basement to get our uniforms. I thought to myself, *What the hell is the receiver's basement?* Turns out it was a warehouse in the basement of Five Cell House with an outside entrance. I learned my first lesson on the job: prison workers have their own language to describe the Castle's twisty, cavernous interior. I knew we had to learn fast or we would not find our way around. KSP is enormous, with five large cell blocks that housed 1,200 inmates in 1978. In subsequent years, two new cell blocks were added, even as the overall population decreased to around 980, because inmates no longer shared cells.

With uniforms in hand, the new hires were directed to report to the hospital for a physical. The hospital, I later learned, was a state-licensed facility complete with infirmary beds, a surgical wing, a pharmacy, and an emergency room. But we had no idea how to get there. After wandering around the sprawling prison yard for what seemed like an eternity, one of the older guards took pity on us and pointed to where we had to go.

A man in a lab coat with a stethoscope led me into an exam room and asked some standard questions about my health. I filled out a medical history as he listened to my heart and lungs, took my blood pressure, pulse, and temperature. I thought he was a doctor. Several weeks later, I saw him in the canteen line and realized the man I mistook for a doctor was actually a convict.

SOMETHING FISHY

A "fish" is a term used to describe a newly hired officer or a new inmate who just got off the bus. Why, I don't know. It is just prison slang. The "fish tank" was a row of cells in One Cell House used to house inmates until they had been given an orientation and a list of the rules. They would also meet the Classification Committee to be assigned a job and a cell.

A fish *officer* is a new hire who has not attended the academy or learned the ropes. These rookie officers are basically useless and treated accordingly. You remained a fish officer until you became familiar with all the ins-and-outs of daily prison operations and earned a small degree of respect. You had to prove yourself, meaning you would not run from trouble and you would back up your fellow officers. You also had to follow orders to the letter.

I was hired in with two middle-aged female employees, Betty Blackwell and Rosy Mitchell. In the late 1970s, only a handful of females were hired as correctional officers. It was still a man's world, but that was rapidly changing for the better. Nora Aldridge was the first female hired as a correctional officer sometime around 1976. Soon after, Judy Groves was hired and had already made sergeant by the time I came aboard. I try to imagine how they must have felt entering such a hostile, male-dominated environment, where danger and violence were the norm. These were courageous and brave women.

As the three of us made our way out to the receiver's basement, we had to traverse a sidewalk just below Four Cell House then Five Cell House. Inmates could stand at the barred windows in the hallways of Five Cell House and look down at the walkway we were on, the cars in the parking lot, and the boat traffic on Lake Barkley. We were about to learn our next lesson.

Betty Blackwell, walking next to me on the winding sidewalk, was a middle-aged blond with an attractive figure, and Rosie Mitchell, a middle-aged person of color, strode alongside Betty as we made our way to the receiver's basement. As we passed under Five Cell House, we could hear a whistle and catcall from somewhere above us on one of the four floors of Five Cell House. "Shake it, baby, shake it!" I was street smart and did not look toward the direction of the voice. Betty reflexively glanced up, however, and that same voice yelled, "Not you, Bitch. HIM." I thought, *Oh my God, they are talking to me!* Another lesson for a fish guard.

TRAINING

Training consisted of a two-week academy at Eastern Kentucky University, the training center for all correctional officers and police officers in Kentucky. After the academy, we endured a week of firearms training at KSP, followed by on-the-job training. Before could be scheduled for the academy, I had to shadow more experienced officers. I was not allowed to work by myself until I graduated from the academy.

TWO

THE CASTLE

Built by Italian stonemasons on the banks of the
Cumberland River in the 1880s, KSP has survived the test of time.
Little has altered its medieval appearance over 140 years, save for the
addition of a cell block in 1937 and a more modern cell block in the
1980s. First called the Kentucky Branch Penitentiary because the original prison was located some two hundred miles away in the state's capital, Frankfort, the Castle officially opened on Christmas Eve in 1890.

When the Cumberland River was impounded to form Lake Barkley
in the 1960s, most of the old town of Eddyville disappeared beneath
Barkley's waves. KSP, situated on high ground overlooking the river
valley, became waterfront property almost overnight. Despite its
picturesque setting, the Castle's stone exterior and cold, foreboding
appearance have always suggested something sinister to the casual
observer. Its gothic architecture hovers over the idyllic scenery of Lake
Barkley like an ominous, misplaced relic of a bygone era. Still, the decision to construct KSP entirely of quarried limestone was a wise one. To

this day, the prison exterior has withstood the test of time (not to mention earthquakes, cyclones, and extreme temperatures) over the past 140 years. There are no signs of cracks or settling anywhere around the structure to this day. KSP is a truly amazing feat of construction, considering that in the 1880s there were no modern cranes, bulldozers, or power tools to cut the large stones. Yet each stone is perfectly cut and fits like a glove.

Legend has it that a sign once hung over the front gate entry that read "Abandon Hope All Ye That Enter Here." The message served as a friendly reminder to convicts that they were entering a place unlike any they had ever seen.

I thought a lot about that old sign over the years. What it must have meant to guards, or "keepers," as they were called back in the nineteenth century. The pay was meager then, just like it is now. Barely starvation wages. Keepers were issued ill-fitting, itchy, prison-made uniforms, and they wore them year round, in the dead of winter and the sweltering heat of summer. It was all they had. Those poor old keepers, walking under that sign every day: "Abandon Hope All Ye That Enter Here." They probably felt as lowly and miserable as the convicts they guarded.

The sign was gone by the time I started in 1978. No doubt removed by a more benevolent administration who believed our profession should be more humane and compassionate. As memorable as that sign was, I'm grateful I didn't have to see it every day!

DEATH REGISTER

One of my favorite artifacts that survives from the Castle's earliest days is the Register of Deaths. Every death was meticulously recorded by hand in a journal starting in 1891. Each entry lists the date of death, full name, age at death, race, crime, county of conviction, date received, term of sentence, hour of death, and cause. The Death Register listed all deaths until it was discontinued in 1979.

As a historical document, the Register is both morbid and endlessly fascinating. As one might expect, convict deaths in the early days resulted from a variety of maladies—some, like influenza, diarrhea, consumption (tuberculosis), syphilis, and gangrene, could be treated successfully by modern medicine. Others, like "murder," not so much. Some inmates were "shot by guards." The over 160 causes of deaths included "Legal Electrocution." As for the crimes that led to incarceration a century ago? Arson. Rape. Murder. Stealing horses and chickens. And perhaps the most troubling of all: selling whiskey to Indians.

I could only imagine the terror of a young man sentenced to prison for selling whiskey, as he was led through the front gate in shackles and handcuffs, past a sign that said "Abandon Hope All Ye That Enter Here."

Adding to the nightmare of a lengthy stay was the fact that indoor plumbing, electricity, and even ventilation were nonexistent at KSP a century ago. In the winter, old potbelly stoves were the only source of warmth, until the addition of a coal-fired boiler that utilized steam to heat the cell blocks. Lighting was provided by kerosene, oil lamps, or candles. Once locked in a cell, a bucket was the only way for an inmate to relieve himself until the next morning, when all inmates would be released to carry their buckets to the appropriately named "dump station" to be emptied and cleaned for the next day's issue.

As if that were not enough, summer temperatures in western Kentucky can easily reach one hundred degrees or more. Temperatures inside the prison, even higher. The luxury of a daily shower, even for law-abiding citizens, did not exist. Most of the modern conveniences that we now take for granted had not yet been invented. Combine this with a lack of basic hygiene and rudimentary medicine, and KSP was a virtual breeding ground for disease. Times were hard—but they were hard for everyone.

THE WHIPPING POST

In those early days, punishment for rule violations was decided by the warden and usually consisted of a trip to the dungeon, with nothing but bread and water to eat. Along with a trip to "the hole," the warden could order an offender to receive up to twenty-five lashes (the legal limit) with a braided leather whip—an incredibly painful ordeal. Repeat whippings often left a recipient both emotionally and physically scarred. This punishment was carried out at one of two places: a whipping post located in the prison yard, for all inmates to witness, or at a second whipping post, located indoors in Two Cell House. The most humane punishment, reserved for minor offenses, was a ball and chain shackled to the convict's ankle.

Excerpts from the Journal of Louis Curry, Chief Warden, Kentucky Prison at Eddyville -1888 to 1896-

Entry 16th *Oct. – Physician Harper appeared for his monthly visit to the prison. I thereupon had Prisoner Berry, #239, brought to the mid-yard post and shackled. After assembling the prison population, I supervised the administration of twenty-five lashes. Keeper Gray wielded the braided whip. Upon completion of this punishment, I inquired of Berry whether he was now ready to resume hauling stone. He cursed me vilely. For this unwarranted affront, I would have personally administered another twenty-five lashes had not the good Physician stayed my hand. Still, I was sorely tempted to ignore the Physician's warning and have the whip again laid to this villainous creature's back. With a great deal of effort, I managed to temper my outrage and await the Physician's next monthly visit to administer the added twenty-five lashes, which are the maximum number allowed. Prisoner Burton, #152, received twenty-five lashes for the recent disturbance he caused in the dining area. Both prisoners were then placed under guard in the prison infirmary. When their wounds have finished festering, they will be returned back to the dungeon.*

THE DUNGEON

Excerpts from the Journal of Louis Curry, Chief Warden, Kentucky Prison at Eddyville -1888 to 1896-

Entry 9th Oct. – Prisoner Penrod, #147, was released from the dungeon after seven months confinement. An incorrigible conniver, Penrod was reported attempting to subvert a newly hired Keeper to bring loose tobacco into the prison. I will not tolerate any prisoner to misuse my Keepers for such nefarious deeds. As an added reminder, I have ordered Penrod's right ankle to be shackled with a ten-pound ball weight. This will perhaps go far in correcting his evil ways.

The interiors of One and Two Cell Houses were still in use until the early 1980s, at which time they were renovated for administrative purposes. As a correctional officer, I often worked in these cell blocks. They are best described as small "dungeon cells" stacked four stories high inside each cell block. An officer would carry a large ring of keys to unlock or lock each padlock in each of the 120 or so cells, and the "slam" lock at the end of each walk—a very labor-intensive ordeal for each officer. Often we would have nonviolent inmates assist as "key boys" to help us get all the locks open/closed.

In Two Cell House, I recall standing on the old concrete platform that was once the whipping stone (the post long since removed), just to get a better view of the inmates milling around during "free time."

The dungeon cells were located just off a tunnel that ran under Two Cell Block, but the tunnel ran under One, Two, Three, and Four Cell Blocks. I was told the tunnels were used to move inmates from one location to another, especially at night. At some point, probably when plumbing and electricity were installed, these tunnels or walkways under the cell blocks became a logical place to construct the infrastructure necessary to modernize the old cell blocks.

One day early in my employment at KSP, I asked Lt. Mitch McKinney if I could see the old dungeon in Three Cell House. It was a slow day, sometime during the winter of 1978. There were not many slow days in Three Cell House—but when the temperature plummeted, inmates would often hunker down and sleep. This was one of those bleak midwinter days.

Lt. McKinney smiled, which was rare, and said, "Let me go get the keys and I will let you in." I could not wait. This was a rare privilege. A short time later, he returned and said, "Come with me." I followed him down to an area known as death row and the "death chamber." This was where the electric chair and the old holding cells for the condemned were located. McKinney keyed open a set of bars, then unlocked a solid steel door I had never noticed before. He handed me a weak flashlight and instructed me to walk straight ahead, through the tunnel. With sewer pipes and steam lines overhead, I had to duck down most of the way until I knew I was under Two Cell House. About the time I found myself under Two Cell House, I heard the steel door slam behind me. I knew I had been had. McKinney had locked me in, and I was not getting out until he felt like it. More than likely the batteries in my flashlight would run out before I got out. Oh well. I made the best of the situation and continued on.

The antiquated tunnel that once served as a passageway under the old cell blocks was filthy from a century of sewer leaks and neglect.

Occasionally, a maintenance worker would wander down to make a repair, but only when things got really bad. Cleanup after a leak was apparently never a consideration. There was no lighting. Not even a single lightbulb. A flashlight was the only way to maneuver around. The only other sign of life down there was an occasional rat, more often than not the size of a well-fed housecat.

There it was! The dungeon.

I approached the first cell. The entry was covered with an old wooden plank door, similar to what you might see on a barn. There was no latch, but it creaked as the old rusty hinges reluctantly allowed the door to open... one more time.

The dungeon cell appeared to be approximately ten feet by ten feet. In the center of the cell was a hole, which served as a drain. No doubt it served as a toilet, too. Around the walls hung the rusty remnants of manacles. A convict was likely chained to each wall and left to suffer for days in silence and darkness, with nothing but a meager ration of bread and water. It must have been a truly horrible experience, which was the point. This punishment was designed to break the most difficult prisoners of their worst behavior. And it usually worked.

I always wondered if I would see a ghost in Three Cell House. After all, there had been over 160 executions and countless deaths from murders, suicides, drug overdoses, and natural causes. If spirits haunted KSP at all, they would most likely be here. Only once when I was giving a tour did I sense a ghostly presence. I was leading a group of guests throughout the prison. I keyed open the door to the electric chair, as I had done hundreds of times. In this moment, however, the hair stood up on the back of my neck, and I felt an otherworldly presence. I saw nothing out of the ordinary, but I felt something unmistakably creepy. Whatever it was chilled me to the bone. As my career progressed, I would oversee executions in the very same room—but I never experienced anything like that again.

Once I had inspected the dungeons, I was satisfied and had no reason to venture further down the tunnel. I was ready to come out. I made my way back the short distance to the steel door on death row where I began. Between you and me, I was scared to death down there with my fading flashlight, the giant rats, and the lingering sense of great suffering that permeated it all.

I could only imagine Lt. McKinney and the rest of the Three Cell House crew having a good laugh. I had been in the tunnel for less than an hour. I banged on the door. I did not have a radio, so I had no way to signal for help. No response. I did not want to rap the door with the flashlight and risk losing the only illumination I had available. I did switch off the flashlight just to see if I was in total darkness. I could see a few slivers of light coming from under the door.

I stood at the steel door and continued to bang. I do not know how much time passed, but eventually I heard keys on the outside rattle and the door swung open. There was McKinney, grinning and welcoming me back to the real world. I am sure I looked as pale as a ghost myself as I emerged from the darkness.

In retrospect, there was nothing much to see of the old dungeon. The real experience was the atmosphere surrounding the place, and that is something I will never forget.

DETERIORATING CONDITIONS

By the time I began work in the penitentiary in 1978, not many attempts had been made to improve conditions at KSP, but that was about to change. An inmate named Gerald Kendrick filed a handwritten lawsuit in the United States District Court alleging, among other things, the conditions amounted to cruel and unusual punishment, in violation of the Eighth Amendment of the U.S. Constitution. It would be several years before a settlement was reached, and money was appropriated by the Kentucky General Assembly to make improvements to the prison infrastructure.

In the meantime, overcrowding continued at prisons throughout Kentucky, and conditions continued to deteriorate. Violence, drugs, and suicides were regular occurrences to those of us who were familiar with the climate at KSP.

Repairs and modernization were badly needed. One and Two Cell Houses were original, except for the addition of a toilet, sink, and electric light in each cell. There were approximately 120 cells in each House. Cell doors were constructed of slats of steel riveted together, not bars. Inside each cell was about forty square feet of living space. There was barely enough room to turn around—yet a second bunk was added above the bottom bunk in each cell to maximize capacity. Add a fan, TV, radio, and civilian clothing for each inmate, and the space was almost inhumanely tiny. Keep in mind there was no air conditioning and no ventilation, and the cell walls were two feet thick. These living conditions could be unbearable in the summertime. Prisoners suffered from the temperatures and the tight living quarters—and changes were a long time in coming.

The *Kendrick* lawsuit, and the resulting Consent Decree, was an order specifying physical plant improvements, as well as changes in the overall management of the prison. The interior cells in One and Two Cell Houses were demolished, and that space was used to create modern offices, a library, visiting area, chapel, and recreation areas. This allowed the razing of many of the old shacks on the yard that served the same purposes. Five Cell House was closed and renovated to meet modern standards. A new cell block (Six Cell House) was built to replace One and Two Cell Houses. Four Cell House was modernized with a new locking system and control center, along with new plumbing, electrical, and heating and air conditioning. At the end of several years of repairs and reconstruction, all buildings would be air conditioned, with the exception of the gymnasium.

On the operational side, the established court order specified only one inmate per cell was allowed. To our relief, the settlement created a mental health unit and professional mental health staff at KSR.

To our surprise, a 20 percent raise was added for correctional officers and other staff. It was estimated the total cost to comply with the Consent Decree was $40 million for both Kentucky State Penitentiary and Kentucky State Reformatory.

ONE CELL HOUSE

One Cell House was the original cell house built in the 1880s. There were four levels of tiny dungeon cells, little more than forty square feet each. The walkways were wooden planks, secured on metal support brackets on each level. The cell fronts were steel slats riveted together to form one cell door, and the walls of each cell were approximately two feet thick. At the end of each walk was a slam lock, which secured each row of cells, but there were also padlocks on each cell. There was a metal staircase on one end of the cell block, and there was a metal spiral staircase on the other end.

For the most part, inmates didn't complain much about living conditions in One or Two Cell Houses when I was a guard, because they knew we would have moved anyone that did complain to the least desired cell block, Five Cell House.

For some unknown reason, the Italian stonemasons who built KSP constructed a large archway in One Cell House that spanned most of the length of the building. At the time of its construction, this was the largest freestanding archway in the world, or at least that is what we were told. It was constructed without a keystone, a feat that might surprise modern engineers. The result was beautiful: the archway still stands out as an elegant architectural feat to those who take the time to appreciate it.

TWO CELL HOUSE

Two Cell House was almost a mirror image of One Cell House, complete with a spiral staircase and tiny, dungeon-looking cells, four levels high. Remarkably, Two Cell House also had a large archway spanning the entire length of the huge cell block.

THREE CELL HOUSE

Three Cell House burned sometime in the 1950s and was then renovated, making it the most modern and probably the most secure cell block at KSP. Of the 156 cells operated electronically, it was single-celled and housed the most dangerous inmates—the worst of the worst. It wasn't until the late 1980s that solid steel plates were fashioned to cover the cell bars. Until then, an inmate could throw feces or urine at a staff member as they made rounds. More than once, I had seen inmates pull the ceramic commode from the floor and throw it at the bars timed for when an officer was walking by. When the ceramic toilet hit the steel bars, it would shatter into hundreds of pieces. It was like an explosion. Sharp glass would go everywhere. If a piece hit you, it would easily cut you. Solid steel plates over the bars solved that problem.

Three Cell House was modern in every way during my time at KSP —except for air conditioning. Only the Administrative Control Unit (ACU) was air conditioned. It housed the most violent, hardcore inmates. A stay on ACU would last at least a year and sometimes longer. Inmates who had been placed there were allowed one hour out of their cells to mill about and an occasional exercise period in a small gym constructed just for ACU. That was the unit I was assigned to most of my time as a correctional officer. Because Three Cell House housed violent inmates, they were known to assault staff with every imaginable object they could get their hands on. I was assaulted more than once, but we had methods at our discretion to make it very uncomfortable for an inmate if he assaulted one of the guards. We carried mace and batons and could respond immediately if necessary. There weren't any hard-and-fast rules or procedures, but common sense prevailed. We knew when it was prudent to get a team together to enter a cell to restrain an inmate. The last thing we wanted was to be injured as we responded. Spraying an inmate with mace was usually enough, but we were required to offer a shower to wash off the mace once the inmate calmed down enough to place his hands out the tray slot to be handcuffed. When mace did not work, we could go in and wrestle the inmate down on the bed in order to restrain his arms and legs to the bedframe with cuffs and shackles.

Life in Three Cell House was not supposed to be pleasant. It was a form of additional punishment within the confines of the prison, and it usually served as an effective deterrent for the rest of the population. Most inmates would avoid rule violations (write-ups) that would result in a trip to the hole.

FOUR CELL HOUSE

I only worked Four Cell House when I was a newbie fish guard in training. The wing was constructed in 1910, and as a result, the cells there were much larger and relatively more comfortable.

The interior of Four Cell House was four levels high, and there was a basement on the side facing the lake. For the most part, Four Cell House housed the cream of the crop—the best-behaved inmates. Most of the men went to work in Prison Industries, either in the furniture plant or the garment factory. Some worked in maintenance or food service. All inmates were required to work or go to school. At some point, it was designated as an "honor unit," and prisoners were granted additional privileges like longer yard time or extra visits. It still serves as an honor unit to this day.

FIVE CELL HOUSE

Built in 1937, Five Cell House is the largest and most complex cell block, but not necessarily the most secure. It was renovated in the early 1980s to comply with the judgment in the *Kendrick* Litigation. Before renovation, Five Cell House consisted of four levels of cells, divided into three separate wings. It housed 560 single-celled inmates, or 1,120 if they were doubled up. By the 1970s, Five Cell House had deteriorated to the point that it was unsafe and unusable. The old slam-locking system did not work properly. Toilets and plumbing leaked at every level, and each cell had a window that was supposed to manually crank open. (Most did not.) To make matters worse, the main kitchen and dining hall was at ground level. All the toilet and plumbing leaks would make their way down and drip from the ceiling, often on the dining room tables. Below the dining room and kitchen was a basement area with an outside entrance that served as a warehouse for the entire institution. It was called the "receiver's basement."

After the lawsuit was settled, money was finally appropriated to renovate the entire unit to modern standards. The redesign combined three individual cells into two, increasing inmate living space to comply with modern standards—but reducing overall capacity to 360. New infrastructure, including electrical, plumbing, windows, and HVAC, resolved most of the problems that had plagued Five Cell House for years. It still was not a desirable living arrangement for most inmates because the cells faced each other, resulting in less privacy.

Two floors of Five Cell House were devoted to housing so-called "protective custody" inmates. Inmates needing protection is a reality in prisons, for reasons as varied as snitching on other inmates or unpaid debts between inmates.

Debt is a constant source of strife between prisoners. Cartons of cigarettes, drugs—pretty much anything can and does lead to inmates becoming indebted to one another. Sometimes the only way to pay a debt is by performing sexual favors. And an inmate's refusal to pay a debt could lead to serious injury or even death. This is a harsh reality of life in the prison system. We coach new inmates to never borrow or fall into debt, but some do anyway. After all, these folks are not serving time behind bars for following the rules.

Another common reason that an inmate might need protective custody is because the nature of their crime demands it. Child molesters fall into this category, as do people who have committed hate crimes or crimes against women. The average person might find it odd that prisoners tend to respect cohorts who commit murder, but they draw the line at hate crimes. It's one of the many mysteries of life behind bars.

My experience is that informants are by far in the greatest risk category needing protection. No one likes a "rat" or "snitch," as they are pejoratively called—even more so in prison. Still, some inmates will inform prison staff of everything going on in hopes of gaining favor or to get a transfer to another prison. Staff are forbidden to exchange favors for information, but I am sure it happens in all prisons, including KSP. Making a drug bust by any means possible is tempting to officers who want to make a name for themselves. Using informants can be productive, but it can have deadly consequences. If the identity of an informant becomes known, protective custody becomes necessary. Needless to say, other inmates view protective custody inmates as the lowest creatures on the totem pole. Words like "lowlife" and "rat" plague the reputation of inmates who violate the social hierarchy, and they almost never earn that trust back.

SIX CELL HOUSE

Built in the 1980s, Six Cell House housed 189 inmates during my tenure at KSP, including thirty-plus death- row inmates in a separate section of the building. I was on the design committee during the planning stage of Six Cell House, and I am still proud of what we built. It is the most secure cell block for general population. Unfortunately, we specified the cells to be constructed with electronically operated bars at the front of the cell. Our thinking at that time was to maximize visual observation from a centralized control center. While this objective was accomplished, inmate privacy was compromised, and we later learned that bars were not as secure as solid walls and solid steel doors. This design would not meet regulatory standards today, when newly designed high-security units across the country now incorporate cells with solid concrete blocks and solid steel doors, with a small window and tray slot that closes and locks. But at the time we built Six Cell House, it was state of the art.

SEVEN CELL HOUSE

Late one afternoon sometime when I was ready to leave for the day, Commissioner Doug Sapp called. I can't remember the date, but it was around the year 2000. I was serving as warden of KSP at the time. Sapp explained that the Clinton Crime Bill had allocated a large amount of federal grant money that would be reallocated if it was not used quickly. He asked if there was anything I needed at the penitentiary.

I lit a cigarette and thought for a minute. Then it came to me like a flash of light. "How about a supermax unit?" I replied. I could tell this piqued Sapp's interest.

"How much would that cost?" He wanted me to give him a monetary figure on the spot. I told him I was shooting from the hip, but I thought it would cost roughly $150,000 per cell for a state-of-the-art high security segregation unit. I wanted one hundred beds. He asked, "Where would you build it?"

Without much time to think it over, I lit another cigarette and said, "In the back lot where the softball field is, next to Prison Industries."

He said, "Okay, Phil, that's all I need." The conversation ended, and I didn't think much more about it.

A day or two later, I got a call from someone in the financial section at the Department of Corrections Central Office, asking for additional details. Details I did not have. I really didn't think this project had any chance of being funded, but apparently it did. Some $5 million dollars was immediately set aside for the project, to my astonishment. It was full steam ahead on the construction of Seven Cell House.

The grant was approved by the federal government, but not by the Kentucky Legislature. More importantly, the media got wind of the project, and it was reported all across the state, often in critical terms. Neither the Kentucky General Assembly nor the governor were fully aware of our intentions to build a fifty-bed supermax unit at KSP (revised from the original one hundred I had tossed out off the top of my head), and funding for the project became a political hot potato. Once built, a supermax unit would have to be staffed. Money for additional staff would have to be appropriated by the state legislature, and it finally was—but not without a fight. Though I retired before Seven Cell House was completed, I am immensely proud of the final product. This new supermax unit has a calming effect on the entire population. Violence actually decreased between inmates. The threat of supermax punishment gave us an addition to our toolbox to deal with the most violent inmates without compromising the safety of staff. KSP became a safer and more secure institution than it had ever been before.

THREE

THE RAGE AND OUTRAGE OF THE 1970S

THE EARLY 1970S WAS A TUMULTUOUS ERA IN THE HISTORY OF THE Castle. Many of the men who began their prison careers at the time went on to achieve leadership positions in the prison system. KSP produced its fair share of lieutenants, captains, senior captains, and deputy wardens.

The Castle functioned as a maximum security institution in the '70s, but the Kentucky General Assembly failed to fund many improvements or programs. Spending hard-earned tax revenue on prisons was not at the top of many bureaucratic lists at a time when record inflation was forcing people to ration gasoline and food.

Not only were politicians hesitant to allocate money for correctional improvements, but prison staff was also resistant to change. Infrastructure, security, and treatment programs suffered from years of neglect and underfunding.

Inmates were no longer provided uniforms in the early '70s. Prisoners actually wore street clothes behind bars. Rules restricting facial hair and hair length were relaxed. Hippie culture slowly but surely made its way to the Castle with each busload of new inmates.

Property limits were also relaxed. Inmates could accumulate as much personal property as they could fit in their cells. Many even brought furniture over from the KSP furniture factory. It was not unusual to see shelves and cabinets, multiple chairs, and handmade tables in cells. At the same time, a more benevolent prison administration decided to permit family and friends to mail monthly packages to the inmate population. Basically, any kind of nonperishable food item, clothing, hygienic supplies, books, and magazines were permitted in the mail. Naturally, this created a new pipeline of drugs that were cleverly concealed in the hems of blue jeans or even crammed into what looked like an ordinary can of food. For prison guards, the task of searching for contraband became almost impossible. Unsurprisingly, the combination of increased drug access and relaxed policies led to a proliferation of violence at KSP.

Examples of institutional chaos are manyfold. In 1972, two inmates died from smoke inhalation when the upholstery section of the furniture plant caught fire. Eighteen inmates escaped the burning plant, only after two inmates battered a hole through a cinderblock wall. Property damage was extensive and was estimated at over $100,000 (over $722,000 today).

That same year, five inmates held three employees hostage in the hospital pharmacy. After almost eighteen hours of tense negotiations, the hostages were released. Strangely, I could not find any record of this event. A few of the older staff recalled it, but they could not provide meaningful details. The only thing everyone seems to agree on is that the incident was motivated by the drugs stored in the hospital. After this event, the pharmacy was moved to its present location in the administration building.

Fights became common, and stabbings and murders increased. In the period of 1972 to 1975, there were ten inmate suicides, nine murders, and five accidental deaths. Escapes from inside the prison were happening frequently. Just in my first six months in 1978, there were two mass escapes. Stabbings and murders continued relentlessly through the '70s and most of the '80s.

The decade of the 1970s was stricken with strife and barbarity. The condition of the penitentiary had deteriorated to the point it was ripe for a lawsuit alleging the totality of conditions amounted to cruel and unusual punishment in violation of the Eighth Amendment. In retrospect, many of us who worked during the 1970s agreed that the old castle should have been bulldozed down and replaced. Doing this would have been more cost effective in the long run, and it would have ended a century of brutality and mayhem.

CHANGING OF THE GUARD

By 1977, the employee classification of guard was changed to Correctional Officer I and II. Correctional Officer I was a classification for officers without a high school diploma, and Correctional Officer II was reserved for those with a high school education. The phrase "fair, firm, and consistent" became the correctional officers' creed. This was being taught in every state, and it is still taught in the academy to this day.

I recall attending the academy at Eastern Kentucky University in Richmond, Kentucky, in 1978. Our academy was shared with the police academy in a state-of-the-art facility. We were taught a variety of skills to do our jobs effectively. This included resorting to the use of force only as a last resort to defend ourselves, defend others, or protect state property. Instructors also insisted that we never use the term "guard" or "convict" to describe prison hierarchy. We were to use "correctional officer" and "inmate." The terminology offered a more humane and professional approach for all involved.

To this day, however, I do not think we ever won the battle to change the public perception and use of older prison terminology.

People ask me if I started as a "guard," and I often see the term "jail" or "prison guard" used in newspaper articles. Most professionals in our business cringe when they hear the title "guard," and as a warden, I used to politely correct politicians, attorneys, and news media when they used the term.

In retrospect, decades after the word "guard" became taboo, I view it with affection because most of my early mentors started as guards. They were not uneducated or brutal. They were tough, but they were professional. They were fair, firm, and consistent, but make no mistake, they were strong when they needed to be. They were proud to be guards.

MY FIRST USE OF FORCE

During one of my early days while I was working with an officer in Four Cell House, two officers and Lt. Mitch McKinney came to Four Cell House and instructed me to go with them. We walked almost casually across the yard to the hospital where inmate Gary Daily was barricaded in a high-security hospital cell, holding a mattress and a piece of Plexiglas that he had managed to shape into a weapon of sorts. A makeshift prison shank. Even though I had just returned from the academy, I suddenly found myself in a position as the number-two man rushing into a cell to disarm and cuff a violent inmate. Officer Gail Doles was the first to go in. He was a physically small man, probably no more than 130 pounds, and around thirty years old. But he had more guts than most of the blackbelts I had sparred with over the years. Lt. McKinney was quiet but had a tall, athletic build, was tough as nails, and was not afraid of anything. I am six foot two, and I would have to look up at him. He must have been six foot seven or more. He was one of the toughest men I had ever met. Lt. McKinney sprayed a burst of mace in the cell's viewport and told us to get ready. After another half a minute, Lt. McKinney keyed open the door, and Officer Doles, the first officer to go in, grabbed Gary Daily in a headlock, and I threw a few punches as we took him to the floor. Officer Charlie Ramey came in behind me with handcuffs. At this point, Lt. McKinney, Officer Doles, and Officer Ramey placed Daily in four-point restraints, which basically restrains each arm and leg to a bed. Hogtied, if you will. The reasoning behind this is that the restraints would encourage the prisoner to calm down without the need for medication or additional force. Then he would be freed from the restraints.

Inmate Daily was a very disturbed young man—the most disturbed individual I had ever met. His nickname was "Monster." He could hurt you in a heartbeat. He had no fear of us or anything. He didn't fit anything I had studied about human behavior in my psychology classes. He might as well have been from another planet. He was a frequent "cutter," meaning he would take any sharp object and lacerate his arms, which bore numerous cut marks and scarring. He was in the state of mind that he would cut himself or the use-of-force team, and it didn't matter to him which. To say Daily was quite a challenge for a new correctional officer facing his first use of force would be an understatement.

On the way out of the hospital, I told Lt. McKinney that he could come get me any time. He could tell that I liked the action. He grinned back at me. In retrospect, this was apparently a test to see if I had the right stuff or if I would let fear cower me in the moment. I think McKinney went straight to the administration building and reported to the warden how I had performed. I must have passed the test, because about three weeks later, I was called to the senior captain's office and was told that I was selected for the E-Squad, along with thirty other seasoned officers, sergeants, lieutenants, and captains.

E-SQUAD

The prison Emergency Squad ("E-Squad") was an elite group of correctional officers. They were the toughest, biggest, bad-asses I had ever seen. Some of them were giants, literally. All would and could fight. All were fearless. I was surprised to be selected for this special group. Normally, only proven officers with at least two or more years of experience would qualify. I had only been there six weeks—just out of the academy, and now going back to the academy for three weeks of additional training in special weapons, riot tactics, and squad formations. And I was joining the elite of the elite, but there was a price to pay for the privilege. Many of these men would drink hard and play hard. I wasn't much of a drinker in those days, but they were, and I learned that drinking and fighting was what they did well. Several carloads of officers were drunk before our caravan got out of Lyon County on the 250-mile journey to the training facility in Richmond, Kentucky.

Once we had checked into our dormitory at Eastern Kentucky University next to the police academy, the heavy drinking began. Feeling out of place, not knowing many on the team, I slipped away to my dorm room. Then there was a knock on the door. A man nicknamed "ROHO" was waiting outside. He said, "Come on and be sociable, come join us," as he handed me a beer. I reluctantly followed him to a room down the hall, where at least fifteen or so drunks were gathered in a dorm room. I couldn't help but notice a wad of cash sitting on a nearby table. Then it hit me. They were placing bets on whether another guy in the outfit, Sgt. Kenny Holloway, could whip me. What had I gotten myself into?

FIGHT WITH A SENIOR OFFICER

Sgt. Holloway was a retired navy veteran and supposedly had a black-belt in Judo. He was the real deal. Holloway was also drunk, like everyone else in the room but me. The place was trashed. About that time, someone threw a whiskey bottle out the door, and it broke against the wall in the hallway. I knew I was in trouble. They wanted Holloway to whip my ass. I was the fish guard that had no business in E-Squad training. It wasn't my fault. I didn't ask to be there. I was selected by Warden Bordenkircher and Deputy Warden L.T. Brown. Still, I began to see I had no way out of the current situation except by defending myself. I wasn't drunk, but I also wasn't a coward.

As I assessed the situation, Sgt. Holloway staggered up to me and said, "I'm fixing to whoop your ass."

I stepped back a few feet and said, "Look, tomorrow when everyone is sober, I will fight any of you in the ring, but tonight we are not going to fight." I was shocked, and somewhat scared, but also pissed. I walked into the hallway.

I heard Lt. McKinney say, "Leave him alone," behind me. And everyone listened to Lt. McKinney. He was a man of few words, but everyone respected him, even when they were drunk. I thought I was in the clear, until Sgt. Holloway followed me into the hallway. Things unraveled quickly from there. Holloway charged at me to try to get me in a Judo hold, and I kicked him in the temple. As he fell to the floor, I kicked him one or two more times. He was out cold. In a split second, it was over. By then, my adrenaline was flowing, and I was ready to fight all of them. Hearing the commotion, everyone came out of the room and saw Holloway knocked out on the floor and me standing over him. The training officer, Tom Presler, ran up to hold me back, and I told him that if he touched me, I would knock his ass out, too. He stopped dead in his tracks.

I looked at all these giants, these seasoned street fighters, and said, "Who's next?" When nobody accepted my challenge, I walked down the hall to Sr. Captain Hendrick's room and knocked on the door. When he answered, I said, "I quit. I shouldn't be here, and I'm going home." He motioned me into his room and asked what had happened.

When I told him I wasn't going to fight every night just to prove myself, he advised me to just give it a day or two. The men, he predicted, would come around. I was pissed off—but I also needed this job. I went back to my room, still fuming, but I resolved to give it one more day. I'm glad I did.

The next morning in the dormitory restroom, I saw Sgt. Holloway walk in sporting a big shoe print on the side of his head and a bruised eye. He came up to me, his hand extended. "I guess I owe you an apology."

Right behind him was big Mike McKinney, Lt. Mitch McKinney's twin brother. He came up to me and said, "Thank you, Parker, for not putting him in the hospital." Several others also shook my hand and thanked me for not hurting Holloway any more than I already had. From that day on, I was one of them. As uncivilized as the experience had been, I earned their respect and secured my place on the E-Squad. I guess part of what impressed the old-school guards was the fact that I dispatched Sgt. Holloway in a very private way, out in the hallway, without making a big show of the encounter to the rest of the group. They appreciated that I wasn't a showboat or a braggart.

Just six weeks after my start date, I was a member of the Elite Squad. Yes, I was still a fish guard. But I was also respected by the old-school guards. They would take me under their wing and teach me how to drink, party, and walk the yard like a seasoned pro. The rest would be up to me. After all, I obviously knew how to fight already.

Reflecting back on that incident, I can understand why I was not trusted from the outset. These guys were not about to accept a fish guard into their ranks. And I don't blame them. I looked like a college kid, a skinny bookworm. So what that I had a college degree and a black belt? What really mattered was whether I could win a pissing contest with these men. Could I fight? Would I have their back when shit hit the fan on the yard? Now they had their answer.

Sgt. Holloway and I became good friends years after I became warden. We would often laugh about that incident. I think we respected each other in ways few could understand. When he became ill and succumbed to lung cancer in our later years, I felt his loss deeply. Holloway was a tough, ol' Navy Vet and a good man. I still miss him.

My journey as a fish guard was just getting started. I was already on the prison E-Squad, I was respected, and my colleagues saw that I could stand my ground. I had been there about three months, and my future was bright. Unfortunately, I was still being paid virtual starvation wages. My take home pay was $210 every two weeks, not much even in 1978. (Roughly $970 today.) Working overtime was a blessing. Working a second job was the only way to pay the bills. But I loved my job at KSP, and I was determined to carry on even though my poverty was now as bad as or worse than when I was in college. I remember when my only meal for the day was an inmate tray, after we served inmates in "the hole," in Three Cell House. My haircuts were from a prison inmate barber. A good cut cost seventy-five cents and a pack of cigarettes for a tip. Carpooling to work was the only way to afford the fifty-mile drive for me. Times were tough for a penitentiary guard. We were poor as dirt, but we had pride. Some days I came to work just to see what the hell would happen next, and I endured some crazy stuff. Years later, some of us were still around, but most officer recruits just didn't make it. New hires typically only survived the academy and then resigned when the reality of the job's risks hit home. The Castle was not a place for the timid. It took fortitude to walk past that entry gate day after day, into the belly of the beast.

A NEW WARDEN USHERS IN A NEW ERA

In August of 1976, Don Bordenkircher took over as warden of KSP. Bordenkircher had earned the reputation as a hard-nosed, no-nonsense corrections line officer and supervisor in California's San Quentin State Prison. He had also managed military prisons in the Middle East. The guy was tough as nails.

One of Warden Bordenkircher's first changes at KSP was to suspend the practice of picnic visits in a dilapidated old pavilion on the back of the prison recreation yard. Bordenkircher was more of a conservative, "law-and-order" warden who would not tolerate the visiting program to be used for smuggling dangerous contraband into the prison. Picnic food would often consist of pies, cakes, fried chicken, ham sandwiches, potato salad, slaw, or anything else that could be carried in containers. The containers were the problem. It was impossible to search most of these items, and there just was not ample time to process hundreds of visitors and all the food they might carry.

This program was a holdover from Warden Cowan's administration, and it was widely known that the picnics were a major pipeline for dangerous drugs. Heavy sexual petting was also allowed during the gatherings, which often escalated into illicit sex as soon as staff looked the other way.

Bordenkircher claimed he had received literally hundreds of letters from inmate families in support of eliminating the heavy petting and lewd conduct, but suspending the picnic-type visits was extremely unpopular with the inmates. After all, this was their only chance to engage in sex with the opposite gender, and it was a very lucrative method of smuggling drugs into the prison. Eventually, the backlot visiting area was spruced up with a coat of paint, a playground for the children, and new bathrooms. After a prolonged uproar, Bordenkircher finally gave in and let picnics resume. The program was staffed better, and more thorough searches were conducted, but the drug pipeline remained intact. Inmates can be very clever and can easily exploit any weaknesses in a security program. The picnics were no exception.

OPEN HOUSE

Warden Bordenkircher excelled in the art of security, and he understood the dynamics of a maximum-security prison. He did a lot to secure the prison. He tightened security around the visitor program. Security was much better on the yard. He developed a rapid-response team of some of the best correctional officers to respond immediately to fights and disturbances. This team would also encourage prisoner informants and search for contraband. It was quite effective, and numerous weapons were confiscated along with homebrew and drugs.

Warden Bordenkircher was liked and respected by staff who appreciated his brazen approach to controlling inmates and his emphasis on security and order. He was not as popular with the prisoners, however. Bordenkircher spent very little time coddling inmates. He often came across as curt and rude in his interactions with them. Bordenkircher could be merciless if inmates created a disturbance, and they knew it. They didn't like him, but they feared him, and to some degree they respected his demeanor.

He also understood that seemingly small decisions could have dramatic impacts on the prison population. He was good at judging inmate morale and tension and would sometimes resort to a carrot-and-stick approach to get the prison population to do his bidding. He would give inmates something they really wanted, while taking something else away at the same time.

Warden Bordenkircher was a master manipulator. He could create a new program that would speak to his benevolence as warden, only to use it to his advantage to maintain order among the prisoners. Perhaps the most infamous example of this was the annual Open House Program.

Open House was an unbelievably bizarre initiative that essentially opened the prison's doors to the outside world once a year and encouraged the general population to invite their families in to gain a sense of daily life at KSP. Each inmate was allowed to have up to four visitors bring a picnic basket into the prison. They could take visitors to the gym, yard, weight pile, classrooms, kitchen, and into the cell blocks. Each inmate could spend up to thirty minutes with visitors inside his cell, and they were allowed to cover the bars with a bedsheet for privacy. Basically, the program encouraged conjugal visits, though this was never actually acknowledged by staff.

As a guard, my job was to help search and process the visitors then patrol to make sure that everything remained civil. The inmates were always on their best behavior. At roll call we were instructed not to enforce petty rules, but to be polite and respectful. We were told not to interrupt family visits in the cells, but we could enforce the thirty-minute time allowance as needed. Yes, these were unofficial conjugal visits, but it was part of the plan. Word got out that if any inmate acted up or caused trouble, he would be dealt with by the other prisoners. In reality, they would have killed anyone who caused the program to fail. Bordenkircher promised that KSP would have another Open House the following year, if the inmates avoided engaging in any major distur- bances or riots. It worked. They didn't want to lose this program—a brilliant maneuver by Bordenkircher to keep the lid on the place. Once I became warden years later, I understood Bordenkircher's carrot-and- stick approach to running KSP. But as a guard, I could not understand why the Open House program was even considered—to relax security and allow inmates and their girlfriends or wives private time in their cells? Permitting food baskets in the main prison? Unheard of. And only Bordenkircher could pull this off without a hitch.

By 1979, Warden Dewey Sowders had replaced Warden Bordenkircher, and I was appointed to the position of Administrative Assistant to the Warden and Institutional Ombudsman. Warden Sowders allowed the Open House Program to continue, primarily because he didn't want to start a riot by abruptly ending the program. It would be much easier if inmates gave him an excuse to end the program. So the annual Open Houses continued despite the fact that it was the most bizarre and unconventional program one could imagine in a maximum security prison. This was essentially a holiday for the inmates—but they were on their best behavior. At least they were discreet. It was a security nightmare, but these gatherings worked to calm a very tense prison.

After Sowders had served a three-year stint as warden, he was succeeded by Warden Al Parke. The Open House Program continued for one more year under Warden Parke, but he had the fortitude to eliminate it. Parke would often walk the yard and took the time to talk to inmates. He would explain his reasoning for decisions, and he would never make an abrupt change in security or programs without first informing them about what he was about to do and why. He would give the inmates times to hash out their feelings and come to terms with pending changes. To our surprise, Parke eliminated the Open House Program without a riot. This is the kind of leadership that inspired me and influenced my interactions with inmates years later when I was warden.

WE MADE IT GOOD TO THEM

Senior Capt. Billy Adams was a legendary old-school guard. He began in 1966, and he was the Senior Captain by the time I started in 1978. He later became one of my mentors when I started climbing the ranks. He was always firm but fair to staff and inmates. He set a good example for everyone, but he was also tough, earning the nickname "Banging Billy." He was one of the few penitentiary employees who didn't smoke or drink. He was another giant that was nobody to mess with. When he told you something, he meant what he said.

Bill Henderson started in the early '70s and was another giant, tough man. Unlike "Banging Billy," Bill Henderson smoked and drank and would get rowdy from time to time. He was enlisted in the

Kentucky Army National Guard and eventually earned a retirement from the military while working a long career in the penitentiary. Everyone referred to him as "Big Foot" because of his large feet. At six foot five, Henderson was another giant of a man, with a personality to match.

Capt. Elwood Bell started his career in the early 1960s, but he wasn't physically imposing like some of his colleagues. He compensated for this by always carrying a "slapjack." A slapjack was a leather strap about twelve inches long that had a good-sized hunk of lead sewn in a pocket on the end. It was an effective defense weapon. Many cops in those days carried slapjacks to beat down unruly drunks or someone resisting arrest. If you were ever struck by a slapjack, you never forgot it. They were more or less as effective as the modern Taser gun. Crude, maybe, but effective.

These three fearless men had already earned their reputations. They had nothing to prove and were "Kings of the Hill." When they responded to a disturbance, the instigators didn't have a chance.

On a warm, sunny day in the summer of 1973, a little before my time, guards reported to roll call and were given their assignments. Most guards were happy to be assigned to a gun tower or a cell block where inmate contact would be minimal. The prison was double-celled, and dangerous contraband was everywhere.

Pills, marijuana, and homebrew could be obtained any day for a few packs of cigarettes. Prisoner-made shanks, or "stickers" as we called them, could also be bought for a few packs of cigarettes. A really good knife could be purchased for a carton of cigarettes. Stabbings and murders were fairly common. Suicides and escapes were also common. To make matters worse, the penitentiary ran on a shoestring budget. There was never enough money to hire more guards or buy additional security equipment like radios or handcuffs.

On this particular day, only two guards were assigned to patrol the yard: Officer Charlie Holt, who was twenty-one years old, and his partner, Officer George Thomas.

Only a hundred or so inmates worked in prison industries, making furniture or garments. There were fifty or sixty inmates enrolled in school, and fifty or sixty more worked in the kitchen helping to prepare meals. Another thirty or so inmates worked in the cannery, canning vegetables harvested from the prison farm. About fifteen inmates worked in maintenance. There simply weren't enough jobs for KSP's 1,300 inmates.

It was typical for all unemployed inmates to roam the yard trying to hustle other inmates. They often kept themselves occupied by making knives or homebrew. Some would work as male prostitutes, offering sex for a price. And of course, some inmates kept their distance from the many vices of prison life and spent their day lifting weights, playing handball and basketball, or just hanging out.

Officers Holt and Thomas were hoping for an uneventful day, but in the backs of their minds they knew it was rare for a shift to end without any fights or drunken behavior. It was this way every day. Some days were worse than others.

The morning in question started out normally. Inmates were released after breakfast to report to work or to go to the yard to hang out. Some of the inmates would spend the day in "one shop," which was an indoor recreation area with pool tables, picnic tables for dominoes, and a TV viewing area. It was also a place where the "tush hogs" or bullies would try to take advantage of weaker inmates. There were many inmates who avoided one shop because it was a hotbed of trouble. Fights were common, and occasionally someone was stabbed by one of the tush hogs. Inmates who were trying to stay out of trouble to make parole stayed out of one shop.

The inmate commissary was also a hotbed of activity. The commissary was just like a grocery store on the street. Inmates didn't carry money, but they could have money withdrawn from their prison accounts and placed on a punch card, which would be used to make purchases.

Cigarettes were in greatest demand, but inmates could also buy canned goods to take back to their cells. Even stamps and envelopes to write home with were sold in the commissary. Every day, inmates would line up at the window in the middle of the prison yard to make purchases. It was easy to observe the loan sharks hanging out near the commissary to collect debts or to make loans to new "fish" inmates. Tush hogs would sometimes rob inmates as they walked away with a grocery bag full of goodies.

That morning, Officer Holt was positioned on the side of the laundry and Officer Thomas was observing from the other end of the row of buildings, including the canteen. It was high ground, where they could observe a lot of the routine activity from an elevated vantage point.

All of a sudden, both Holt and Thomas could hear blood-curdling screams rising from the commissary. They knew right away these were coming from the two civilian female canteen workers. Three inmates workers were used to stock shelves and unload trucks. Only the female employees were allowed to sell commissary items out the window.

Apparently one of the working inmates had a scheduled medical appointment, and one of the female employees keyed open the barred gate to let him out. This presented an opportunity for five intoxicated inmates waiting at the door to rush in and take over the commissary. The inmate workers tried to fight off the five intruders, but they were no match. The female employees were yelling for help. It sounded like they were being beaten or perhaps even raped.

Officer Holt grabbed a shovel from a nearby work crew and Officer Thomas grabbed a broom. They got close enough to assess that there was a prisoner takeover, and KSP employees were in grave danger.

As this was unfolding, Capt. Adams entered the yard from the administration building. An inmate ran up to him and said, "You better get over there."

"Where?" asked Adams.

"At the canteen," said the inmate, "and you better hurry."

Adams cautiously approached the canteen, and he could hear the screaming. A radio call went to Deputy Warden L. T. Brown, who was in Warden Cowan's office meeting with security supervisors.

About a year before this incident, a similar takeover had occurred in the canteen. Negotiators worked for eighteen hours to end the standoff peacefully. Warden Cowan and Deputy Warden Brown had already decided if a takeover was to ever occur again, there would be no negotiation.

They were about to make good on that promise.

The lockup bell sounded, which should have signaled to all the inmates to return to their cells. It didn't work. Roughly two hundred inmates gathered and remained on the grassy bank looking down at the commissary. They were sitting on the ground, waiting to see all the action.

As the situation rapidly deteriorated, Warden Cowan and Deputy Warden Brown rushed to the armory below one stand and issued a 37mm gas gun to Capt. Bell and a 12-gauge shotgun to Lt. Henderson. They filled their pockets with 12-gauge ammunition and 37mm penetrating projectiles, designed to release tear gas after piercing glass windows or plywood barricades. The warden grabbed a snub-nose pistol and several riot batons. Dep. Warden Brown also grabbed a 12-gauge shotgun. No one bothered to grab gas masks in the heat of the moment.

As Warden Cowan and his armed team arrived on the scene, Deputy Warden Brown pointed a shotgun at the two hundred or so inmates milling about on the grassy bank and said, "I'm gonna start shooting if you don't get your asses back to your cellblock." That did the trick. They all took off running.

Outside the barred door of the canteen, Warden Cowan asked, "Who has the key?" There was no answer. He realized that they had failed to check out the key from the captain's office.

Deputy Warden Brown looked around and saw the old slop truck parked nearby. The slop truck was used to haul all the food garbage from the kitchen to the farm to be fed to the hogs. Thomas McCormick was assigned to make the daily trip with the kitchen slop, and he had the truck keys in his pocket. McCormick was another beast of a man. He had the largest hands and feet I had ever seen. He rarely spoke, but everyone was intimidated by him.

McCormick backed the slop truck up to the barred gates and began hooking a log chain to the axle of the truck and the other end to the bars of the gate. Meanwhile, Capt. Bell fired one round after another from the 37mm gas gun, filling the canteen with tear gas. Soon, the air in the canteen was thick with smoke.

Warden Cowan grew increasingly impatient as this was unfolding. He finally yelled, "Go, go!" McCormick floored the gas pedal on the old truck, which easily yanked the barred gate from the wall. By then, several other staff responded, including Recreation Supervisor Everett Cherry, who was armed with a baseball bat. Better than nothing.

Officer Sam Hooks was working six wall stand that day. Six wall stand was the gun tower overlooking the sallyport, a portion of the wall, and prison yard. At some point in the past, Officer Hooks had placed a one hundred–yard shot from his Winchester 30-30 dead center into the head of inmate Phillip Draffen as he held a knife to an officer's throat. Hooks was a self-trained sniper. One of the best. And he was in position with his 30-30 rifle to neutralize a threat if needed.

As the door was yanked off its hinges by the slop truck, Adams, Henderson, and Bell began to breach the gas-filled building. Inmates had barricaded the door with a desk, a table, and a filing cabinet. It didn't work. As the team plowed through the barricade, they began using batons and their fists to force the inmates to lay down on the floor.

Lt. Henderson struck an inmate with one hand while still holding his shotgun. Several shots were fired at the ceiling, but not at the inmates. Once Henderson had the inmate on the floor, he held him at gunpoint and looked around at the bloody scene that Capt. Adams (a.k.a. "Banging Billy") had created beating inmates down on the floor. It was not a pretty sight. Meanwhile, Capt. Bell was using his 37mm barrel to beat another inmate when the gas gun accidently discharged and hit the stock of the shotgun Lt. Henderson was holding at hip level. The projectile penetrated Henderson's shotgun stock and lodged in a can of coffee on a shelf. Tear gas had already filled the air with suffocating smoke. All Henderson could say was, "Well, shit."

Once Henderson's shotgun stock was hit, it was over. Everyone wanted out. The officers' failure to put on gas masks before the breach finally caught up with them. Tear gas has a way of creating panic—it's hard to breathe, the gas burns your eyes, and it makes you feel like you are on fire. Needless to say, the focus in that canteen quickly shifted from subduing prisoners to escaping the painful effects of the tear gas.

One inmate was unconscious after the fracas and had to be dragged out of the building by Capt. Adams. The other four crawled out on their hands and knees where the warden, deputy warden, and others were waiting. The four conscious inmates eventually stood up with their hands behind their heads, and were escorted at gunpoint to Three Cell House, "the hole." As they began the walk over, Sr. Capt. R. O. Long arrived on the scene with a double-barrel 12-gauge shotgun. It was his day off, but when he heard the news about the takeover, he high-tailed it to KSP. He didn't want to miss the action.

Capt. Long joined Warden Cowan and the others escorting the inmates to the hole. As they passed Five Cell House and then Four Cell House, inmates began yelling insults and cursing the warden and the escort crew.

Without saying a word, Sr. Capt. Long shouldered his double barrel and began firing shots at the cell houses. That had the desired effect of quieting the screaming inmates fairly quickly.

Almost fifty years after this event, I interviewed Capt. Adams about that day. Everyone else had passed away, save for Officer Holt and Capt. "Banging Billy" Adams.

I couldn't help but ask Banging Billy about the beating the inmates received in the hostage rescue. He didn't want to share that part of the experience. Some things, he implied, were better left unsaid. I could understand his position. Yet so much time had passed—over fifty years —that I didn't think it was necessary to protect the innocent or guilty. So I kept pressing him to give me additional details for this book. What happened to the inmates involved in the hostage takeover? Finally, Billy looked at me with a grin and said, "We made it good to them."

"How good?" I asked.

Banging Billy looked at me, still grinning, and repeated, "We made it good to them."

I knew that was an old-school guard's way of telling me they beat the living hell out of them. So be it. The beatings ensured that it would be a long time before inmates ever tried to take hostages again. When another hostage situation did unfold at KSP years later, I happened to be in the position of hostage negotiator, while Banging Billy Adams was at my side as a coach during the entire eight-hour ordeal.

In that case, we had a green light to kill William "Snake" Woolum as he held a gun to the head of Officer Jasper. Thankfully, that never happened.

Snake Woolum eventually made parole after forty-four years in prison. He frequently calls former Kentucky Supreme Court Justice Bill Cunningham and me to let us know how he is doing. Woolum is now a senior citizen, and in retrospect, I'm glad we didn't "make it good to him" the day he decided to take a hostage at KSP.

A WARDEN TAKES HIS SHOT

Within my first six months at KSP, I learned that Warden Don Bordenkircher had been shot by his "houseboy," Johnny Fulton. At the time, wardens and deputy wardens were required to live in one of the state houses on prison grounds. Houseboys were selected as trustees to clean house, do laundry, and sometimes cook meals. They were servants, but they lived a privileged life compared to the convicts behind bars. Most houseboys could be trusted to even babysit on occasion. They knew that any misstep would result in a trip to the hole and back to life in the prison. For the most part, the system of trustee or houseboy worked. There were exceptions, of course, like the time the governor's houseboy took a state police cruiser to get pizza and ended up driving through the state capital town of Frankfort with blue lights. Another incident a few years later resulted in Warden Bill Seabold's wife getting shot in the hand after she struggled with a houseboy at the Kentucky State Reformatory. Following these events, the days of houseboys were over in Kentucky.

As I mentioned earlier, Warden Bordenkircher was respected by staff but hated by some of the inmates. The warden's short time at KSP had been marked by murders, stabbings, escapes, and disturbances. There had been ten escapes in 1978 alone under Bordenkircher's watch. Now, to top it all off, his houseboy, Johnny Fulton, had shot him.

Fulton had no reason to dislike Bordenkircher. After all, he was treated well and lived a privileged life outside the penitentiary. But, like so many men behind bars, Fulton could not handle hard liquor. He had gotten into the warden's liquor cabinet and took a drink, then another, then another. The warden also kept his loaded pistol locked away in the liquor cabinet. Before long, Fulton took the warden's wife and daughter hostage in a drunken stupor. He waited for the warden to get home from work. Fulton was going to kill Bordenkircher. Warden Bordenkircher asked Fulton if he could at least kiss his wife. Fulton agreed but continued to hold the gun on him. This created an opportunity for Bordenkircher to wrestle the gun away, but not before Fulton shot him in the leg. It was a close call.

After the shooting, Fulton suffered a skull fracture when he "accidentally" fell into the bars at the entrance of Three Cell House. This happened after he was cuffed with his hands behind his back and marched through part of the prison with a shotgun aimed at his head by Captain Deboe. Fulton survived the skull fracture, but the Kentucky State Police investigated the incident. They recommended felony charges for Fulton and assault charges for Captain Deboe. Lyon County Attorney Bill Young refused to prosecute Deboe, suggesting that he would never get a conviction on a penitentiary captain given the circumstances. Commonwealth Attorney Bill Cunningham, however, disagreed with Young's assessment and stepped up to prosecute Deboe. Deboe pleaded not guilty, and the case went to trial. He was eventually found not guilty in a jury trial but resigned a short time later and moved out of state to leave this saga behind him.

MASS ESCAPE FROM THREE CELL HOUSE

By the time I started as a correctional officer in July 1978, Warden Bordenkircher only served another six months. The time we overlapped at the penitentiary was marked by two mass escapes at KSP. The first of these occurred on my very first day. Three inmates in Four Cell House cut out of their cells and managed to crawl out through the air ventilation system. The next escape, on November 14, 1978, occurred when three inmates cut out the vent in the back of their cells in Three Cell House then crawled out the ventilation system onto the roof. Two of the inmates, Donald Mayo and Michael Holland, made it all the way to Indiana, where they hijacked a van at a gas station and took shelter in a barn, where they were caught. They received felony charges in Indiana but were eventually paroled back to Kentucky to finish serving their time. Escapee Michael Holland, incidentally, had been a high school student of my mother-in-law's, Carolyn Goodin, when she taught in Pineville, Kentucky.

The third inmate, Robert Styles, fell to the ground as he was scaling down the outside of Three Cell House. As he propelled down the escape rope, he let go after suffering severe rope burns to his hand. The fall resulted in a compound fracture. At this point, he could barely crawl. Styles' escape attempt then became a cry for help. He managed to drag himself about one hundred yards to the prison doctor's doorstep. Unable to wake the doctor, he just lay on the porch in agony until Chief Engineer J. C. Butts came out of the house next door and spotted him. So much for his great escape.

MURDER ON THE YARD

The most disturbing events during Warden Bordenkircher's final six months were a series of prison murders.

One day in the fall of 1978, while working Three Cell House (the hole), we could hear radio traffic that warned of a serious incident on the yard. Several of us gathered at the entrance door in Three Cell House to see who the officers would bring in for us to process into segregation. It wasn't long until we heard Officer Mike McKinney outside. The cage officer opened the door, and Officer McKinney walked in, dragging inmate Chauncey Baldwin with one hand and a weight bar in the other. He had not even taken the time to cuff Baldwin. He just grabbed him by the scruff of the neck and began the walk to Three Cell House. As McKinney walked through the door, he shoved the prisoner toward us and said, "Lock him up. He just killed somebody." The murder was a vicious attack on inmate Billy McGee, who had taken Baldwin's towel while he was in the shower. A furious Baldwin had finished his shower and went to the weightlifting area (called the weight pile). He retrieved a heavy-duty weight bar and went looking for McGee. When he found him on the other side of the yard, he hit him one time in the back of the head, all but decapitating him. Blood and brain matter were everywhere. Baldwin then entered into a defensive posture, ready to attack anyone who approached. This didn't stop Officer McKinney. As Baldwin swung the heavy bar, Officer McKinney timed his takedown as the bar barely missed him. He grabbed Baldwin by the collar of his shirt and took the bar in the other hand, and started toward Three Cell House, where we were waiting. No cuffs, just muscle and fortitude. Officer McKinney probably saved the lives of several inmates because Baldwin was in a state of mind to attack anybody. Baldwin remained in Three Cell House for years.

SIT-DOWN STRIKE

Another event during Warden Bordenkircher's final days was a sit-down strike by approximately two hundred inmates who refused to go to work in prison industries. Things were tense. Kendrick's lawsuit in federal court was gaining traction with hearings scheduled. Violence was an everyday occurrence. The inmates fought for control of the yard. The penitentiary was overcrowded, often with two inmates in each cell. Cellblocks One and Two, built in the 1880s, did not meet modern prison standards, and the square footage space was well below the minimum for one inmate, much less two inmates, in each cell. Five Cell House (1937) housed one inmate per cell, but it was probably in worse condition than One and Two Cell Houses. Several floors of Five Cell were closed due to poor conditions. Five Cell was a huge building with a warehouse in the basement, a kitchen and dining room on the ground level, and four floors of cells above. It housed approximately five hundred inmates. The total population at KSP at the time was now over 1,200.

During the sit-down strike, inmates refused to work at any job, and a large crowd gathered on the recreation yard near the old cannery.

They were yelling, and it appeared a riot was imminent. I was working Three Cell House, and was told to get ready because the warden was going to attempt to lock down the yard by calling out the E-Squad to deal with anyone who did not comply with orders to return to their cells. I left my station to retrieve my E-Squad gear and meet the other E-Squad members at the sallyport. Shortly thereafter, a small group of some of the bravest, biggest men I had ever seen walked into the middle of the disturbance. Among them was Captain Billy Adams, Captain Bill Henderson, Captain Pat Kilgore, Captain Harry Barnett, and Sr. Captain Robert Hendricks. Capt. Adams ordered everyone to settle down and explained to the crowd that he couldn't talk to hundreds of inmates at one time. He assured them he would talk to a few individuals who could speak on behalf of the rest. He also told them he would only meet with the inmate representatives if everybody else returned to lockdown first. To everyone's surprise, this tactic worked. Inmates began to slowly walk back to their cells. As this unfolded, the assembled E-Squad members waited by the gate, ready to go in with tear gas, batons, and shotguns. It was all unnecessary.

Capt. Adams and the other supervisors had miraculously defused the incident and led five of the inmate spokesmen to the yard office. One of these was Johnny B. Preston, a singer-songwriter who had written several bluegrass hits. He was also a convicted murderer. Preston had also recorded songs, but none had made the top charts. In prison, he had developed a reputation as a writ writer, also called a legal aide. Preston had studied law in prison and was often allowed to represent inmates who appeared before the prison disciplinary board for rule violations. A legal aide would charge for their services with payment in the form of cigarettes or canteen items. It was a profitable racket, and legal aides enjoyed a certain status among the inmate population.

Preston was a ringleader in the sit-down strike, and once the prison had returned to relative normalcy with the lockdown, the warden brought in the E-Squad to round up all the ring leaders—Preston included. I was given the assignment to go to Preston's cell and transport him to segregation. First, I gave him enough army surplus duffel bags to pack up his property. Once he bagged his property, I wrote his last name and prison number on masking tape and affixed it to each bag so he could claim his property from storage once he was released back to the general population. He had a lot of property, filling a dozen or so bags. Once it was all tagged for storage, I placed him in cuffs and escorted him to the hole. He cooperated, but he was running his mouth as he passed other cells. I vividly remember him stopping to engage in conversation with other inmates, as I repeatedly nudged him along with my baton. In retrospect, I found myself escorting the life of the party to the hole that afternoon.

KSP administrators decided to segregate every one of the two hundred inmates who had participated in the sit-down strike. It fell to the E-Squad to move these individuals from Two Cell House to Five Cell House, which had been closed due to poor conditions. After working around the clock for two days to reopen parts of Five Cell House and prep them for occupation, we moved the Two Cell House inmates there to segregate them. For good measure, the administration decided to move all the inmates from Four Cell House to One Cell House, and the inmates already in One Cell House were moved to Four Cell House. We were instructed to destroy all the old makeshift furniture and junk from the cell blocks as we moved inmates, which was a massive job in and of itself. We worked the better part of a week to make this happen, with little time off. Most of the moves went off without a hitch, though there were a few who resisted and were dealt with quickly. The whole episode was a headache for the staff, and I was glad when it was finally over. Or so I thought.

As it turns out, my headache was just beginning.

TRIAL AND TRIBULATION

Warden Bordenkircher's tumultuous tenure was finally nearing its end. Murders, escapes, and disturbances had plagued his time in office. Then he was shot by his houseboy. By January 1979, Bordenkircher had had enough. He resigned and was replaced by Warden Sowders. As this all unfolded, Johnny Preston decided to sue me in federal court. To my surprise, he accused me of violating his civil rights. He claimed I had misplaced or purposely taken a notebook of songs he had written when I placed him in segregation in the aftermath of the sit-down strike. He also alleged that I was forceful and physically abusive when I transported him to the hole. I never laid a hand on him.

The case went before Judge Edward Johnstone, the same federal judge who had combined other complaints and lawsuits into a class action. My case, however, he agreed to hear separately through a jury trial. Linda Cooper, a young attorney who had only recently joined the Department of Corrections' General Counsel Office, was assigned to defend me. She was an excellent and highly skilled attorney who was respected at all levels in our department. I felt that I was in good hands. Johnny Preston acted *pro se*, meaning he was allowed to proceed as his own attorney. He had nothing to lose but time. (He did not have to even pay filing fees.) It was a joke, as far as I was concerned. I wasn't particularly worried, because I had simply been following orders to pack his property and lock him up . His accusations of theft and physical abuse were baseless. The problem was that in those days, we didn't inventory an inmate's property when it was placed in storage. The only record was a simple log in the property storage room, with the inmate's name and number and the total number of bags.

The trial lasted a few days, and the jury came back with a finding that I had in fact violated Preston's civil rights. If I remember correctly, the jury awarded compensatory and punitive damages for a total of $5,000. I couldn't believe it. They took a convict's word over mine.

Given the benefit of hindsight, I came to realize he was a notable song-writer, and I was just a lowly prison guard at the time. The jury was likely swayed by Preston's celebrity (minor as it was) and gave him the benefit of the doubt. To add insult to injury, Preston won the case without an attorney. Yet I had done nothing wrong. I didn't even know who he was when I took him to the hole. All I had was his last name and prison number, and I knew he was the ringleader in a prison disturbance.

As we rose to allow the jury to exit the courtroom, I asked my attorney, Linda Cooper, what the verdict meant. She waited until the jury exited and briefly explained that the state was responsible for the compensatory damages, and I had to pay the punitive damages. My mind was about to explode. I told her that there was no way I would pay a convict six months of my wages. I couldn't and wouldn't do it. I was ready to go to jail before I would pay Johnny Preston a single penny, and I meant it. I insisted she carry my message to Judge John-stone, but she had the good sense to reason with me. She assured me that she would try to take care of it if I would go back to work. As soon as I smoked a few cigarettes outside the courtroom, I calmed down enough to heed her advice. I'm glad I did. A month or so later, I learned the state had sent Johnny Preston a check for $5,000, thus covering the state's part and my part of the verdict. I moved on, wiser and perhaps a bit more world-weary from the whole experience.

FOUR

THE HOLE

Working Three Cell House was my favorite assignment. It was the prison's segregation unit—in effect, a jail inside the jail. Inmates and staff referred to it as "the hole," a carryover term from days of old, when punishment was administered by placing inmates literally in a hole in the ground or in a dungeon on a bread-and-water regimen. At KSP, the hole was where the action was. It housed 156 of the most dangerous inmates in the state of Kentucky. A large percentage were mentally ill, some were psychotic, and many were undiagnosed but very disturbed. Many of these individuals had no hope of getting out and nothing to lose. Some were gang members, and some were just mean to the core. A guard's day overseeing the hole was filled with activity. Violence was commonplace, especially during the mandatory exercise period when we would release ten to twenty inmates at a time to exercise on the walk.

We made rounds at least every hour up and down the walks in the huge cellblock. In those days, before renovation, the cell fronts were bars instead of a solid surface. Today the construction of new cells requires solid concrete walls and solid steel doors. Bars are not used in modern prisons. In the old Castle, an officer making rounds had to walk past each cell to take a count or pass out medication or food trays. An inmate could reach out and grab an officer as he walked by or, as I mentioned before, he could throw food, water, or feces at the officer through the bars. Incidents that involved reaching through the bars to grab an officer were relatively rare, because most of us would have made sure the result was a broken arm. More often than not, inmates would just stand there and cuss at us or throw something at us. We called them "cell warriors." If you opened their cell to let them have a shot at you, they always chickened out. I did this a few times but never had an inmate use the opportunity to hit me.

SUICIDE

On one occasion, as I was passing out food trays on 13 Left, inmate Fred Dunn moved his food tray through the tray slot and threw it back at me, covering me with food. That was considered an assault. Dunn was already in the hole for assaulting staff at Kentucky State Reformatory, which landed him a trip to the Castle. (One of his assault victims was a future warden, Glenn Haeberlin.) On the two hundred–mile, high-speed transportation trip from Kentucky State Reformatory (KSR) to the Castle, inmate Dunn spit on the back of the head of Officer Tucker, who was driving. Tucker, a gentle giant most of the time, was in no mood to play. He pulled the car over, got out, opened the rear door, and struck Dunn one time on the left side of this face. By the time he arrived at the Castle, Dunn's eye was swollen shut. Predictably, he didn't spit on Tucker again that trip.

Only a day or two after we received inmate Dunn from the Reformatory, he assaulted me with the food tray. I left the scene to change my shirt and didn't have time to deal immediately with inmate Dunn because I was needed to handle several other disturbances in the cell block. By the time I got back to Dunn, I discovered him hanging in his cell. I thought he was probably faking it and would jump down and attack if I opened his cell to check, so I called for a supervisor and waited for backup before going in. Lt. Tim Barnes and Officer Steve Galusha responded. Still not sure if he was going to ambush me, I cautiously entered, ready to strike with my riot baton. I nudged him with the end of my baton. When there was no response, we realized he was dead. Suicide.

This was another hard lesson for a fish guard. Had I not been called off to help with several other disturbances, my first reaction would have been to go in with my baton. After all, I had been assaulted, and I was a young hothead at the time. One of us would have gotten hurt, and I was pretty sure it would not have been me. I think he was trying to provoke me into violence. When this didn't happen, he turned his rage and aggression on himself. This was the first death I had seen in the prison, but it would not be the last. I always wondered how I would have felt if I had gone in and used force. Would he still have hung himself? If so, I would have probably felt responsible. His death still left a mark on me, but it was an important lesson. After having time to reflect on this event, I believe that nothing I did led directly to his decision to end his life.

A WORLD OF VIOLENCE

My early days at KSP were filled with violence. I went to work every day knowing I would probably face situations where the use of force was necessary, because I worked in the segregation unit where such incidents occurred regularly. Most of the time the segregation unit worked as a team, but there was no policy regarding how we should react to assaults and random violence. We were expected to exercise good judgment and ask for a supervisor and backup, but sometimes we were just expected to handle it ourselves. Some days we were short-staffed, and I would have to cover half the cellblock. On these days, you didn't always have a backup, so we just tried to handle things as best we could. It was dangerous, and violence was commonplace, but somehow you grew accustomed to it. After a while, it no longer shocked me to see someone cut themselves to the point of almost bleeding to death. It was not unusual to stand at a cell and talk an inmate out of hanging himself. When a fight broke out during exercise breaks, we would stand behind the gate and order everyone to return to their cells. Most of the time, the uninvolved inmates would do as we ordered, leaving only the instigators for us to deal with. Usually, we would use mace to break up the fights then render first aid. Violence and danger were the rule, not the exception, and those of us who continued to work in Three Cell House grew to like our assignment. To us, any other jobs inside the prison were boring by comparison.

As I previously mentioned, the prison was managed on a shoestring budget. We were issued surplus Air Force uniforms or worn-out prison guard uniforms, and there were never enough handcuffs or radios. Before roll call, officers could check out handcuffs and a radio, but only if you arrived at work thirty minutes to an hour early. There were only fifteen to twenty radios to cover a day shift staff of about one hundred officers. It was the same with handcuffs. Some officers bought their own cuffs, but I was stubborn. I reasoned that if the prison wanted to equip me with a radio and cuffs, they would do so. I wasn't about to get there an hour early, and I wasn't going to buy my own equipment. In segregation, we had plenty of cuffs in the unit, but not the other cellblocks. On more than one occasion, while working in other areas of the prison, I would find myself involved in an incident without any cuffs to restrain somebody after a takedown. In those cases, all I could do was pin the inmate to the ground and hope that backup would arrive quickly.

In one instance I recall vividly, a prisoner had written a letter to

Federal Judge Edward Johnstone, claiming that another inmate had stolen his TV. The court magistrate, Judge David King, called the warden and asked him to look into it. The warden passed the letter to me. I interviewed the inmate and found out he had traded his TV to another inmate, but the TV he received was bad, and he wanted his old TV back. I told the inmate I would try to resolve the problem, but he would have to go back to his cell while I checked out his story. The inmate refused to go back to his cell without his TV. I said, "Yes, you will." I took him by the arm. He began to resist. I fought the inmate, trying not to hurt him. Eventually, I pinned him to the floor. Unfortunately for the inmate, while I had him pinned, he spit in my face. I must have snapped, because I hit him several times in the face. I wasn't playing—I hit him hard. The guy's lesson for the day was never to spit in an officer's face when he has you pinned to the floor. He was a quick learner.

I wondered if I would lose my job for hitting an inmate who was pinned down. I went straight to Warden Sowders and told him what had happened. He just shrugged it off, but I could tell he wasn't happy about it. The warden told me to call Magistrate David King and tell him exactly what happened. When I did, Magistrate King didn't sound too surprised that an incident had occurred. He knew the inmate in question was part of our Special Needs Unit, which housed mentally ill inmates. To my surprise, Magistrate King apologized because he felt somewhat responsible for putting me in a position to take drastic action and defend myself. I couldn't believe that a federal magistrate was apologizing to me, but he was. That was the end of it. I told Warden Sowders about the conversation with Magistrate King. The warden smiled and asked, "Did you learn anything?"

I smiled and replied, "No, not really, but the inmate learned something."

As I said before, during this period, each day I reported to work I knew there would be violence and that I would probably be involved.

At first this work was exciting and unpredictable. I didn't mind responding with my fellow officers. We had each other's backs. Eventually, though, the endless cycle of violence began to take a toll on me physically and mentally. It was no longer fun or exciting—in fact, quite the opposite. I began to dread the work. I found myself slowly but surely getting burned out by the stress of the job. None of us ever complained, though. We just soldiered on as faithful defenders of the Castle.

FIVE

A NEW ROLE

On a cold winter morning sometime in February 1979, I attended the routine roll call for officers in the basement of the administration building. This was where we received daily briefings on any developments and current events. We also would get our day's assignments. Captain Kilgore was often the man in charge at these briefings. Kilgore was shorter than many of his colleagues, including me, and he was stocky. He always had a grin on his face, even when he was clearly unhappy or mad. Kilgore was quiet—a man of few words—and he meant business. For some reason, I never thought he liked me very much. Whenever he was shift commander, I would get stuck with an assignment that was excruciatingly boring—like occupying the Number Three Gun Tower, where one could only sit and struggle to stay awake. All things considered, it probably shouldn't come as a surprise that I tried to avoid interactions with Captain Kilgore.

As Kilgore called roll that morning, he finally got to my name. "Parker," he said monotonously.

I responded, "Here."

"Report to the warden's office."

I couldn't believe it. I must be in trouble, I thought—or I was about to get fired. Warden Sowders had been appointed only a few weeks earlier, and everyone was very apprehensive. We knew he was a powerful, intimidating man who didn't suffer fools gladly. Sowders was tough, smoked cigarettes constantly, and could change from friendly and charming to loud and mean in the blink of an eye.

What in the hell did I do? I thought. Then it occurred to me I had used force against an inmate, Gary Dailey (a.k.a. Monster), in Three Cell House the day before. This was the same disturbed inmate I had used force on when he was barricaded in the prison hospital. Fortunately, all I had actually done was spray mace at him. The previous day, I had Dailey out of his cell to help me pass out drinks from a water pitcher, as I and other officers passed out food trays. It was routine. For some unknown reason, Dailey started arguing with one of the other special needs inmates, and he refused to serve him a drink. When I went to get the pitcher of water from him, he turned and positioned himself to throw the water on me. I reacted by drawing my mace canister and spraying him in the face and chest as he threw the water. I got wet, and some of the mace must have traveled back with the water, because I suddenly felt the full effect of the chemical hit me. The effect mace has on the body is awful. Instantaneous burning of the eyes causes temporary blindness—or blurred vision, at best. It releases a flood of mucus from your nose. You may feel like you can't breathe, and your gag reflex kicks in. For some reason, mace never seemed to bother Gary Dailey very much. In fact, it often just made him madder and more difficult to deal with. I always wondered if he was somehow immune to mace. He certainly had his share of it.

In any event, during this particular episode, Dailey capitulated. We returned him to his cell and continued our work. I wrote the appropriate reports. I was sure my use of force was justified. Maybe the new warden didn't like what he'd read, though. There was nothing else I could think of that would result in a trip to the warden's office. His assistant, Vicki Patton, was a young, highly professional secretary at the time. Years later, when I made warden, Vicki was my secretary. She told me to have a seat. When she finished what she was doing, she said, "It will be a few minutes. Someone else is in there." I didn't know Vicki back then, but I knew she was a force to be reckoned with. I certainly wanted to stay on her good side. I didn't say anything because she looked busy, but I was scared as hell. Finally, the door to Warden Sowder's inner office opened, and someone walked out. Vicki picked up her phone and pressed the intercom button. She asked if he was ready to see Officer Parker. Sowders replied, "Send him in." I thought, *Oh shit, here we go.*

I walked in and stood at attention. He looked up and very politely invited me to sit down in a seat close to his desk. He asked, "Do you want a cup of coffee?"

I said, "No, thank you. I'm fine." I tried not to show my nervousness and anxiety. I was waiting for him to lower the boom. He began with a little small talk to break the ice, but I had the feeling he already knew all about me and what kind of officer I was. Finally, he got around to it.

"The reason I called you in is because the senior captain and deputy wardens have recommended you to be my administrative assistant. I want someone who has a college degree, who can write memos and procedures, and someone who doesn't have a long history here. I prefer somebody who is flexible and has not let this place become all that they know."

I was relieved and honored that I had been recommended, but I said, "Well, I really like what I am doing now, and I'm not sure I've been here long enough to fit the bill."

Sowders replied, "Oh yeah, I think you have." I started to ask if it was a promotion with more money, but before I could finish the question, he said, "I want you to understand this is not a promotion, only a title change—and no pay raise. You will learn a lot, and somewhere down the road, I will promote you to a new position."

I inquired, "Do I stay in uniform?"

He replied, "Sure, if you want." I think he realized I had recently graduated from college, and my street clothes were not much more than blue jeans and T-shirts. That was about all I had. I couldn't afford a new wardrobe for work. I asked what I would be doing. He explained that I would write letters for his signature to inmates or inmate families. More importantly, I would write policy statements and directives to all staff. My working title would be Administrative Assistant/Ombudsman. Furthermore, I would be investigating inmate complaints, including complaints against staff.

This sounded like a big job. I was intrigued. I needed more money, and I thought a promotion to sergeant or lieutenant was in my future if I stayed on shift assignment. I had already turned down an offer from the deputy warden of treatment, Charles Eastland, to fill a case manager position. That would have given me a 10 percent raise, but I wanted to stay in security.

After thinking it over for a day or two, I took the job the warden was offering. Sowders immediately gave me a few inmate letters and told me to write a response for his signature. I didn't have an office, a desk, a typewriter, or pen and paper. He told me just to sit on the couch and write. So, after gathering up a few pens and a few legal pads from the business office, I went back and started writing. I asked how I was to type it up, and he told me to give it to Vicki and she would type it.

My writing must have fit the bill, because Sowders started piling it on. Every morning I would have a stack of letters to investigate and respond to. I was soon overwhelmed. I had more than I could possibly do, and more and more was piling up. As it turned out, Sowders really disliked paperwork. He enjoyed dealing with people. The warden was building relationships, figuring out who he could trust and who would be loyal to him. Furthermore, he had a keen ability to detect corruption. Sowders seemed to already know who was stealing, who was having affairs, and who was covering up past deeds.

Warden Sowders could be very charming. But I soon discovered that he would use whatever talent I had and take full credit for the work I did. Sowders always felt slightly insecure because he didn't have a college degree, though you would never guess it in regular interactions with him. We did become close in our working relationship, and he would invite me over to his house to visit after work. His wife, Inga, and three daughters, Ina, Debbie, and Andy, treated me like part of the family. I never forgot the fact that he could be ruthless, if provoked. He had no qualms about firing employees at the drop of a hat. All in all, I learned a lot from Warden Sowders. Like all of us, he had some really admirable qualities, and he had some bad qualities. I worked with him as his assistant most of his three years as warden at KSP, until he was promoted to deputy commissioner.

CONSENT DECREE

As I settled into my new job, the *Kendrick* litigation was center stage in federal court under the jurisdiction of Judge Edward Johnstone and Magistrate David King. As I mentioned before, the *Kendrick* litigation was a handwritten lawsuit by inmate Gerald Kendrick, who alleged that the conditions in the prison amounted to cruel and unusual punishment. It was combined with other inmates' lawsuits to form a single class action.

In my role as the warden's administrative assistant and ombudsman, I was often called upon by our department's attorneys to produce documentation and investigate inmate claims. As the scope of my responsibility grew, I was also called to testify on occasion. When a settlement was reached, it became known as a Consent Decree. It became my full-time job to document our progress in compliance. Much of the information I provided to our department's attorneys was used to support this process. We had some very good lawyers: Paul Isaacs, Barbara Jones, and Linda Cooper. They often used me as their "go to" when they needed information. Their offices were some two hundred miles away in Frankfort, and a trip to Eddyville required an overnight stay.

The Consent Decree was the latest blow to staff morale. Everything we were taught and everything we did (or didn't do) was questioned. Inmates would often write letters of complaint to Judge Johnstone or Magistrate King. It appears they had gained the ear of the court. While I believe Judge Johnstone was a good person and tried to be fair to both sides, there was no doubt in our minds that he gave credence to inmates' embellished stories.

Part of the problem was that Judge Johnstone had been a state judge in Kentucky's 56th Judicial Circuit before he was appointed to the federal bench by President Jimmy Carter. He had also served in the army during World War II and had earned a Silver Star and a Bronze Star in the Battle of the Bulge. A popular and respected figure, Johnstone knew everyone in the local area, and everyone knew him. He would often hang out in the local barbershop on Saturdays and was known to shine shoes just for the heck of it.

Long before he was a federal judge, Johnstone would overhear small talk in the barbershop about things transpiring in and around the prison. Some guards couldn't help but brag and embellish stories about how they handled inmates. This exposure probably led Johnstone to suspect that guard brutality was commonplace at KSP—whether the stories were true or not. But times were different in the '60s and '70s. Guards (yes, they were officially called guards) would often handle bad situations with brute force. Guards would carry slaps, which as I mentioned earlier, was a leather strap with a piece of heavy lead sewn in at the end. The weapon would hurt like hell and often knock the recipient out cold. Sometimes guard–inmate physicality would get out of hand, but use of force was occasionally necessary to maintain control. Johnstone heard these anecdotes, true or not, and likely concluded that the system needed to change.

BRUTALITY AND HARRASSMENT

Because we had not yet reached a settlement in the *Kendrick* litigation, inmates were bombarding the court with handwritten letters complaining about everything—especially situations that involved a use of force. Judge Johnstone finally decided to give the inmates their day in court. I don't recall the date, but this was sometime in 1979 or 1980. He set a hearing on the issue of brutality and harassment and allowed over fifty inmates to testify. To my surprise, I was one of the twelve named defendants in the complaint. This all stemmed back to my time on the E-Squad and my assignment to Three Cell House, the segregation unit.

I had been involved in the use of force almost daily, but I always justified my actions in reports, and I never did anything that I considered "brutal" nor did I "harass" inmates. At least, not much.

In any situation where I was faced with a highly unstable, convicted felon, it was my job to use force to control the inmate—and then to go home in one piece at the end of shift. Thankfully I was injured only once during a use-of-force incident in my years on the job. The physical injury I suffered was minor, but I was momentarily knocked out as Captain Henderson and I forcibly entered inmate Prentice Duncan's cell to restrain him to his cell bed.

PRENTICE DUNCAN

Prentice Duncan was a special needs inmate who would often act up just to get attention. In segregation, there is no radio or TV. Inmates are provided with plenty of things to read, but violent and/or mentally challenged individuals rarely ever sit peacefully and read. The boredom they experience is tremendous.

Three Cell House was rocking and rolling on this day, as we used to say. It must have been a full moon that night, because there was definitely an uptick of activity. Self-mutilators were cutting themselves. Anxious inmates were becoming more so, and I sensed open hostility throughout the cell house every time I made a round. This was usually when inmates would throw spitballs or wet toilet paper out on the walk. Since those were the days before we outlawed smoking, matches and tobacco were readily available. In fact, we used tobacco many times to calm inmates—not to mention ourselves—and it worked. I would often light a cigarette to calm my nerves. Most of the staff smoked.

While filling out the logbook at the end of Thirteen and Fourteen Right Walks, I noticed smoke coming out of Duncan's cell. There was the usual yelling and banging bars, but nothing particularly serious. In less than the time it took me to get up from the desk and stand at the crash gate, the smoke was rolling. Now it was serious.

I summoned the control center cage operator and told her we had a fire and I needed backup. I grabbed the nearest water fire extinguisher and went in. As I got to Duncan's cell door, Capt. Henderson and one other officer joined me. I immediately pulled the pin and began extinguishing the fire. I thought I might as well wet Duncan down while I was there. The fire was easily extinguished, and Duncan had turned his back so the water wouldn't get in his face. When I thought he had had enough, I stopped. He turned around, grinning, and said, "You didn't get this." He brought up a lit, rolled-up cigarette to his mouth and blew a big puff of smoke. Instinctively, I emptied the fire extinguisher to make sure I got the cigarette out and everything else.

Capt. Henderson knew we would have to do a cell entry and subdue Duncan. It was common practice for us to use four-point restraints as a method to control highly agitated inmates. Basically, as I described before, we would forcefully place an inmate on his bed and restrain each arm and each leg to the bedpost using shackles. We would leave them in this position for a few hours or until they calmed down. These were the days before the restraint chair was in use, which basically does the same thing except that a restrained inmate is in a sitting position. Either way, an inmate would be immobilized and no longer capable of hurting himself, setting fires, or flooding the walk by deliberately stopping up his commode. It is a very effective method of control, and most of the time there are no injuries.

Inmate Duncan was highly agitated as we entered his cell. Capt. Henderson was first through the cell door, and I followed. The third officer stayed just outside the cell. Capt. Henderson used his baton to jab Duncan in the stomach. It wasn't a hard blow, just enough to make him bend over. As soon as he bent over from the baton jab, I took him down to the bed. I don't remember hitting him, but I do remember forcibly taking him down to the bed and pinning him so we could restrain his arms and legs.

As this was happening, I saw a starburst, and I was temporarily out. I don't think I went out cold, but my bell had been rung, and I was addled. What in the hell happened? I tried to shake it off and came to enough to hold him down while Capt. Henderson and the other officer finished restraining him to the bed. It was over as quickly as it began, and Duncan was no longer a threat. I got up and checked myself for injuries. I had a large knot right on top of my head. A "goose egg." All I could say was "Damn!" as I rubbed my head.

Capt. Henderson said, "What in the hell is wrong with you?" He had no idea I was injured in any way.

"Why did you do that?" I asked.

"What?"

"Hit me," I replied. He gave me a bewildered look. I said, "Here, feel this," motioning to rub my goose egg.

We both thought for a second, and he said, "Oh. When you took him down, I threw my baton down to help you, and it must have ricocheted off the wall and hit you." We both had a good laugh about it. I didn't mention it in my report, and he didn't, either. This was the only time I suffered a physical injury in all the use-of-force incidents I was involved in. And it wasn't even from an inmate. Just another unpredictable day in the belly of the beast.

JUDGMENT DAY

After months of hearings in federal court and transporting over fifty of the worst inmates in the entire prison between KSP and the courthouse, the ordeal was finally coming to an end. But not before an escape attempt was made during one of the all-day hearings. We had placed dozens of inmates in the three or four cells in the U. S. Marshal's office, and we relinquished custody to the marshals. We knew there were some bad actors in the cells, but the marshals had full custody— and full responsibility. They truly thought their cells were secure and nothing would happen.

Sometime in the late morning, one of the inmates managed to gain access to the attic of the courtroom. As he was crawling around, we could hear strange noises above us. It dawned on us about the same time that one or more inmates were in the attic. What to do? We didn't have custody; the marshals did. As we were looking up at the ceiling, one of the marshals came in from a side door, went straight behind the bench, and whispered to Judge Johnstone. The judge declared that court was in recess. The bailiff ordered all to rise. The judge vanished to his chambers, and about twenty of us went out in the hallway to see what was going on. To most of us, this was comical. We could have predicted this, or something worse, would happen. All we could do was sit back and see how the marshals handled this mess. With physical force? Brutality? Were they going to politely talk the attic crawler down from his perch? All in all, we were more than a little pleased to see the court get a taste of what we had to deal with every day. Actually, we thought it was hilarious.

After a while, one or two of our staff who were familiar with the inmates went in and talked the crawler down. Of course, we knew the marshals had snipers on the rooftops surrounding the courthouse, and they were just looking for a reason to respond. An escape out of the building would have resulted in the inmate's death. In the end, however, and to the marshals' embarrassment, it was our staff who calmly handled the situation and resolved it without any use of force.

The trial was a bench trial, meaning that the proceedings were heard in their entirety by the judge and not a jury. The plaintiffs were represented by Oliver Barber, a young, likeable attorney from Louisville who had not yet established much of a practice. This was his big break. He would become a well-known lawyer when this was over. We couldn't stand him, because he was like a bird dog who sniffed out every lead and allegation. He piled on hour after hour, billing for months and years. Looking back, he was just doing his job. We thought he was the enemy at the time, but he really wasn't. We were our own worst enemy. We had suffered through years of political appointments at all levels of Corrections, from the top to the bottom. Though it may be hard to believe now, in those days there were no standards or written policies and procedures. We relied on memos and oral directives from lieutenants and captains. Not much else. Sometimes staff did not write reports after being involved in use of force. (Incredibly, more than a few officers could hardly read or write.)

I recall a particular lieutenant on the midnight shift who could not write. When he was forced to write a report, he would sit beside an officer and tell him what to put in the report then sign his name to it. He was one of the few African Americans who had made rank, which was probably due in part to his genuine skill at handling inmates. He was another giant of a man and could calmly walk into a situation and defuse it with just his mere presence. A good man, but nobody to mess with.

This lieutenant was one of the twelve defendants, and Oliver Barber played him like a fiddle when he was on the stand. Fortunately, we learned that Judge Johnstone knew him from his days as a lawyer and had represented him in a legal matter. Since this was a bench trial, the judge could decide how much credibility should be afforded in weighing his testimony. To those observing the proceedings, however, it looked like game over. The lieutenant was destroyed on the stand by Oliver Barber, which was a foreshadowing of things to come.

The trial ultimately ended in a guilty finding. The decision found "substantial evidence of a pattern of brutality and harassment." I was one of the twelve defendants. One of the "dirty dozen." I suffered no repercussions, but the judge ordered limitations on Sr. Captain Hendricks, Captain Billy Ashley, and Captain Bill Henderson. Basically, he ruled that these captains could no longer sit on the Adjustment Committee, which is the prison's disciplinary board. They could also no longer make decisions involving cell moves and were forbidden from offering privileges to informants in exchange for information. The decision was basically a slap on the wrist—but it was nonetheless embarrassing, and it was perceived as a win for the inmates. Of course, it could have been a lot worse. The decision really didn't change much.

All the defendant-officers went on to other career gains. Captain Ashley became a deputy warden and eventually the warden at Western Kentucky Correctional Complex (WKCC). Capt. Henderson was promoted to senior captain, and then to deputy warden of security at Kentucky State Penitentiary, and Captain Hendricks continued a long and respected career as senior captain at the penitentiary before finishing his career as senior captain at WKCC. In many ways, these individuals were my mentors, and I had tremendous respect for each one. They were among the best in the business.

This court proceeding was one of the worst experiences of my career. Sitting in that courtroom, listening to lie after lie spoken about me and my colleagues for months, was unbearable. Of course, not *all* of the allegations were false. Mistakes had been made along the way. Sometimes force was used unnecessarily, and occasionally there was a coverup by somebody who should have known better. The twelve of us who had been named in the lawsuit, however, were the movers and shakers. We were easy targets. I was glad when the whole ordeal was over.

SIX

A NEW ERA

Warden Al C. Parke was the deputy commissioner of the Kentucky Department of Corrections before coming to the penitentiary in 1981 as warden. He held a coveted position that many wardens aspired to, including Warden Sowders. It was always Sowders' dream to serve as deputy commissioner. Why, I'm not sure. I turned down the position several times later in my career. Sowders made some very powerful political friends in Frankfort. He played all the right cards to secure a promotion to deputy commissioner. I know this because I was his right-hand man and his administrative assistant for the three years he was warden. Al Parke was the opposite when it came to playing politics. He did not like the game. Instead, he relied on his education, professional experience, and reputation.

Sowders had the experience and reputation, but lacked higher education. For some reason, Sowders hated to attend training sessions. Later in my career, I was deputy warden of security at Northpoint

Training Center, where Sowders had been demoted back to warden. In my seven years of working closely with Sowders, I never knew him to attend much training. If he did go to a convention or training session, he would slip off at the first break, not to be seen again. How he got by with this attitude is a credit to his humor and charm. Sowders' superiors never held him accountable for the gaps in his training or slowed his career advancement, even though he never attended the minimum of forty hours of in-service training each year. Go figure.

Reluctantly, Al Parke accepted the demotion to warden at KSP, and Sowders assumed the position of deputy commissioner. As Sowders' righthand man, this left me in an awkward position because Warden Parke made it clear that he did not need an administrative assistant. During our first meeting, he assured me that he would find another position for me to continue my career. In short order, I applied for the position of program director and was selected. The job came with a nice pay raise. I supervised all inmate programs, including legal services, job assignments, and religious services, and I served as chairperson of the Classification and Adjustment Committees. I also wrote new procedures for the programs I oversaw in the prison. The experience I gained through this position would help prepare me for the next step in my career as deputy warden.

Warden Parke immediately set out to transform KSP and bring it out of the Dark Ages. Under all the previous wardens, there had been very few written policies and internal directives. Whenever the administration wanted to change a policy or procedure, a memo was simply issued with the warden's signature. This had the same effect as law. Violate this memo, and you might be fired. The problem is that staff would misplace an older memo or not even be aware the warden had issued one. It was a very haphazard and ineffective way to manage the prison. Warden Parke set out to develop written policies and procedures in all areas of the prison operation—a massive undertaking. I think I wrote the very first procedure for the inmate property operation. This is where we would store an inmate's property while he was hospitalized, away on a court trip, or until he was released from segregation. There were always lawsuits in small claims court alleging we misplaced or lost something belonging to an inmate. Prior to the policy, there had not been a formal procedure for officers to follow when it was necessary to store inmate's property.

Warden Al Parke read the procedure I had written and signed it right away. He now had a model policy to show staff how it was done. Parke began giving assignments to department heads, pushing them to draft policies for his signature. At the same time, he established a procedures office and tapped Jack Wood to head up this monumental task. Jack had practiced law before coming to KSP, and he was a perfect fit for the position. KSP began to run more efficiently, and people took notice. In just a few short years, we were ready to be accredited by the American Correctional Association, thanks to the leadership of Warden Parke.

Warden Parke was educated, experienced, and was a proven leader at several institutions before running KSP. At thirty-six, he was the youngest warden in the history of the Castle. He also had a master's degree in psychology. For the next three years, Warden Parke led KSP through some of the most tumultuous events in the prison's history. Warden Parke had to move quickly to develop policies and procedures while setting a goal to have the prison accredited by the American Correctional Association. An enormous task to take on, especially as he oversaw the implementation of the Consent Decree. Several major construction projects commenced, including the renovation of Five Cell House. And to top it off, several horrific and dire events occurred around the same time in rapid succession.

Warden Parke's first six months were marked by a major arson fire that destroyed the furniture plant. He had only been the warden for about two weeks before an arsonist started the blaze. Thankfully, all the inmates managed to escape the fire and were placed back on the yard. We suspected the fire could have been a diversion for an escape attempt or a takeover. I was on the yard giving a tour of KSP to three attorneys from Frankfort when this happened. As I was leading the tour, I spotted smoke suddenly rising behind four wall stand, and I knew the fire was in the furniture plant. Without any way of knowing whether it was safe to return the visitors to the administration building where our tour began, I made the decision to shelter them in the prison hospital. They would be safe there, and I would be free to respond to the emergency. Deputy Warden Mike Samburg radioed me and asked me to retrieve the video camera and film the event—and whatever else developed. I positioned myself on four wall stand with a good view of the furniture plant and the prison yard. The inmates were following instructions to go back to their cells. In any kind of disturbance, the first order of business is to "ring the bell," which was the signal to lock down. Most inmates always complied with lockdown orders, not wanting to get in trouble. Any inmates that did not comply would have to be dealt with. Everyone was on full alert. All the gun tower officers were positioned on the catwalk, with rifles locked and loaded.

KSP had an old firetruck that would run, and someone, I believe Billy Baker or Jerry Phelps, hooked it to a fire hydrant and pressurized a long fire hose. I was filming as responders held the hose nozzle, but only a trickle of water squirted from the hose. More impressive was the sight of the hose bursting in five or six places along its length. Nobody had ever bothered to check the thing, and it had dry rotted. Worthless. I couldn't help but chuckle as I filmed the debacle. By then, the furniture plant was completely engulfed. A volunteer fire department was called from nearby Eddyville, but it was too late. The most they could do was contain the blaze and keep it from spreading to the garment factory. Fortunately, the inmates didn't have plans to attempt an escape or takeover. We were lucky.

Several hours later, as things began to calm down, I remembered the attorneys I had stowed away in the safety of the prison hospital. "Oh, shit!" I muttered as I made my way back to them. When I arrived, the nurses told me they had escorted them to the administration building after the inmates were safely locked down. This was just the first of several events that marked Warden Parke's first six months.

Warden Parke handled the prison fire like a pro, using the event as a learning lesson.

In the follow-up investigation of the fire, we learned that an inmate set the fire to a trashcan in the lumber storage area, not thinking it would be a big conflagration. For whatever reason, he wanted to get off work early, and a fire, he reasoned, would shut down the plant for the afternoon. Unfortunately, it was a very windy day, and the small trash fire quickly spiraled out of control and engulfed the dry lumber.

The fire was just the start of Warden Parke's headaches. It was as if he was being tested. As the new man in charge, perhaps he was. Soon afterward, we experienced several escapes. Johnny Johnson escaped from the industries area, and Larry Dale broke out from One Cell House. Inmates Bobby Cole and Johnny Sullivan escaped from Five Cell House, which had been closed for remodeling.

During Warden Parke's first six months, there were also three inmate murders, a hostage situation, and a staff murder. Even in a place as eventful as the Castle, this was over the top. Parke had more setbacks during his first six months than I had in twelve years as the warden. None of it was the result of Parke's leadership, however. In fact, quite the opposite—he excelled at leading us through these events. Human behavior is unpredictable. One never knows what is in store at a maximum security prison. Warden Parke would always carefully analyze these events afterward and use them as a learning tool to implement new procedures that improved the safety and security of KSP for all involved.

ONE WARDEN TO ANOTHER

In September of 1987, Warden Bill Seabold reluctantly accepted the wardenship at KSP, replacing Gene Scroggy. Scroggy had been at the helm for about three years, which was roughly the average term for a warden at a maximum security prison.

Warden Scroggy had seen his share of problems. His predecessor, Al Parke, had transformed the penitentiary into an accredited institution despite a term hampered by escapes, inmate murders, hostage situations, and the murder of an employee. He handled each incident with the confidence of a pro. Unlike Parke, Warden Scroggy came from outside the Kentucky system. Most of his corrections experience stemmed from his time as a commanding officer in a Marine Corp military brig, as well as some civilian experience in a civilian jail.

Staff at the penitentiary was a combination of retired military veterans with combat experience and a larger percentage of civilians with no military experience. The veterans understood Scroggy and his no-nonsense demeanor. At times he treated staff like marine recruits, dressing them down or making insulting remarks. At other times, he could be genuine and helpful. He was never bashful about making decisions, and he looked for innovative ways to make progress with programs and security.

Unfortunately, his approach didn't work with civilians. Once line staff are insulted or talked down to several times, they feel defeated and give up. They resort to doing the minimum amount necessary to get through each day. Scroggy's approach led to poor morale, and it quickly became contagious. Staff felt beaten down and welcomed a change in leadership.

Warden Seabold's management style was the polar opposite of Scroggy's. He was experienced, friendly to all staff, and could relate well with inmates. He was also a disciplinarian when he needed to be. Staff respected and liked him. Morale began to improve.

As fate would have it, Seabold had been warden for less than a year when the worst escape in Kentucky Corrections history occurred. The date was June 16, 1988.

Everyone who has worked up through the ranks in a prison system knows that a new warden has a "honeymoon" period the first year. He needs time to learn the ins and outs of the prison, who he can trust, who works hard and who doesn't. Each prison has its own personality and set of quirky traditions. There is always a learning curve at a new institution. Warden Seabold was in his "honeymoon" period when the escape of 1988 occurred. It immediately made national headlines and was quite obviously a huge embarrassment to Kentucky.

Warden Scroggy was long gone and bore no responsibility for what happened. Warden Seabold hadn't been at the helm long enough to make changes that could have prevented a total breakdown of security. So it was difficult to pin the blame for this disaster on any one person.

In the aftermath of the event, it was determined that staff error led to the escape. Quite simply, staff members in key positions at multiple levels simply weren't doing their jobs. Procedures were in place to prevent escapes, but they had not been diligently followed. Complacency had taken over. Staff assaults, drugs, gang problems, suicide attempts, and fights were still commonplace. Morale was improving under Warden Seabold's leadership, but the process took time.

It was common knowledge at the time that an inmate on the yard could obtain a prison-made knife. You just needed to know who could sell you a knife, and you had to pay up front, usually in the form of cigarettes. (This was long before tobacco was outlawed in prisons.) Selling knives was a racket, similar to selling drugs or arranging for a male prostitute. If there was money to be made involving one of the many prison vices, someone would step up and fill the role. Inmates ended up controlling the prison yard instead of staff. In an unhealthy work environment, staff could grow numb to all this. Low morale led to employees ignoring minor problems until they became major crises. This was the climate at KSP as Warden Seabold took over. His honeymoon was about to come to a screeching halt.

BREAKDOWN IN SECURITY

A perfect storm of circumstances led to the mass escape of June 16, 1988. Staff handled matters reactively rather than proactively. Drugs, weapons, and assaults were commonplace. In Three Cell House, the 156-bed segregation unit, chaos was the rule rather than the exception, arguably more so than when I was a fish guard in 1978. Now everything was videotaped, unlike the old days when the only record of prison incidents involved eyewitnesses and written reports. New procedures were implemented that governed all use of force.

Use of force in segregation had become more predictable. Inmates soon learned what we could and could not do to quell a disturbance. We could not predict what the inmates would do, but they could predict how we would react. Gone were the days when we could respond quickly and proportionately to violent behavior.

In 1978, an inmate wouldn't dare throw feces or urine in an officer's face. It never happened while I was an officer, but in 1988, it was occurring more frequently. We didn't have procedures in place to deal with these situations in 1978, and our response could be swift and unpredictable. A decade later, there was a prescribed procedure to deal with inmate behavior, but there was no longer any deterrent. The consequences were predictable, and inmates knew they could get away with more. It was not until the local commonwealth attorney, G.L. Ovey, pushed for legislative changes to make prison staff assault a felony that inmates once again considered the consequences of their actions. These legislative changes would take several years to enact. In the meantime, assaults continued and steadily grew worse.

A strong, by-the-book correctional officer posed a threat to inmates who did not like authority. Though it may seem counterintuitive in retrospect, one way to get rid of these alpha officers was to pummel them with food or feces. There wasn't a lot an officer could do, so often he would request reassignment to another part of the prison—or quit. Staff learned, perhaps subconsciously, to get through each shift without making enemies. Rules were not enforced. Over time, counts were not taken properly, and security checks were not performed. If an officer performed his duties haphazardly, the inmates stopped behaving badly, which made the officer look like he was getting along and doing a good job. In this way, inmates manipulated those who worked in their units right under the nose of supervision.

For at least two months, inmates had been laying the groundwork for their escape. The plan was to manipulate staff assignments so that aggressive, by-the-book officers worked elsewhere in the prison, leaving more complacent staff to work segregation. Inmates also secured a steady supply of hacksaw blades, which they smuggled into their unit slowly to avoid detection. And finally, the perpetrators made sure that only inmates they could trust were in their unit on Eleven Walk and Thirteen Walk in Three Cell House. Any inmate suspected of being a rat would be assaulted during exercise periods. Staff would relocate the injured individual to another part of the prison, away from the conflict. In retrospect, it was appallingly easy for inmates to manipulate cell assignments by simply assaulting their peers if they were suspected informants. Inmates even recruited other strong but trusted inmates to violate prison rules, so they would be moved to the hole in Three Cell House. Once in segregation, they would get moved to Eleven or Twelve Left Walk to become part of the escape plot. It took at least two months to manipulate the system and coordinate everything before the real work began: cutting their way to freedom.

Hacksaw blades were broken into three-inch pieces and smuggled into Three Cell House either by inmate legal aides, who were approved to represent inmates in disciplinary proceedings, or by taping them to the bottom of food containers sent to segregation for each meal. Once the hacksaw blades made it inside Three Cell House, they made their way to one of the designated inmates. A three-inch blade would be heated with a cigarette lighter and fused to a plastic toothbrush handle, creating a perfect tool for cutting through bars.

Several years earlier, KSP inmates had learned how to make small cuts on the door track at the bottom of each cell door, which would allow the door to hinge out from the top track. Once the metal holding the bottom of the door in place was cut, the door would still open and close as it was supposed to, but it would *also* swing *outward*. The only way to detect that the door track had been cut was with a mirror fashioned on the end of a rod. Officers knew that this was a possibility— and they were supposed to use the stick-and-mirror approach to check for cuts each day. But morale was poor, and officers used a minimal amount of effort to make it through each shift. Cell door tracks were not being checked, even though officers signed a form each day indicating that these security checks had been completed.

Officers were also required to "beat the bars" by taking a rubber mallet and hitting each cell bar. If a bar had been cut or compromised, it would sound different. This was an effective technique for singling out cell bars that had been compromised—but it was very labor intensive and time consuming. Beating the bars was required on each shift. It was one of those things that just didn't get done, especially if there were distractions like fights, suicide attempts, and so on occurring elsewhere.

At the time of the escape, seventeen out of twenty cell doors had been cut with hacksaw blades in Twelve Walk, so that the door would hinge outward but still appear to be operational and secure. A simple security inspection would have deterred this breach, but the inmates knew that staff simply was not paying attention.

In addition to poor staff morale and a failure to perform basic security duties, other factors came into play. Supervision and management also suffered from burnout. More and more demands were being placed on supervisors by the warden and deputy warden of security. Management of the segregation unit was a combination of security and program staff. A captain was assigned to the day shift. A lieutenant and sergeant were assigned to all three shifts. For the most part, security supervisors were competent—especially on the day shift. But it was a demanding responsibility. Daily schedules consisted of exercise outside the cell, mail call, sick call, showers, committee meetings, and haircuts that consumed almost every hour of the day. Then there were three meals to pass out. On top of all these activities, there were the constant disturbances: inmates flooding the walk by deliberately stopping up their commodes, inmates setting fires, fighting during recreation periods, assaulting staff with urine and feces, and more. Occasionally inmates would cut themselves to initiate a trip to the hospital, just so they could get the attention of nurses. There were also suicide attempts. All these incidents required a tremendous amount of paperwork, which was scrutinized by the warden and deputy warden. The workload for all staff assigned to Three Cell House was almost impossible. Things were left unfinished, neglected, and ignored. Unfortunately, security inspections were one of those things.

Jack Wood oversaw the segregation unit in Three Cell House. His official position was unit manager, and his background and experience at KSP was on the program side. Wood had a law degree, though he had long ago given up the practice of law. He was intelligent and very capable and administered the various schedules, classification committees, and mountains of paperwork effectively. Although Wood was technically in charge of all aspects of the unit, the security of the unit was overseen by a captain. In addition, there were lieutenants and sergeants assigned to each shift who should have foreseen the mounting security problems. Furthermore, breakdown in security should have been resolved by a sergeant or lieutenant. Wood couldn't do it all, and he had to depend on security staff to do their job. Unfortunately, they dropped the ball.

SHOOTOUT ON THE PARKWAY

I'll come back to the Great Escape of 1988 later. This was hardly the first time a group of KSP inmates tried to break free from the Castle during my tenure. One of the most infamous incidents in the prison's history, in fact, occurred less than a decade earlier. October 13, 1980, started like any other day at KSP. The night before had been quiet, and everyone was hoping for an uneventful day. Plans had been made in advance to pick up thirteen troublemakers from KSR in the new "short bus." The new bus could transport up to fifteen inmates and still have room for an extra officer to ride shotgun in the front passenger seat.

Officer Richardville was appointed to the transfer team that fateful day. He had a reputation as a reliable officer and a levelheaded member of the E-Squad. Warden Sowders called him into the office and told him to supervise the trip to KSR to transport thirteen inmates back to the penitentiary. Officers Sidney McDaniels and Buck Owens were to assist in the transfer.

Officer Richardville warned Sowders that the bus wasn't ready because the bus had not yet been fitted with security screens and bars over the windows. Sowders rebuffed his officer, saying if Richardville didn't have the balls to do the job, he would find someone else. That's all it took for Richardville to acquiesce and hightail it out of the warden's office. Everyone knew not to challenge Warden Sowders. He could be ruthless if he was questioned—a personality flaw that would come back to haunt him and those who followed his orders.

Early the next morning, the three officers reported in and began gathering all the shackles and handcuffs they would need for the trip. All three officers would be armed. Officer Owens would drive the bus, armed with a standard issue .38 revolver. Officer McDaniels checked out a .38 revolver, as did Officer Richardville. For whatever reason, they decided not to bring a shotgun or extra ammunition. Speed loaders for the .38 revolvers were available but not required. Officer Richardville was tasked with driving a Ford passenger van to serve as a chase car and to haul the inmates' property. It was standard practice to use a chase car if it was a high-security transport of more than two prisoners. All in all, it was a routine transportation trip, save for the new, poorly outfitted bus.

Later that morning at KSR, thirteen inmates were loaded on the new bus, and duffel bags with all the inmate property were loaded in the van. Under normal circumstances, the transportation of inmates was executed at a high speed of at least eighty miles per hour on the Western Kentucky Parkway. Occasionally a Crown Victoria cruiser would reach speeds of ninety miles per hour. We were trained to not allow cars to pass or pull up beside us if we were transporting high-security prisoners. But the bus in this case could only reach speeds of sixty-five to seventy miles per hour safely—and that was traveling downhill. Going uphill, the bus would slow to a relative crawl of fifty or sixty miles per hour.

Officer Owens, the bus driver, was an older man approaching sixty-one years of age from Cadiz, Kentucky. He was a hard worker who would do his best at any assignment delegated to him. Owens was liked and respected by staff and inmates. Officer McDaniels was thirty years old, from the nearby town of Princeton, Kentucky. McDaniels was a quiet man, both mild-mannered and friendly. Like Owens, he took his job seriously, though he did not fit the mold as a rough-and-tumble prison guard. All three men projected dependability and professionalism. They would do their jobs to the best of their ability.

The bus was loaded with the typical problem inmates: some with life sentences and others who wanted to be transferred to the penitentiary just to make a name for themselves as tough convicts. Some inmates would punch a staff member at a medium-security prison just to earn a trip to the Castle. At the other end of the spectrum were inmates who were scared to death of what might await them at KSP.

The trip between KSR in LaGrange and KSP in Eddyville was a little over two hundred miles and would take about four hours. With a loaded bus that traveled more slowly, the entire ordeal could take even longer.

After driving through Louisville and the short distance to Elizabethtown on I-65, the caravan headed west on the parkway. It would have to stop several times at tollbooths, but the traffic was normally very light. At times traveling the parkway, you wouldn't see a car in either direction even though it was a modern, four-lane highway. The road meandered through the hills and valleys of central and western Kentucky. It was an easy, often boring drive.

Sometime after the bus left LaGrange, one of the inmates produced a handcuff key he had concealed in his mouth. In short order, inmates Gene Harpool, John Batowsky, and Raymond Helm freed themselves from their restraints. Harpool was a forty-four-year-old career criminal with a forty-year sentence for robbery, malicious shooting, and assault. John Batowsky was fifty-four, serving sixteen years for possession of burglary tools, storehouse-breaking, promoting contraband, and escape. Raymond Helm was thirty-one, serving ten years for robbery. From their position at the back of the bus, it was easy for the inmates to key open their handcuffs, belly chains, and leg shackles without being noticed. Just after passing the Beaver Dam exit, they made their move. It was still a two-hour drive until the parkway ended near the town of Eddyville then just a few additional miles to the Castle.

All three transportation officers had strip-searched, cuffed, and shackled each inmate prior to departing from KSR. The only way an inmate can beat a strip-search is to place a handcuff key in his mouth or rectum. Typically, drugs would be placed in small balloons and keistered. More than likely, a handcuff key would be concealed in the mouth between the gum and cheek. During a strip-search, an inmate is required to bend over and cough while the officer visually inspects his rectum, then the inmate is required to face the officer and open his mouth, and then raise his tongue. It is not foolproof, but it is about all that can be done short of using a gloved hand to probe those areas. Typically, a body-cavity search requires a court order based on probable cause.

A subsequent investigation determined inmate Batowsky had made a cuff key from scrap material he somehow obtained at KSR. He hid the key in his mouth carefully enough to evade detection and used it to free himself on the parkway. Batowsky then slipped the key to Harpool and Helm.

Once freed of their restraints, the three inmates staged a fight then overpowered Officer McDaniels when he responded to the back of the bus. Harpool grabbed his gun and shot him in the stomach. The bullet entered his stomach, ricocheted around his rib cage, then exited and lodged in his right arm. Wounded and unarmed, he was helpless. Next the gun was turned on Officer Owens, who by that time was making an emergency stop. Another shot rang out, and Officer Owens was shot in the face. The bullet entered his cheek and blew out most of the roof of his mouth.

Officer Richardville, in the chase car, knew something was wrong. The bus was weaving all over the road as Harpool pulled Officer Owens from the driver's seat and commandeered the bus. Then the bus stopped, and Richardville watched as Officers Owens and McDaniels were thrown out the door.

Both men were writhing on the side of the road in mortal agony, unsure if they were about to die. Owens was on the ground, but he managed to stand up. About that time, he felt the bullet in his mouth and spit it out. He was bleeding profusely, as was McDaniels. Neither would survive long without emergency medical intervention.

The entire ordeal lasted less than a minute, and the bus sped off—

but not before inmate Batowsky jumped from the vehicle and started running across an open field.

Stunned at what was unfolding before him, Officer Richardville watched as Batowsky took off running. He lowered the passenger window in his car and fired one shot at Batowsky, but it was too late. The escapee was already out of range. Richardville quickly turned his attention to Officers Owens and McDaniels. Owens was waving his pistol, saying, "Go get them! We will get help."

Officer McDaniels agreed, mumbling, "I'm okay. Just go get them."

Richardville made the gut-wrenching decision to leave his wounded colleagues to fend for themselves and pursue the remaining twelve inmates. Inmates who now had an escape vehicle and a gun.

Richardville had no way of knowing how many inmates were out of their restraints—perhaps all of them. All he knew for sure was that two of his fellow officers had been shot, perhaps fatally, and a group of violent criminals were now on the lam. Nothing like this, on a scale this large, had ever happened before in Kentucky. A few inmates had escaped while on court or hospital trips, but never thirteen inmates at once. Richardville was now on his own. It was up to him to stop the escape or die trying.

A mile or two down the parkway, the chase car caught up with the transport bus. As Richardville closed in on the vehicle, he watched it suddenly slow and cross the median. It was now heading eastbound, back toward Elizabethtown and Louisville. The bus was loaded and sluggish, and Richardville decided to try to get in front of it and force it to stop. Easier said than done. While Richardville could easily pass them, the bus was swerving badly, trying to force him off the road.

After several miles of this, Richardville managed to pull up close just as inmate Helm shot two rounds through the back window of the bus. One shot penetrated the right side of the hood on the passenger side. The next shot was dead on. It hit the windshield just above the steering wheel. Richardville ducked just in time, narrowly avoiding being struck in the face. He was busy trying to get a shot off at Helm, but it was too risky. There was a good possibility that Richardville would shoot an uninvolved inmate. He just couldn't get a clear shot with the bus weaving back and forth.

As Richardville kept up his pursuit, a badly wounded Officer Owens flagged down the first car that came along. A middle-aged lady in a late-model Cadillac slowed as she approached, trying to piece together what she was looking at. She stopped, rolled down her window, and before she could say anything, Owens told her they were both shot and needed an ambulance. He just wanted her to get to the nearest telephone and call for help. (This was a world before every man, woman, and child carried cell phones in their back pockets.) Owens wasn't expecting this stranger to do more than call for help.

"Get in," she said.

Officer Owens thought for a second, looked over at Officer McDaniels laying on the ground, and said, "Okay."

After helping McDaniels into the back seat and sitting down, he was close to passing out. The Good Samaritan told them she was taking them to the nearest hospital, which turned out to be nearby Ohio County Hospital in Hartford, Kentucky. She made sure both officers got to the emergency room, then she left, probably to go wash the bloodstains off her white leather seats. Owens and McDaniels never knew her name, but she was a genuine hero. Her actions saved both officers from bleeding to death. Owens would later express regret that they bled all over her beautiful Cadillac.

Officer McDaniels underwent five hours of surgery to repair internal damage, and Officer Owens required reconstructive surgery and a long, agonizing recovery period. Both were fortunate to be alive.

As Officer Richardville chased the inmates down the parkway, the frantic bus driver began to swerve more and more erratically in an attempt to force Richardville off the road. The inmate's maneuvers backfired. The bus hit a guard rail and careened down a steep embankment, rolling over in the process. When the bus finally came to a stop on its side, two inmates, Gene Harpool and Raymond Helm, crawled out of the wreckage and began running away.

Richardville got out of his car at the top of the bluff, looking past the guardrail and down at the bus wreckage. He quickly drew his gun and fired a single shot at the escaping inmates. Inmate Helm stopped dead in his tracks and put his hands up. Harpool kept running and was quickly out of range. Helm slowly walked back to the wreckage, hands in the air, as the other inmates struggled to escape the overturned bus. They were all still in full restraints. Now Officer Richardville had to find a set of restraints for Helm and help rescue inmates from the wreck. Smoke began wafting out of the damaged front end of the bus, and within a minute or two, the front was fully engulfed in flames. The fire quickly spread to the bus interior.

Most of the ten remaining inmates were out of the bus as Richardville cuffed Helm with his hands behind his back and ordered him to lay face down on the ground. Once Helm was secure, Officer Richardville looked in the bus and saw four injured inmates, including one who was unconscious. The fire was engulfing the vehicle quickly, and there was no time to waste.

Richardville now faced another life-and-death decision. He was holding a group of men at gunpoint, but several more were in imminent danger. Luckily, he knew two of the inmates: Thomas Brown and Clay Ambrose. He told Brown and Ambrose to step forward and said, "I need someone to go in and pull those inmates out."

"No problem, boss. We can do it," Ambrose replied. Still holding his gun, Officer Richardville used his cuff key to uncuff Brown and Ambrose, leaving them in shackles. He still had not recovered Officer McDaniels' firearm, but he didn't have time to worry about that now. Every second counted. One by one, Brown and Ambrose pulled all four inmates from the burning bus. All four had sustained cuts and bruises when the bus rolled over. They were not able to brace themselves for impact because of the restraints.

The last man pulled out of the bus was inmate Bobby Ross, age forty-five, serving a life sentence for murder. He was unconscious and had multiple contusions. Richardville didn't think Ross would make it. Inmate Wilson, serving time for receiving stolen property and a string of other crimes, was also severely injured, but he was conscious and talking. Two other inmates suffered burns on their arms and faces, but their injuries were not serious.

Once the four inmates were pulled to safety, Richardville placed Brown and Ambrose back in cuffs and thanked them for their help. Now it was just a matter of waiting for the state police and ambulance.

The inmates had made their way up the embankment and were sitting on the ground, propped up against the guardrail. Bobby Ross, the most severely injured, was carried up the embankment by Brown and Ambrose. The fire continued to spread, and a plume of thick, black smoke could be seen for miles in every direction. Drivers were beginning to slow and stare, but no one came close or offered assistance. A Department of Transportation officer was first on the scene, and he called in to radio dispatch for ambulances and backup. The Ohio County Sheriff's Office and the state police responded within minutes.

Ross and Wilson were transported to the nearby hospital where Officers Owens and McDaniels were being treated for gunshot wounds. The remaining nine inmates were transported to the Ohio County Jail temporarily until KSP could arrange transportation to Eddyville.

Once all the inmates were in the custody of the state police and sheriff's department, one of the sheriff's deputies took Officer Richardville to a nearby rest stop to call KSP and report the incident.

The state police immediately began a manhunt for Harpool and Batowsky. Warden Sowders sent all available staff and supervisors to the scene to assist in the manhunt.

Despite a massive ground search involving the state police, a police aircraft, and KSP staff, there was no sign of the two escaped inmates for several days. The search expanded to a heavy patrol of the surrounding area. Still, nothing.

Then suddenly, on Thursday, October 16, 1988, three days after the escape, Gene Harpool was spotted hitchhiking on Highway 70 about four miles east of Morgantown. He was taken into custody without incident by the sheriff's department. Harpool was held in the Ohio County Jail until KSP could come take custody. Batowsky, meanwhile, was still on the lam. There had been no sightings—not even a single lead. Authorities believed he was traveling on foot, at night, and would try to steal a car to get further away if given the chance. Yet no cars in the area were reported stolen. Law enforcement was stumped. After a prolonged effort, they suspended their manhunt.

Bobby Ross, the most severely injured inmate, was transferred to Caldwell County Hospital in Princeton so that KSP could post a guard by his bed 24/7. After his condition failed to improve, he was moved to Lourdes Hospital in Paducah. Ross eventually recovered, but it was a long, hard road. Officer Owens never returned to work and took an early retirement. Officer McDaniels did report back to KSP following his recovery, but an ongoing bout with "nerves" forced him to retire soon after. These were the days before post-traumatic stress disorder (PTSD) was a recognized medical condition.

Fast-forward to February 5, 1995, almost fifteen years after the bus escape. I had been the warden at KSP for two years. Vicki Patton, my secretary, was exceptionally good at screening calls and always knew which ones to prioritize or reroute to my office. Vicki had served as the warden's secretary for six of the previous administrations, and she had mastered the job long before I arrived on the scene.

I always knew from Vicki's demeanor whether a phone call was serious enough to answer immediately. She said, "Phil, you need to take this call from the state police. It's about an escaped inmate." My mind raced. Did KSP have an escapee that I did not know about? It had been a normal day. The count had cleared before the day started. An escaped inmate?

I answered the phone in my usual tone. "Warden Parker. May I help you?"

Lt. David Osborne from the Henderson State Police Post said, "Warden, your escaped inmate has been found."

I told him he must be mistaken because no one had escaped from KSP. He replied that they had found John Batowsky, now age sixty-nine, after he died from a heart attack in Jacksonville, Florida. I didn't recognize the name, so I repeated that no one had escaped from KSP and assured Osborne that I would know about it if somebody had. I think he was being patient with me, but I was getting a little agitated. Then it hit me like a ton of bricks. "Wait a minute. You mean the inmate who got away in the bus incident, all those years ago?" Osborne confirmed that was the one. We both got a chuckle out of it. I told him I would note this in our records, and I didn't guess there was anything else to do at that point.

According to Lt. Osborne, Batowsky had been living under an assumed name and was identified by his fingerprints. After his name was run through the nationwide computer system, it came back as wanted, and Florida officials notified the Kentucky State Police. We will never know how he made his getaway and how he managed to remain under the radar. He never had so much as a speeding ticket after the escape. To my knowledge, Batowsky was the only successful escape in the history of Kentucky State Penitentiary.

Several policy changes were instituted in the wake of this horrific ordeal. One was the use of "black boxes," or handcuff covers, to prevent the use of a handcuff key until after the black box cover was removed. The black box covered the handcuffs, and it was padlocked. It essentially provided an extra layer of security. Most transportation of maximum security inmates would now require the use of a black box at the supervisor's discretion. Another change was that all maximum security transports of two or more inmates would now require a minimum of two officers. For the transfer of four or more individuals, a chase car is automatically added to the convoy. The transport of a death-row inmate to court or a hospital now usually involves a supervisor driving a lead car, followed by two officers in the transport car, and a chase car bringing up the rear. The route is meticulously planned before the trip, sometimes utilizing backroads.

In addition to increased security during transportation, all transport vehicles must have a security screen, and the back seat must have the childproof locks activated.

Officer Richardville, a.k.a. Hooterville, continued his career and earned the rank of sergeant. The shootout would not be his last life-or-death incident. He always used good judgment, and his knowledge of inmates proved to be an asset his entire tenure, until his retirement in 2006.

I asked Richardville how he got the nickname "Hooterville," which stayed with him his entire career. He explained that when he started in 1976, he was early to work one morning before roll call, when Captain Alexander asked where he was from. Before he could answer, someone said Hopkinsville, someone else said Lynnville, and still another colleague said Nashville. Captain Alexander looked around, smiled, and said, "Oh, well, hell. He's from Hooterville." The name stuck.

THE JOE CRAIG INCIDENT

Officer Richardville found himself facing another life-or-death decision soon after the events on the Western Kentucky Parkway. As a result of his heroic actions during the bus incident, Richardville was permanently assigned to transportation if he wanted the job. He accepted the challenge. Following roll call, on an otherwise normal day later that same year, Richardville started preparing for a court trip. He was to take inmate Joe Craig to the Lyon County Courthouse for a hearing on pending charges. Joe Craig was a dangerous inmate. He was one of the hostage takers who had taken over the prison canteen several years earlier. After serving a year or so in segregation, he was returned to general population. Then he escaped from Four Cell House, along with two other inmates. This was my first day as a correctional officer in July 1978. Once he was captured and returned, Craig was assigned to the Administrative Control Unit (ACU). The ACU housed the worst of the worst. This unit only allowed one hour a day out of the cell, to mill around on the walk. It was higher security than death row.

Fast-forward to 1980. Knowing he had a court trip that day, Craig had time to plan an escape. He managed to fashion a crude but effective soap gun, which he either (1) had planted in the transport vehicle ahead of time, or (2) taped to the back of his head, concealed in his shoulder-length hair. (In the early 1980s, inmates were still permitted to grow their hair as long as they wanted. They could also wear personal clothing, even in segregation.) During the short six-mile ride to the courthouse, he managed to slip his handcuffs off, but not his shackles. His plan was to pull the gun on the officer as he opened the car door to escort him to the courtroom. Once he had the officer at gun point, he would take his gun, grab his handcuff keys to release the shackles, and steal the vehicle. He would either kill the officer on the spot or put him in the backseat as a hostage.

The plan almost worked, but he underestimated his escort that day: Officer Richardville.

Richardville had two options when he saw the realistic-looking gun pointed at his stomach as Craig got out of the car. He could fight and probably take a bullet, or he could surrender and give inmate Craig his gun and car. Richardville's instincts kicked in. He fought for a second before he realized that what Craig was holding was a soap gun. Not taking any chances, Richardville pulled his revolver and put it to Craig's head. "I will kill you, motherfucker!" he snapped. Craig knew Richardville was not bluffing. He handed Craig the handcuffs and told him to put them on. Craig did as he was told as Richardville aimed the gun at his head. At that point, Richardville had to make another decision. Did he escort Craig on to the courtroom, or did he take him back to KSP? With adrenaline still coursing through his veins, Richardville thought, *What the hell. We're here. We might as well go on.*

Gun still drawn, he told Craig to proceed to the courtroom and warned he would shoot if the inmate tried anything else.

Once they arrived at the double glass entry doors to the courthouse, Craig hesitated as though he was about to try something else. Richardville encouraged him forward with a firm shove on the shoulder. Craig could not catch himself as he stumbled from the push, and he fell face first through the glass door, shattering it. Now Richardville had to take him back, if for no other reason than to treat Craig's face lacerations.

Warden Sowders assigned me to investigate this incident, to make security recommendations based on my findings, and to possibly recommend disciplinary action for the officer on duty.

Given the totality of the circumstances, I could not in good conscience recommend disciplinary action for Officer Richardville. While he may have pushed inmate Craig a little too forcefully when the latter hesitated at the door, Craig was lucky to be alive. Second-guessing an officer's actions in a life-and-death situation is never straightforward. In the end, my recommendation was to give Richardville a commendation. As best I can recall, Warden Sowders just let the entire incident go, and Richardville remained on his transportation assignment.

We never could determine with certainty whether the soap gun was planted in the car prior to the trip or if it was concealed under Craig's long hair. It could have been either. The car was not examined prior to departure. Searching transport vehicles prior to any trip, even short ones to a local courthouse, was added to the security procedure. My best guess was that the soap gun was fashioned by Craig in Three Cell

House then moved in the only place that offered concealment, his long hair.

I recommended to Warden Sowders that we institute a new policy requiring all inmates to have a haircut of no longer than two inches. Sowders disagreed and dismissed my recommendation, but I later implemented it when I became warden.

This would hardly be the last time that Sowders and I would fail to see eye to eye during our long and colorful careers.

SEVEN

MURDER AND MAYHEM

As a maximum security prison, the Castle has always been a dumping ground for all the misfits, gang members, protective custody inmates, and generally dangerous criminals facing lengthy sentences. To borrow a phrase from Obi-Wan Kenobi in *Star Wars*, you will never find a more wretched hive of scum and villainy anywhere in the universe than the motley crew of inmates at KSP. It has been this way throughout the history of Kentucky's corrections system.

Once a recalcitrant convict reached KSP, he would find himself among others who were just as bad or worse. There was always someone tougher and meaner there. The Department of Corrections' leadership had no qualms with allowing other prisons to transfer sworn enemies to KSP together. Once at the Castle, we did our best to quickly evaluate an inmate's potential for violence or his need for protective custody. Most of the time, we were very successful in managing all the problem inmates, including all the conflicts that arose from day to day. Yet, despite our best efforts, violence could still erupt at any time, leaving someone critically wounded—or dead.

In 1981, some of the cell blocks were still double celled due to over-crowding in the prison system. A new prison was in the works, which was later built in eastern Kentucky. The commonwealth was considering contracting with several private companies to build new facilities then manage the prisons. Private prisons were more economical, and several states had already paved the way.

Meanwhile, because of overcrowding and double celling at the penitentiary, prison life grew more violent than ever. A new breed of inmates arrived with every busload. Urban street gangs were popping up in Louisville and Lexington. White supremacist gangs thrived in rural communities like Harlan County, Kentucky, and the Hatfield and McCoy territory of Appalachia. While each region boasted its own distinct culture, identity, and set of traditions, people everywhere struggled to escape the clutches of poverty and drug addiction. And sadly, many succumbed to this struggle and ended up behind bars.

These diverse groups were confined to a relatively small area inside prisons like KSP. To say that the urban black gang members and the rural white inmates were intolerant of each other would be a gross understatement. It was like mixing oil and water. Their close proximity created a hostile and often violent environment in prison.

The days of racial segregation were gone, but there was no way we could house these vastly different and violent groups together in shared cells. Housing inmates of different backgrounds together inside a prison was one thing, but forcing inmates into cells together, without regard to their race or creed, was a recipe for disaster.

We did our best to sort out inmates to be housed together in cells designed for single occupancy. The solution was relatively simple. Like-minded men should share cells. Even despite our best effort, conflicts between cell partners often arose in the blink of an eye. We couldn't spend all our time playing musical chairs with inmates who chose to fight for the most trivial of reasons. Nevertheless, inmates would occasionally resort to violence just to force us to move them to different cells.

WOOLUM WOES

William Woolum was an example of this new breed of inmate. Woolum hailed from Barbourville, Kentucky, in the Appalachian foothills. He was one of nineteen children, born into a very poor family. William, along with some of his brothers and sisters, were placed in foster homes because his parents were unable to provide for that many children. He once told me he felt like a piece of trash, thrown away like garbage, as he moved from one foster home to another.

For many who grew up in Woolum's corner of the world, poverty was a generational way of life. Sometimes the only way for a young man to escape poverty was to work in the coal mines or join the military. Some resorted to crime. Many of the lucky ones found jobs up north in the steel mills or in auto manufacturing. They were often the exception to the rule, however. Most were trapped in the mountains, with few options to choose from.

Mountain families share a number of ancestral values and traditions, and many of those focus on the family as a source of strength and pride. This strong, family-centric heritage often informed how the people of Appalachia approached everyone and everything they encountered. Insulting someone's family was a sure way to start a fight, and doing so repeatedly was a good way to get yourself killed.

A new inmate named Danny Ball arrived at KSP in 1981. Ball grew up in the Appalachia region of Kentucky, so naturally he gravitated toward other inmates from that area. One of these men was Ben Reed. Woolum and Reed were already close friends, and looked out for each other on the yard. Ball, the new kid on the block, was assigned to a cell with Lester Rhodes. After the first night together, Ball found Reed on the yard hanging out with Woolum. Ball approached them almost in tears because Rhodes had tried to have sex with him in their cell. He feared Rhodes might try to rape him when he returned to his cell that night or the next.

Reed and Woolum tried to resolve the problem. Woolum went to a captain he knew on the yard to get Ball moved out of the cell. It didn't work. Woolum also told Ball he could request protective custody, which would be provided in the segregation unit, or Ball could violate a rule, which would do the same thing. Ball didn't want to go to segregation, so Woolum and Reed said they would talk to Rhodes and try to get him to stop harassing the boy.

The conversation between Woolum, Reed, and Rhodes did not go well. Rhodes got mad and told them to mind their own business. Woolum stood up and told Rhodes more sternly to leave Ball alone. The confrontation got heated, and Rhodes left the area. He came back a short time later and stabbed Woolum twice in the back. None of the staff saw Rhodes stab Woolum. As Woolum returned to his cell block after the lockup bell sounded, an inmate slipped him a knife and said, "Here, you might need this." Woolum went in and treated his wounds by applying pressure to stop the bleeding. The stab wounds weren't life-threatening, but the attack was meant to serve as a warning from Rhodes to back off.

When the cell blocks were released to the yard for the next meal, Woolum, now armed with a knife, found Rhodes under the water tower where the confrontation had occurred earlier. Rhodes approached Woolum and pulled up his shirt to display his knife as a warning. Woolum pulled his own knife and went after Rhodes, knocking him down and grabbing his knife. He stabbed Rhodes several times then sat down on his stomach and stabbed him repeatedly in the chest. At one point before Rhodes died, he cried out to Ball, "Danny, please make him stop!"

Woolum later said that once he started, he "snapped" and stabbed Rhodes again and again in a blind rage. As he pummeled Rhodes, Woolum heard a warning shot fired from a nearby gun tower. He threw the knives down and waited for the officers to respond. Lester Rhodes was stabbed fifty-six times. He died almost immediately.

We had seen some brutal violence at KSP through the years, but this topped them all. Rhodes' chest was ripped apart. The incident was horrific, even by prison standards. Woolum later expressed heartfelt sorrow that he had to call his mother to tell her what he had done that September day in 1981. It was her birthday.

Kentucky State Police Detective James Potter investigated the homicide, and Commonwealth Attorney Bill Cunningham prosecuted the case. Woolum was charged with murder, and he received a life sentence. The tragedy also resulted in prison administrative charges, which landed Woolum on the Administrative Control Unit (ACU). We made sure Woolum would not see the light of day for years. He had demonstrated he was far too dangerous to walk the yard again anytime soon.

BLOOD ON MY HANDS

In 1982, I was escorting Sue Wiley, a reporter from a major TV station in Lexington, Kentucky, and her cameraman on the yard to interview a noteworthy escape artist, Don Tate. Tate had escaped from prison more than once and was quite willing to tell his story. During his most famous getaway, he sneaked out from Five Cell House by cutting a windowpane from his cell window and using a rope woven from heavy thread that he and his buddies smuggled from the garment plant to climb down two stories to the prison yard. He then used the rope and a grappling hook to scale the wall of Four Cell House and ran across the roof. Finally, he used the same rope to climb down the outside of Four Cell House. This occurred at one or two o'clock in the morning. Tate vanished into the night and eventually made his way to California, where he started a new life—for a while. As almost always happens in these cases, the escapee was eventually caught and returned to the penitentiary to serve out his sentence.

While reporter Sue Wiley was interviewing Tate on the yard, I started hearing frantic radio traffic, and knew something serious was going on. My first instinct was to get Wiley and the cameraman off the yard and somewhere secure as soon as possible. I interrupted the interview and said, "Come with me. Hurry!" By then, I knew there had been a serious stabbing. Just as we reached the yard office, a young inmate ran right in front of us. I didn't know he was the stabbing victim until he dropped right at my feet. I told Wiley and the cameraman to stand back out of the way, and I started looking the inmate over for a wound. As he slowly lost consciousness, I found a small puncture wound in his ribs on his right side. It wasn't bleeding much, but I applied pressure on the wound in a futile attempt to save his life. Nurse Mary Smith arrived a few minutes later with two inmates to carry a stretcher. One of the inmates started CPR as I continued to hold the wound. Every time the inmate gave mouth-to-mouth, the air pressure would blow blood bubbles in my hand from the wound. I knew that a single stab had hit an artery and his lung. Once his lung filled with blood, it was over. He was gone. I looked up and saw Wiley holding her hand over her mouth. She had just witnessed something most people never see. I also noticed the cameraman with the camera on his shoulder. He had not turned off the camera and had gotten everything on tape.

As the yard was locking down, I cleaned up the blood on me and got what little information we had. The victim was Billy Teeters, a young twenty-one-year-old from Bardwell, Kentucky, imprisoned for arson. He had burned down the Carlisle County Courthouse. The perpetrator was Claude Plumber, an older mountain man from eastern Kentucky. Claude was already serving life for murder.

Teeters was new at KSP, and Plumber, a loan shark, offered to loan him a carton of cigarettes until he could have money placed on his account from home. Several weeks had passed, and it was time to pay up. He found Teeters in the gym playing basketball. Plumber walked up to him and told him he owed him two cartons. Teeters allegedly replied, "Fuck you, I ain't paying you two cartons." Without saying a word, Plumber stepped out on the yard and bought a prison shank. He walked straight back to the gym, approached Teeters from behind, and stabbed him once. Plumber casually walked away and threw the shank in the trash can at the gym entrance. Teeters must have suspected he was mortally wounded because he ran to the nearby yard office, where officers are dispatched. It was the safest place on the yard. The officer supervising the gym called in the stabbing, alerting all staff of the emergency. I held Teeters' head in my lap as I put pressure on the wound. I tried to comfort him as he died, but it was too late. I'm not sure the boy ever heard me. It was a terrible moment that haunts me to this day.

In the early 1980s, incidents of violence and murder were getting worse at KSP. The violence was fueled by racial and cultural disparity, younger inmates serving out longer and longer sentences, and overcrowding that resulted in double celling. There weren't enough jobs and programs to keep inmates busy, so large numbers roamed the yard looking for trouble. *Idle hands are the devil's workshop; idle lips are his mouthpiece. Wickedness loves company—and leads others into sin.* Proverbs 16:27-29. So it was in the 1980s. The old Castle was, in so many ways, the devil's workshop.

RACIAL DISCORD

Byron Jasis was twenty-two years old in 1982 when he was hired as a guard. One look at him and we knew he would fit right in if he had the fortitude to run toward trouble in the heat of battle. He was a strapping six foot six and weighed 325 pounds. Jasis had potential to be a star in the world of corrections. But first he had to prove himself.

Jasis was hired July 29, 1982. After completing the academy, he was assigned to the evening shift at KSP. Within a few short months, he had earned respect from his supervisors and fellow guards.

October 15, 1983, had been a fairly uneventful day by the time the evening shift came on duty at three p.m. Jasis, Johnny Boyd, Tommy Stewart, and Bill Holloman were assigned to patrol the yard before the general population was turned out after count. Inmates would roam the yard after supper until final lockup. Captain Jim Travis and Lt. Herb Mayfield were the supervisors on duty.

Suddenly, a panicked radio call came out from the Five Cell House officer that a fire was spreading on the first floor. Jasis and other officers prepared to respond with air packs and other gear, only to find out the "fire" was a small appliance that had overheated. It was no big deal, and the reporting officer had overreacted when he smelled smoke.

Just as Jasis and the other officer were standing down, another frantic radio call went out from Officer Tommy Stewart reporting a stabbing in progress in front of the laundry. By the time Jasis and the other yard officers got to the scene, a crowd of inmates had gathered. Jasis and Stewart found Ben Higgins laying crumpled on the asphalt in front of the laundry. Higgins was lying in a large pool of blood, and there was a trail of blood and vomit leading back a short distance to where the assault began. Soon, Capt. Jim Travis, Lt. Herb Mayfield, and nurse Mary Smith arrived on the scene. The captain ordered a lockdown, and Nurse Smith realized there was nothing she could do. Blood was still oozing from the multiple stab wounds to Higgins's chest. She then felt around his head and realized his skull had been crushed from the force of a blunt instrument. Yet another brutal and senseless murder at KSP. Only this time, the victim was a black inmate, and the perpetrators were white.

Normal protocol required all cell block officers to stand at the cell block entrance while the inmates lined up to return to their cells. The officers examined each inmate's hands, clothing, and shoes for blood. The perpetrator was almost always easy to find. And there were always witnesses. Some inmates were all too eager to snitch. Inmates Jackie Reffitt and Gary Dale were identified as the killers. There was enough evidence to charge them both with murder.

Reffitt was a longtime member of the violent, racist prison gang known as the Aryan Brotherhood. Dale was a young inmate trying to earn a reputation and join the Brotherhood. But first he had to "make bones," which meant he had to kill or severely injure a non-white inmate. The two found their next victim in Ben Higgins.

Higgins was a Black inmate who worked in the legal office as a legal aide. I was the program director at the time, and part of my responsibility was to oversee the legal office and the grievance procedures. Higgins, I must say, always behaved somewhat hatefully toward me. Our interactions were very strained. If Higgins crossed my line, I would have given him a write-up, which would result in a trip to the hole. But Higgins was smart enough to avoid getting written up. My memory of him was that he hated white people—staff, inmates, everyone. This attitude was what eventually led to his murder.

The Brotherhood made an example of Higgins. Officer Jasis, who was one of the first responders, agrees that the Brotherhood targeted Higgins because he was black. The murder was racially motivated.

Higgins was bludgeoned to death with an eighteen-inch-long piece of flat steel that was a quarter inch thick and two inches wide. Reffitt struck him one time on the back of his head, which was all it took. He was most likely dead before he hit the ground. Dale then stabbed Higgins seventeen times in the chest, even though it was obvious he was already gone.

The knife Dale used was an ordinary table knife, a butter knife, that had been sharpened to a point, with a handle wrapped in electrical tape. Prisons don't allow table knives, so this was probably stolen from a guard's lunchbox. For his part, Reffitt's choice of a lengthy piece of flat steel proved to be a deadly weapon. We never knew where it came from, but the most likely place was the maintenance shop.

Some of the guards in segregation teased Dale for stabbing Higgins after he was already dead—essentially killing a dead man. But Dale's actions nonetheless earned him a coveted membership in the Aryan Brotherhood.

Both Reffitt and Dale were indicted by the Lyon County Grand Jury. Reffitt maintained he was innocent. His public defender was Alan Stout, who later became a top-notch bankruptcy lawyer and was eventually appointed to a federal judgeship. The prosecutor was future Kentucky Supreme Court Justice Bill Cunningham.

During plea negotiations, Dale confessed to the stabbing and using the piece of steel to bludgeon Higgins. He took the rap, which absolved Reffitt of the charges. Dale was already serving time for robbery and kidnapping. He accepted a plea deal for a fifteen-year sentence on the charge of manslaughter. The case was resolved without a trial, and Reffitt got off the hook.

Criminal charges and convictions in the court system had little bearing on administrative charges in KSP—charges that we would use to keep Reffitt and Dale in the hole for months. Our standard was merely "some evidence," not evidence beyond a reasonable doubt. Reffitt and Dale were thus easily found guilty of administrative charges for the murder.

Well aware this was a racially motivated crime, KSP's black population waited patiently for the two Aryan Brotherhood members to serve out their time in the hole. They were dead men walking, and the prison administration knew it. The only solution was to transfer Reffitt and Dale to another state, where they would not be known. This scenario is called an Interstate Compact. We would trade these inmates for two from another state—convicts who were just as bad or worse. The program minimized the likelihood of further violence, at least in theory, and it enabled two disparate prisons to move past volatile situations that threatened the safety of prisoners and staff.

SCARFACE

It was a normal Saturday in October 1982 when the penitentiary's school principal, Barry Banister, reported in to open the school library. Most of the time inmates spent their Saturdays out on the yard, playing handball or lifting weights at the weight pile. Only a few browsed in the library to kill time. Unless it was rainy, most inmates wanted to be outside. The fall weather was beautiful, so Banister didn't expect many to show up in the library. It promised to be a slow day.

Banister unlocked the school entrance and went to his office to read a newspaper. The office had large, plexiglass windows so that he could observe all activity. Eventually only a few inmates drifted in to browse the library. Mostly, they would look through the assortment of magazines to find something interesting.

Inmate John Mays was the first to enter the library, followed by one or two others who went about their usual reading and researching activities. After making a mental note of who was there, Banister went back to reading the paper. At ten fifteen a.m., Banister watched as Samuel Straface strolled in. Straface was a loner. He could always be seen wandering around the yard by himself and often looked unkempt with uncombed hair and a short beard. He never smiled or engaged in conversation. Everyone was afraid of him.

Straface had done federal time but had escaped from the Fayette County Jail where he had been held for the U.S. Marshals. While the details remain murky, we knew that he had escaped and stolen a jailer's official car to make his getaway. A high-speed chase ensued, then a shootout. Straface was wounded and captured. As soon as he was sentenced for those crimes, Straface found himself at the Castle.

Banister watched Straface carefully, because he could tell the inmate wasn't there to read. Straface was looking for someone. As soon as he spotted John Mays reading a magazine across the room, he pulled a shank and went after him. Mays saw him coming and ran around a rack of books, but not before Straface stabbed him in the cheek. The blade penetrated and cut his tonsils. Banister tried to call the yard office for help from his office phone, but the line was busy. As was usually the case, there were no radios available to check out that day. The prison never had enough radios for staff, and the school was low priority. Besides, administrators reasoned, Banister had a telephone if he needed to report something to the yard office.

Mays ran to the office, trying to get away from Straface. Banister locked the door behind him, but Straface used his shoulder to easily break through the plexiglass panel in the doorframe. Banister grabbed the only weapon he could find, which was a piece of the trim from the door, and he hit Straface over the head. Straface turned to Banister and said, "You hit me again, and I will kill you."

He stabbed Mays again in the back. As this was unfolding, inmate and frequent library patron Charlie Walker quietly entered the office and handed Banister a coatrack. He liked Banister and was annoyed that prison violence had spilled over into the relative peace and quiet of the library. The coatrack had been made in prison industries on a lathe. It was roughly five feet long and three inches thick. Banister swung and hit Straface on the head, which cut him from his hairline to his lip. Straface shook his head and made a swipe at Banister, who was trying to hit him again. Unfortunately, the coatrack had broken in half after the first hit.

Fighting for his life, Banister swung wildly with the broken chunk of wood. He managed to hit almost everything within striking distance, whether it deserved it or not. At one point, Mays said, "Goddamn, man. You're hitting me!"

Stabbed again in the shoulder, Mays ran back out in the library with Straface in pursuit. Banister took the opportunity to use his phone again to call for help. This time a desk sergeant at the yard office answered the phone and quickly radioed all yard officers to report to the school.

It took less than a minute for Captain Jim Travis and several officers to respond and enter the library. Travis radioed five gun tower to come out on the catwalk and shoot Straface as the officers tried to lure him outside. Travis took the broken coatrack from Banister and began taunting Straface, trying to get him to attack. It almost worked. Straface chased Travis to the exit door but would go no further. Five gun tower was ready to shoot Straface, and he knew it. As Straface paused, Mays seized the opportunity to run out of the school and seek help at the yard office. Captain Travis kept ordering Straface to throw down the knife, but the inmate was not about to give up without a fight. Travis swung at him with the coatrack, and Straface lunged back, not paying attention to the two officers who had snuck up behind him. Travis managed to hit him on the head with the piece of wood, which gave the officers the split second they needed to take Straface down. They managed to wrestle the knife away from the furious inmate and cuff him. It was over.

A natural leader, Captain Travis was a tough Vietnam veteran who earned the rank of master chief petty officer, one of the highest ranks available to enlisted members of the United States Navy. He retired and came to work at KSP, where he quickly climbed the ranks to captain. He was also the commander of E-Squad. Travis proved himself time and time again. Then suddenly, as he was attending a meeting in Deputy Warden Morgan's office, Travis suffered a massive heart attack and died almost instantly. It was a terrible loss for the KSP community.

The violent incident at the school could have easily resulted in multiple deaths. Mays was stabbed three times, but he survived. Banister was shaken but uninjured. Travis's actions saved Banister and inmate Mays from certain death. As for Straface, the head injuries he received from Banister and Travis healed into a prominent scar that ran the length of his face. From that day forward, he would be known as Scarface.

In retrospect, this event was a perfect example of the old adage, "You never know what the day has in store for you." I was on call that morning as the duty officer. It was my job to follow up and make sure all the reports were in order and to report the incident to the warden. From that day forward, a radio was issued to the school so that emergency help could be summoned instantly.

Captain Travis and Banister were both heroes, in my opinion. Their brave actions that day illustrate why it is so important to know who you can count on in a place like KSP. Our lives depended on men and women who would run toward danger, unarmed, and without hesitation.

THE LOSS OF PAT ROSS

Officer Patricia Ross was a thirty-seven-year-old food service instructor at KSP. She taught food service classes, enabling inmates to learn a vocational certificate. She was an excellent employee and was respected by staff and inmates alike.

Pat participated in all employee activities and often volunteered to help with staff picnics and potlucks. She was divorced and had a fourteen-year-old son, Bryan Crawford.

Little did I realize as I woke up on March 1, 1984, that it would end up the worst day of my career. I was in training most of the afternoon, but I returned early and proceeded up the front gate steps to turn in the keys to the state car I had checked out. As I drove up, I could tell something was wrong because I saw administrative staff trickling out the door, and the workday was far from over.

On the steps, I bumped into Officer Lawrence Newsome, and I asked him what was happening. He was crying, and all he could do was shake his head and gesture toward the front gate. Several secretaries were walking down the steps in front of us, in tears. I repeated my question to anyone who would listen, until someone replied that Pat Ross had been murdered. I was stunned.

The prison was already in lockdown by the time I arrived. I went straight to the warden's office to see if there was anything I could do. Mike Samburg, the acting warden at the time, explained that we didn't have a suspect yet. He asked if I would help to escort inmates to Internal Affairs for interrogation. Captain Billy Ashley was the Internal Affairs officer, and he had begun interviewing each inmate assigned to food service that day. I only saw one or two officers standing guard over the dozen or so inmates waiting to be interviewed. I positioned myself by the control center and middle gate, in case one of the inmates became combative. An eerie quiet had settled over the administration building. Muffled sobs echoed everywhere. It was a surreal scene. How could this happen? Who did it? We all wanted answers.

Ross's body was still at the crime scene, awaiting state police to begin their investigation. The murder had occurred in the food service storage area, where bulk supplies were stored along with pots and pans, trays, and silverware. It was usually locked, but not always, because inmate cooks would occasionally need supplies for preparing meals. On the day in question, the storage area had been locked.

Officer Richardville was one of the first officers to respond to the murder scene, and he was given the gruesome task of guarding the body until the coroner arrived. It was a couple of hours before the body was removed. Richardville had asked for a sheet to cover the body, but it was denied. Prison investigators did not want the crime scene disturbed, so Richardville sat alone, guarding the scene. He would later say that it was the toughest assignment of his career

Captain Ashley interviewed food service inmates, one at a time, in a small private office on the first floor of the administration building.

Ashley had a lot of experience investigating inmate crimes. He could usually get to the bottom of any incident.

It only took about thirty minutes for Ashley to find a culprit. He opened the office door and stepped out with inmate Fred Grooms. "Take this inmate to the hole," Ashley said. "He did it."

All the inmates lined up to be interviewed were already handcuffed, so it was just a matter of escorting Grooms through the hallways to Three Cell House to be placed in segregation. I stayed with the other inmates. Ashley would still need to interview everyone to determine if they were witnesses or had any information that would be helpful.

I asked Ashley if Grooms had confessed to the murder, and he answered affirmatively. Apparently, Grooms had grown impatient at the interrogation process. He walked into the office and without sitting down exclaimed, "I don't know what's taking you so long. I did it." Ashley asked him directly if he killed Pat Ross. He responded, "Yeah, I did it. Now take me to the hole." The interview was over before it started.

The dozen or so other inmates who worked in food service were visibly shaken. They had worked with Pat Ross and liked her. Each one was interviewed to see what they knew or if they suspected somebody else had also been involved. None of them knew anything was wrong before the murder occurred. Grooms, for the most part, blended in with the workforce and didn't cause any problems. He seemed to be a loner, but that is not unusual in prison.

Inmate Larry Lehner, a kitchen worker, entered the storeroom as Grooms was attacking Pat Ross with a commercial can opener that was about sixteen inches long and weighed about ten pounds. Grooms had already fatally injured Ross before he turned on Lehner, hitting him at least once in the head and knocking him unconscious. The injuries to Ross were so severe that there was blood splatter on the walls at the crime scene. It was the stuff of nightmares. Whether or not Lehner tried to intervene to stop the attack is not known, but we surmised he just walked in on the scene at the wrong time. Lehner was severely wounded, but would survive his injuries after a long stay in the hospital. He suffered lasting impairments from a brain injury, but at least he survived. He was unable to remember anything after the fact.

Suspect Fred Grooms had worked in food service, helping to prepare meals, for years. He was a loner and rarely caused any problems, though he occasionally received write-ups for disrespecting staff. Grooms had never assaulted staff before. After the incident, Warden Parke reviewed Grooms' record only to find he had a history of assaulting women on the street. His plan was to sexually assault Pat Ross after she unlocked the storage room door to let him in, but she turned and confronted him before he could. Grooms snapped without making any sexual advances and hit her twice in the head just as inmate Lehner walked in carrying the silverware. It was over almost as quickly as it had begun. Ross and inmate Lehner never had a chance.

Grooms was tried in Lyon County Court and received a death sentence. Future Circuit Judge and Kentucky Supreme Court Justice Bill Cunningham was the prosecutor. Grooms spent most of the remainder of his life on death row, but eventually his sentence was reduced to life without parole. Cancer claimed his life as an old man at KSR.

Warden Parke had just been named commissioner of the Department of Corrections when Ross was murdered, but because his replacement at KSP had not yet been named, he traveled back and forth from Eddyville to Frankfort, fulfilling the duties of both warden and commissioner.

Parke was at the Leitchfield toll plaza on the Western Kentucky Parkway when he was notified of Ross's death. These were the days before cell phones, so his secretary, Vicki, began calling the toll plazas on the Western Kentucky Parkway to try to locate and advise him of the emergency. Some 150 miles or so away, he heard the news and quickly returned to KSP.

Once Parke arrived, he was briefed on everything we knew. The investigation was now being handled by the state police, but it was a straightforward case. We had the suspect in custody, and he was admitting his guilt. He also had blood spatter on his clothes and shoes. We ultimately concluded that this was an isolated incident and no other inmates were involved. In fact, most inmates were very respectful, and many expressed their condolences.

The staff was still in shock long after the crime scene was processed and the lockdown was lifted. It was as though a dark cloud hung over the Castle on the shores of Lake Barkley. Inmates were unusually quiet and respectful, and correctional staff went about their required duties with heavy hearts. An inmate dared not provoke a staff member while we were grieving. In fact, most wouldn't even make eye contact, for fear we would take it as disrespect. I recall helping to patrol the yard during meals and walking through the cellblocks, almost hoping someone would go off or disrespect me so I could unleash my fury. After all, one of them had killed one of us, and the prison was as tense as I had ever experienced. It took a long time for things to return to some sort of normalcy. Eventually, of course, inmates started behaving like inmates again, and staff began doing what staff must do to maintain order and survive. One thing was certain: Ross's murder served as a harsh reminder to all of us that we worked in a place full of danger. We could never let our guard down, even in the best of times. Pat Ross might have been any one of us.

Warden Parke eventually made the decision to release inmates from lockdown the second day after the murder. Most of us followed orders day in and day out without grumbling, but this was a little hard to swallow. It felt disrespectful. We believed the inmates should remain in lockdown, at least until Pat Ross's burial. Parke remained steadfast in his belief that we should not punish all the inmates for the actions of one bad actor. Deep down, we knew he was right, but emotions were raw. Looking back now, I can honestly say that all the inmates were on their best behavior in the immediate aftermath of the murder. I think if we had to use force on one of them, which was routine, we would have overreacted. In fact, I know I would have. I think the inmates sensed that. The Castle remained unusually calm and uneventful, at least until our colleague was laid to rest.

Godspeed, Pat. You were a friend and a good employee. We have never forgotten.

EIGHT

A SNAKE HOSTAGE

In the wee hours of October 3, 1982, I was awakened around one thirty a.m. by a phone call from the control center at KSP. A female voice on the other end sounded frantic as she blurted out, "Get here quick. Woolum has taken a hostage in Three Cell House!" Before I could ask any questions, she had hung up. She was busy calling the E-Squad and other staff. Warden Parke was out of town and had left Deputy Warden Samburg in charge.

I threw on a clean shirt and a pair of blue jeans and hightailed it the short half mile to the prison in my car. The front gate was already open when I arrived, and Lt. Billy Adams was waiting for me. His job was to brief me as we rushed through One and Two Cell Houses and finally into Three Cell House.

I could hear Woolum, a.k.a. Snake, on an officer's radio yelling for the warden. Deputy Warden Mike Samburg met me and explained that he wanted me to be the hostage negotiator. No one had begun negotiations, and Woolum continued to call out on the officer's radio for the warden. "Warden, you better talk to me," he snarled, "or I'm gonna kill me an officer."

Samburg handed me his radio, and I told Woolum the warden wasn't available. He would have to talk to me instead. He was quick to reply, "I don't want to talk to you. I want to talk to the warden."

Woolum was housed in Three Cell House on the ACU (Administrative Control Unit). ACU was a separate enclosed walk. It had nineteen cells. There were no windows to the outside, and because ACU was enclosed without external ventilation, it was the only unit in the entire prison that was air conditioned at the time. ACU, as I have mentioned before, housed the worst of the worst. It was completely cut off from the rest of the prison population. The only news coming from the other parts of the prison was either through carefully monitored correspondence or the occasional, approved visit from an inmate legal aide.

Inmates were permitted one hour of exercise outside their cell on the walk, five days a week. Occasionally when we had enough staff on duty, we would restrain them and escort them to what was called the "mini gym," just a short walk down the staircase in the rear of the cell block. But even in the mini gym, there was no access to the outside world—no view of the outdoors, no direct sunlight, no fresh air. The mini gym was almost not worth the trouble it took for the guards or inmates to access it, but the inmates still used it occasionally.

There were three "special cells" on ACU that housed a cage in front of the cell. The small cages, roughly six feet by six feet, were built just to give the inmate some time out of his cell. They were hardly large enough to do any meaningful exercise, but they were constructed to provide inmates with an option to "exercise outside the cell," as required by law. Inmates who occupied a cell with cages were either deadly enemies with some other inmate or they were too dangerous to be allowed out to mingle during the exercise periods. Looking back, it was a bad idea to construct these cages, because they obstructed the view of the guard who was always positioned at the end of the row of cells just outside the crash gate. Whenever the officer went in to pass out medicine, food trays, or take a count, he was required to call for a backup. This rule would often be relaxed if everything was peaceful and quiet or if we were short-staffed. We were short-staffed more often than not, and that fateful autumn night in 1982 was no exception.

As previously mentioned, William "Snake" Woolum was born into a poor Eastern Kentucky family with nineteen children. He was in and out of foster homes, which had a profoundly negative effect on his formative years. Woolum grew up unloved and rebellious. His early life was a classic study in how to damage the emotional and psychological health of a human being. Woolum first entered prison facing a twenty-year sentence, but repeat offences would eventually extend his time behind bars to seventy years.

By late 1982, young Woolum had already received a life sentence for killing inmate Lester Rhodes. He had to serve a year or more in ACU before we would even think about returning him to the general population. In so many ways, Woolum was a desperate young man. He had no hope and no future—a tragic situation that was entirely of his own making. He lacked self-control and was extremely dangerous, just like a riled rattlesnake. Woolum had no qualms about killing Rhodes after the latter made sexual advances toward his new friend, Danny Ball. The brutality of Rhodes' murder was something we had not seen before. Once Woolum had Rhodes down and mortally wounded, he continued to stab Rhodes over fifty times, literally mutilating his entire chest. It was brutal beyond words. This attack and other instances earned Woolum the apt nickname "Snake."

Officer Paul Jasper, a Vietnam vet, was assigned to ACU on the midnight shift. He would do what he was told and didn't make waves. Inmates had no reason to dislike him or like him for that matter. He was reliable in making rounds and following post orders.

Officer Jasper was making his second round down the walk counting inmates. He was unarmed, but had an institutional radio for communication with other staff in the unit. He was by himself making rounds, but the cage officer who operated the cell doors and crash gate was safely standing by the control panel observing while he made his count. Officer Jasper was required to count once per hour. All seemed quiet throughout the cellblock.

As he made his way down the walk, he was counting, but he was also checking to make sure everyone was breathing. This was to make sure he was not counting a dummy. It was a standard post order in all the cellblocks.

As he passed the second cage about midway down the walk, Woolum called him over to the bars, nonchalantly put a gun to his head, and told him he was dead if he didn't do exactly as he was told. Officer Jasper got a glimpse of the gun in the subdued lighting. In a split second, he was now a hostage held by the most dangerous man in the penitentiary. There was no doubt that Woolum would kill him. Jasper was forced to turn around with his hands up. Woolum told him to radio the cage officer to open his cell. A few seconds later, the cell opened and Woolum stepped out with the gun still on Officer Jasper's head. Woolum took the radio and forced Officer Jasper to walk in front of him with his hands up.

The cage operator knew something was wrong but didn't see the gun until they got closer. Standing at the crash gate, Woolum ordered the cage officer to open the gate. Officer Jasper said, "You better do as he says. He has a gun." The cage officer was behind a set of bars beyond the crash gate. The cage officer could control any of the 156 cell doors in the cellblock as well as the entry and exit doors to the unit. Woolum was gambling the cage officer would open the gate since he had a gun against Officer Jasper's head. When the officer hesitated, he turned the gun toward the cage officer and demanded he open the gate. The security of the entire cellblock was at risk. Potentially all 156 cells could be opened in short order which would result in an instant takeover of the entire unit—a riot in the worst possible scenario.

Instead, the cage officer retreated and ran down the set of steps to safety. Now Woolum was trapped on Thirteen Walk with an officer hostage. His gamble failed thanks to a quick-thinking officer who did not give in to Woolum's threat.

Woolum had no choice but to go back to his starting point and take cover behind the cage in front of his cell. He still had Officer Jasper at gunpoint, and by now officers were responding to the unit but stayed behind cover. The shift captain was notified. He ordered the control center to notify Mike Samburg, who was not only the duty officer, but was also the acting warden. Deputy Warden Samburg responded to the institution, but not before ordering the control center to notify me first then the entire E-Squad.

I arrived as quickly as humanly possible. My adrenaline was off the charts when I learned Woolum had a gun and had taken an officer hostage. I realized the situation was isolated, thanks to the cage officer that retreated rather than opening the gate while under duress.

There could easily have been 156 inmates rioting in Three Cell House, a complete armed takeover. It was a close call, but the situation was dire. It was up to me to negotiate with Snake to save the officer's life.

Deputy Warden Samburg gave me a pep talk on the way over to Three Cell House. He said, "Phil, you can do this. Stall for time while we get the E-Squad here. I don't have a green light from the warden to kill him, but if he does anything to harm the officer, we will go in and kill him. Just be calm and talk to him, but don't agree to any demands until you check with me. This will help stall time until the E-Squad can get in position."

While I began negotiations, Deputy Warden Samburg was finally able to get a call through to Warden Parke, who was two hundred miles away in Frankfort. After a short briefing from Deputy Warden Samburg, Warden Parke gave the green light to kill Snake if we could get a shot. We already knew we could take him out if he were to harm the officer, but now we were authorized to kill him if we could get him in our sights, even if the negotiations were going fine. A license to kill, as they say.

So, now in my mind, my job was to try and defuse the hostility and anger Woolum was displaying. I could end this if I could lure him out in the open so a sharpshooter could take him out. On the scene, I positioned myself behind cover in the cage. I was standing behind the control panel that electronically opened and closed cell doors. Capt. Bill Henderson crawled around the corner of the cage and took up a position lying on the floor armed with a .223 caliber Ruger mini 14. Henderson was a good shot, but he was not a trained sniper. In fact, we did not have a trained sniper on the E-Squad during that time period. At a range of about twenty-five yards, it would be an easy shot if only we could lure him out from behind cover.

From my position, I could see Woolum and Officer Jasper sitting on the floor behind the makeshift exercise cage. Woolum was behind Officer Jasper. I could see the gun against Officer Jasper's head.

I continued to talk to Woolum over the officer's two-way radio. Woolum didn't believe me when I continued to tell him the warden wasn't there. Next, he demanded to talk to Mike Samburg. I told him that he had to give me something first. I told him I wanted to talk to Officer Jasper. Woolum agreed and keyed the microphone. I could hear a voice say, "I'm all right." Not knowing if that was really Officer Jasper's voice, I told Officer Jasper to wave to me. Officer Jasper held up his hand and waved. This was a breakthrough. Woolum had given me something, so I told him to stand by while I called Samburg.

On the phone, Samburg again gave me a pep talk, telling me I was doing great. He said, "Tell him I can't talk right now because I have the warden on the phone." I relayed this message to Woolum, and it seemed to satisfy him.

About the time Capt. Henderson positioned himself for a possible shot, Sr. Captain Adams came inside the cage to my position and said.

"Phil, you're doing good. I'll stay with you." I asked him if he wanted to take over, but he said no, since Woolum was talking to me, and to just keep going.

I could not have asked for a better coach than Capt. Adams. I had the utmost respect for this man. He was fair, but he was tough and had more common sense than anyone I knew. He had been in many major disturbances for the past twenty-five or more years. He probably had more experience than anyone before or since. As Woolum and I continued the back-and-forth negotiations, Capt. Adams would offer suggestions. He would say tell him this or tell him that. It was reassuring to have someone to bounce an idea off of before I perhaps gave the wrong response. I was worried that if I said the wrong thing, Woolum would kill Officer Jasper. I had my doubts that Officer Jasper would get out of this situation alive, no matter how well the negotiations proceeded.

About three a.m., Woolum started to calm down. He said he wouldn't hurt anyone if they wouldn't hurt him. I felt this was a good sign. He was worried we were going to kill him even if he gave up the hostage. He kept demanding to talk to the warden, and I kept telling him the warden was on his way. I asked him what he would say to the warden if he were here. He said that he wanted a transfer to a federal prison, and he wanted to talk to a TV crew.

This started a whole new series of back-and-forth negotiations. It was about this time the officer's two-way radio began to break up. The batteries were dying. Eventually, I just yelled down the walk and told him I was going to slide a fresh battery down the walk so we could continue to use the officer's radio. He was nervous about this and yelled back that he would kill Officer Jasper if we tried anything. I told Capt. Henderson to get ready because he might get a shot. I slid a fresh battery down the walk just far enough away that he would have to leave his cover to get it. A minute or two went by, and then suddenly, without warning, he moved to get the battery but used Officer Jasper as a shield. My ploy for a shot didn't work, but I think it helped continue our negotiations because he had developed some trust in me, however slight.

By three a.m., the State Police Special Response Team (SRT) and the E-Squad were staged in Two Cell House, ready to come in. Woolum kept insisting he would let the officer go if he could talk to the warden and if he could have Channel 6 local news come in and film his surrender. He reasoned that without a TV crew filming the surrender we would come in and kill him, or at the very least we would drag him out to Fifteen Walk or an office and beat the shit out of him. By then, I was told the warden was in the prison but to not to tell Woolum. I was also told the warden was not going to let the TV crew in to film the surrender. The warden also sent me a message not to outright deny a demand but to try to find a way around it or an alternate solution.

It was the middle of the night, and everyone was tired. There were long periods of time that neither Woolum nor I had anything else to say. I knew the longer this lasted, the less likely he was to kill Officer Jasper. I had learned this from training.

Woolum once again said, "Parker, are you making any progress in getting the warden on the radio? And where is Channel 6 News?"

I said, "No, we are working on it." Then I changed the subject. I said, "Woolum, we have some fresh coffee out here if you want some."

He said, "That would be great."

I told him okay, but first he had to show me the hostage was still okay and have him wave at me. Officer Jasper raised his hand and moved. I told him to stand by and I would slide a coffee thermos to him. Once again, I told Capt. Henderson to get ready. Again, I deliberately slid the thermos down the walk, and once again he retrieved it using Officer Jasper as a shield.

Woolum was getting impatient and asked why he kept repeating himself. "Get the warden here and Channel 6 News. If you do this, I will release the officer," he stated. I was not allowed to agree to either demand. I had to come up with some other solution, so I sent a message to the warden asking if we could agree to transferring Woolum to a federal prison or out of state. The warden sent back a message to tell him we would transfer him out of state. Woolum wanted to know what state, and I told him those arrangements would have to be made later.

Behind the scenes, the warden and Deputy Warden Sandburg were trying to find a way to meet his other demand to talk to a news outlet. We were still stalling for time.

It was another slow time when negotiation had stalled. I made contact and asked Woolum if he would like a pack of cigarettes. He eagerly accepted the offer, so once again I said, "You're going to have to give me something. Have the officer stand up and wave, and I want to hear his voice on the radio." They both stood up and Officer Jasper waved and said he was okay on the radio.

I got an unopened pack of cigarettes from someone and told Woolum the cigarettes were on the way. Once again, I told Capt. Henderson to get ready. I could hear the safety click off on Henderson's gun. I slid the pack of cigarettes down the walk. Again, it was out of reach, and he would have to move about ten feet to retrieve them. Maybe thirty seconds went by, then suddenly Woolum darted over and got the cigarettes and sat back down in his position behind Officer Jasper. I was pissed. I looked at Capt. Henderson and asked him why the hell he didn't take the shot. I couldn't believe it. It was less than twenty-five yards, which would have been an easy kill. No one said anything. Capt. Henderson gave me a go-to-hell look. It was a long night. I had worked so hard to give him a good clean shot, and then he didn't take it. Oh, well. What could I do? I never brought it up again. I guess Henderson had his reasons.

The night dragged on. Probably about seven in the morning, I was called from the command center which had been established in the warden's office. The warden still would not allow a TV news crew in, but I was to offer a solution, which was the hostage situation to be reported to the local radio station.

I made the offer to Woolum that we would report the situation on the radio and would provide him an AM radio so he could hear it. He did not like that idea at all. I also had to tell him we could not reach the warden. He didn't like that, either, but he was wearing down. I finally told him, "Look, I will give you my word, if you write down on paper everything you want the TV crew to know, I will personally hand deliver it to a reporter." I think he realized this was about the best deal he would get. I said, "Remember, you will get a transfer to a federal prison or an out-of-state prison, and your demands will go to the media. You have my word on that, and Mike Samburg gives you his word as well." Woolum still wasn't convinced, so I changed the subject again. "Let's work out the details of your surrender. There is an empty cell down the walk. I will go ahead and open that cell. When you are ready, drop the gun and run down to that cell. I will close the cell, then we will come in and get the officer. You will not be harmed." He didn't like that plan, so I said for him to tell us his plan. He didn't have a plan. I told him that if it were up to me, I would have the news crew here and I didn't think he was going to get a better deal. He still wasn't happy, and I didn't think he was about to surrender.

He said, "How do I know you're not going to kill me or come in here and beat the shit out of me?"

I said, "I guess you are just going to have to trust me. We haven't rushed in yet, and now the state police are here to witness everything we do. Just follow my plan, and you will not be hurt."

Woolum then spent roughly twenty minutes writing a four-page letter to the media. He described that his original plan was to escape, but when that didn't work, he tried to use a hostage to improve conditions on the Administrative Control Unit. I think more than anything, the letter helped Woolum save face. At least the media would know ACU had some issues. When the document was finished, he told me where I would find the letter, and he reminded me that I promised to take it straight to the media. I agreed and said, "The cell is open whenever you are ready." Another five minutes went by. I knew we had a deal, and I told the command center it would be over soon.

Without warning, I saw the gun hit the floor, and I saw Woolum run down to the empty cell. I was at the controls, so with the flip of a switch, I shut his cell door. The standoff was over.

I then opened the crash gate, and a small army of heavily armed E-Squad members and state police troopers stormed the unit and took up positions. My job was done. Standing there almost in disbelief the nightmare was over, I lit another cigarette and waited for Officer Jasper to walk out. I stepped out of the cage and gave him a handshake. He was visibly shaken, and neither of us knew what to say, so nothing was said. He continued walking toward the exit. He wanted out of there, and so did I. I walked with him through Two Cell House then One Cell House. As we entered the administration building, I could see a gauntlet of state police officers and administrative staff waiting for us. Everyone started clapping and shaking our hands. Officer Jasper was taken to an office and debriefed. I went to the warden's office, had a seat, and lit another cigarette. Warden Parke and Deputy Warden Samburg both complimented me for the safe release of Officer Jasper, and I sat for a while just replaying some of it in my mind. It was now nine in the morning, and all I could think was about going home to be by myself. I was all used up.

Before I left the warden's office, I believe it was Capt. Travis, the E-Squad Commander, walked into the warden's office with the gun. I could tell in the bright light that it was a soap gun. None of us, including Officer Jasper, could tell it was a soap gun in the dim light of the cell block. He handed it to the warden then to me. I didn't know what to think. I almost wish it had been the real thing. I said, "A soap gun? Really?" Then I said, "The hell with it. I'm going home."

WOOLUM'S DEMAND LETTER

First of all, I William Woolum would like to say that the first reason for this hostage situation was to escape from the Kentucky St. Prison. The plan was to escape, however if the escape wasn't successful, the next plan was to hold hostages and force the Administration to contact the news media so that my complaints would be heard.

First of all I've been in lock-up in three cellhouse since Sept. 1981. I have constantly been harassed. The conditions of the Adm. Control unit are a health hazzard [sic]. There are no windows and the ventilation is very poor. The A.U. goes outside in a bullpen once a week for one hours' excercise [sic], when the weather permits. The Administration has been aware of the situation for a long time. Don Tate has a civil suit in federal court as to the conditions at the present time. Also, the Administration was aware that this situation would make the convicts desperate enough to make a desperate attempt to change the conditions. Don Bailey was housed in 3 cellhouse on 14 cell 14 when Lt. Mike McKinney came to his cell and stated to him that they didn't want to put him on the A.C.U. because the convicts on the A.C.U. were getting ready to break out of their cells and take hostages, and that the officers were ready for it.

Instead of trying to improve the situation they harassed the convicts even more, for example: 1. Tommy Alford had all his property taken his bedclothes and mattress taken his cloths [sic] were taken and he had to sleep on cold steel for 3 days. 2. Woolum, Gibson, and Reed, were placed on 15 walk, naked with no personal hygine [sic] items, no paper, envolopes [sic], or material to write letters, wasn't allowed to brush teeth, no running water in the cell, the tolits [sic] didn't flush because the water was turned off. This lasted 21 days. On another occasion, Whittaker, Gibson, Reed and

Woolum were placed on 15 walk in the same conditions for 10 days. At one time while on 15 walk, Woolum was penalized his food ration. He was given a sandwich 3 times a day. At one point while on this sandwich diet, Officer Roy Cridder kicked a large cockroach into his cell and stated that since he wasn't getting much to eat, to eat the cockroach.

The A.C.U. is supposed to be a non-punative [sic] unit. Recently to have the hot water for coffee after midnight was taken. The convicts are taken to 15 walk when a search of the cells is done. The convicts on the A.C.U. are not allowed to be present when their cells are searched. The officals [sic] can easily deny these allegations, however if an investigation was held and all the convicts on the A.C.U. and have ever been on the A.C.U. were interviewed you will find that all the story's [sic] will be the same. These complaints may seem small to someone not in the same conditions and situation, try putting the shoe on the other foot for a while. We here on the A.C.U. are human beings too. All we ask is to be treated like humans. Also I demand that myself and anyone else housed on the A.C.U. that wants to go, be transferred to a federal prison and to stay in the federal prison until paroled, or serve out. The reason for is this because the lives of these convicts will be in grave danger because of this hostage situation. Their are convicts on the A.C.U. who were not involved in the attempted escape, or the hostage situation. However, we believe that everyone on the unit will be held responsible.

As promised, we released Woolum's letter to the press. It never made much of a splash in the news, I believe, because it was overshadowed by the hostage crisis itself. As for Woolum, he continued to be housed in segregation in Three Cell House until he was transferred as quickly as arrangements could be made to an out-of-state federal prison. He eventually returned to the Castle.

NINE

ACCREDITATION

Before we move on from the Warden Parke era, it should be noted again that in just a few short years, KSP's administration evolved from management-by-memo to management through written policies and procedures. Our objective was to meet the many standards promulgated by the American Correctional Association head on. Warden Parke set his sights on this goal from day one, after taking over the reins from Warden Sowders.

At first, middle-management supervisors were skeptical after witnessing some of the standards that completely altered the way we did business. The old-school staff viewed this effort as just another new trend that would fade away in time. Standards compliance meant two things: First, we would have to write policies and procedures for every area of the prison. Second, we would have to accept the responsibility of maintaining compliance with all the policies and procedures. It was a big job.

Some of us, myself included, supported the accreditation process.

As long as we were following policies and procedures, we would have a good defense in all the lawsuits inmates filed that criticized prison conditions and the way they were treated. Accreditation essentially meant we had to comply with nationally accepted standards for prisons. From day one of Parke's appointment as warden, he delegated assignments to all management staff and supervisors to begin drafting prison procedures. Throughout this process, KSP was inundated with violence. We had a staff murder, three escapes, three murders, a major fire, and a hostage situation in Parke's first six months. This number does not include all the fights, assaults, and stabbings. It was a rough period, but Parke moved forward, pushing and pulling us toward accreditation.

Finally, after three years of hard work, we were ready for an audit team to come in and examine each of the four hundred or so compliance standards to determine if we met the accreditation threshold. We knew going in that we could not comply with a handful of standards surrounding the physical plant. Physical plant standards included minimum requirements such as square footage of cells, maximum noise level, and other environmental concerns. These standards basically specified requirements for the structure itself. After all, KSP was built in 1884. We were still occupying Cell Houses One and Two, which didn't come close to meeting the minimum for cell size and space. But, if we didn't fail one of the forty *mandatory* standards, we had a good chance of passing inspection.

A team of three auditors came from different states, and all were experienced wardens or management staff. Though we were hopeful we had done the work necessary to modernize KSP, we failed one of the mandatory standards regarding fire safety. One of the auditors, Gene Scroggy, noted that the mattresses issued to our inmates were not fire retardant. So he conducted his own burn test in one of our parking lots. He chose a random mattress for the test. It took a little effort to light the material, but once lit and turned into the wind, it continued to burn and smoke badly. Scroggy concluded that our mattresses presented a significant fire hazard, and KSP failed accreditation.

CELEBRATION FOR LOSERS

We took the news hard. I had only once seen staff morale at a lower point, and that was after the murder of Pat Ross. We had worked so hard, and the result was devastating. Warden Parke had planned a big celebration party at Kentucky Dam Village State Park. He had rented one of the executive houses and provided cold cuts and hors d'oeuvres, along with several cases of beer. It was too late to cancel the event.

I really didn't want to attend the festivities under false pretenses. Like many others, I wasn't in the mood to party. But I went anyway to show solidarity with the staff. As I opened the venue door, the first thing that caught my eye was the spectacle of two female correctional officers fighting with each other. I have no idea what they were at each other's throats about, but the fight was a good one and spilled out onto the lawn. They were separated, and one of them left. I sat down with a beer and drank about half of it before another fight broke out between two male officers. There were probably thirty or forty staff there, and more would arrive after dark. . It wasn't a great vibe. Everyone was pissed off. Add some booze to the equation, and I knew I would probably be in a fight before long.

I didn't even say goodbye or tell anyone that I was leaving. I just got the hell out of there. These folks would not back down from a show of force inside the prison, so I knew damn well they would fight until the bloody end at that party. The moral of this story is to celebrate your wins—and, when necessary, cut your losses.

AN APPEAL

A short time after the failed audit, Warden Parke appealed the auditors' decision. He argued that the test conducted by Gene Scroggy had not been valid. Parke had done his homework and demonstrated how a fire test would be conducted properly, in a laboratory. In addition, we provided documentation that proved KSP mattresses had been treated with a fire-resistant chemical. Parke maintained we had done our due diligence in preparation for the audit, and the "field test" was not scientific and therefore invalid.

The American Correctional Association Commission reviewed the appeal and, ultimately, agreed with Parke. KSP was granted accreditation.

Parke was promoted to commissioner of the Department of Corrections soon after the audit, and he was in a position to hire his replacement at KSP. Apparently Gene Scroggy, the auditor who failed us, expressed interest, and Parke appointed him after obtaining the governor's approval.

TEN

THE SCROGGY ERA

Gene Scroggy was warden from April 1984 through June 1987. He was well-known and respected in Corrections, especially the American Correctional Association (ACA), where he attended national conventions and workshops. He had an impressive résumé to accompany his stellar reputation at ACA.

KSP needed a warden with proven leadership qualities and experience. Scroggy fit the bill. Staff at KSP were hoping that Deputy Warden Mike Samburg would be selected, but for reasons that have been lost to history, Commissioner Parke didn't believe he was the best candidate. Shortly before Scroggy was appointed, I was promoted to fiscal manager. Warden Parke wanted me in this position to give me experience managing a budget and to learn the multitude of regulations that control purchasing and service contacts. I was a fish out of water, but I accepted the position.

Once he took over, Warden Scroggy quickly fell back to what he knew best, which was delegating work through a strict military chain of command. He wanted all supervisors to report up that chain of command. Gone were the heady days of Parke's "open door policy." I had been used to reporting directly to the warden when I needed an answer to anything that required his approval. There were individuals along the chain of command who were either incompetent or didn't want to be bothered. Scroggy told me that, as fiscal manager, I should report to Deputy Warden Willard McLean. Scroggy "didn't have time to deal with the little people." That's a direct quote. Deputy Warden McLean, however, spent working hours in his office with the door literally and figuratively closed. He wanted no part in managing this area of the prison. McLean was a military veteran who was hired straight into a senior management position just to fulfill a minority quota. He was nice enough and intelligent, but he didn't have a clue how the prison operated, and gave everyone the impression he didn't want to learn.

Scroggy's strict chain-of-command protocol put me in an untenable position. I could only report to Deputy McLean, and all decisions to and from the warden would likewise have to go through McLean. In a perfect world, that would have been fine, but McLean really had no idea what he was supposed to be doing. With no other option, I reported to McLean when I needed the warden's decision on a matter. Naturally, I never got answers. This was a frustrating time in my career. I had no direction and could not get the answers I needed to do my job effectively. My morale plummeted. I finally decided that if the warden didn't want to deal with "the little people," to hell with it. I would let the warden sit in his ivory tower, totally isolated from my help and advice.

This was happening to other supervisors and managers as well, and most of us took the path of least resistance. Scroggy's interaction with line staff also left them demoralized. There were times when he would address line officers at roll call like a military general talking down to his troops. (Scroggy once said he could hire monkeys to sit in a gun tower all day.) No one wanted to ask questions of a man who treated them with such disdain, and staff quickly grew detached and discouraged. Whatever message Scroggy was trying to communicate got lost in the translation. Scroggy would inevitably fail without input and advice from his advisors, or the support of his staff, but that was the way he wanted to manage KSP.

Soon after Scroggy began his stint as warden, I got a call from Warden Sowders. The latter had been demoted from deputy commissioner to warden of a new medium-security prison in Danville, Kentucky, called Northpoint Training Center. Sowders had two deputy warden positions open and asked if I would come aboard. I interviewed and was selected as the deputy warden of security. My days with Warden Scroggy were over, and I could not have been happier to get away from him. As for Scroggy, he eventually left KSP and moved on to another state, but not before KSP experienced a major riot under his watch.

THE RIOT OF 1986

Tensions were high in June 1986. Many inmates were complaining and filing grievances about the food. Racial tensions were seething just below the surface. At least two black inmates had been murdered by members of the Aryan Brotherhood by the end of 1984. Black gangs such as the Bloods, Crips, and Gangster Disciples were constantly at odds with the Aryan Brotherhood and with each other. Each gang had their "turf" on the yard, where they would hang out. If those boundaries were respected, bloodshed was kept to a minimum.

Word quickly spread throughout the prison on Friday, June 20th that a hunger strike was in effect. Inmates had been stockpiling canned food items and snacks from the commissary. This did not go unnoticed by the staff. Unusually brisk food sales were often an indicator that inmates were planning on being locked down for one reason or another. The spike in sales was reported to the administration.

Beginning Saturday morning, and continuing through Sunday, only a handful of inmates ate meals in the mess hall. Those who did eat in the kitchen were reportedly harassed by the rest of the inmate population. Everything was eerily quiet that weekend. Inmates were not interacting openly with officers. Fights broke out occasionally, but no weapons were involved. The tense atmosphere spooked everyone. You could feel it in the air. Something was going to happen.

On Sunday, June 22nd, staff members overheard conversations between inmates in which they threatened anyone who ate in the mess hall. The warden received word that inmates were on a hunger strike and that "something" was going to happen at the evening meal. The warden ordered all inmates to return to their cells if they were not going to eat that evening. Normal yard time after dinner was cancelled without incident.

Overnight, inmates began spreading the word that no one was to report for work. In addition to the hunger strike, there would be a work strike.

Administrators decided to open the yard for inmates to have an opportunity to eat breakfast and report to Prison Industries and other jobs. Only fourteen inmates showed up.

Fights started to break out on the yard in several locations, targeting inmates who chose to eat breakfast. Officer Henderson in Five Wall Stand fired a warning shot with a .223 caliber mini-14. Then a second round. Officers responding to the fights were able to separate and cuff the inmates, then escort them to Three Cell House segregation.

As they were being escorted across the yard, a group of inmates circled the officers and inmate Danny Tetrick, who had chosen to eat breakfast that morning. They attacked the group, but Officer Choat was able to break away from the chaos and escort Tetrick to Three Cell House. Officer Coursey stayed behind, trying to fight off the inmates. He was hit several times as other officers arrived to help. Another officer, stationed in Ten Gun Tower, fired warning shots throughout the ordeal. The threat of gunfire finally worked; inmates began to back off their assault of Officer Coursey and ran to the opposite side of the yard.

By seven a.m., multiple fights were occurring simultaneously. A group of five inmates ganged up on one inmate at the door of Six Cell House, then ten more individuals started kicking him while he was down. An officer in number Four Wall Stand fired a warning shot, which dispersed the crowd. As the violence spread, Major Henricks radioed to lock down the yard.

Instead of returning to their cells, the inmates gathered in a large group on "the hill." When ordered again to lock up, they sat down defiantly on the ground. Inmates across the yard continued to defy officers' orders.

Those who were passively sitting down began moving around and throwing rocks at officers. Sgt. Peek reported that inmates were ransacking the recreation shop and gathering pool balls to throw at officers. Officers were told to seek shelter in a safe place. The E-Squad was staged just outside the sallyport, waiting for orders to go in and restore order.

By 7:20 a.m., a full-scale riot had erupted. The recreation shop was destroyed. Windows were broken out, toilets were ripped from the floor, and a large-screen TV was destroyed. A fire was set on top of a pool table.

The officer in number Ten Gun Tower reported he was under attack by pool balls and rocks and could not return fire because of flying glass from the windows that were being broken out. Meanwhile, other inmates had broken into the legal office and set it on fire. A large group of inmates moved toward the yard office where Officers Marie Harper and George Aldridge were locked in. Officer Jack Smith had locked himself inside the laundry and was radioing for help because a group of inmates was trying to break in to kill him. Inmates also started fires in the caseworker's office and the property room, and inmates in Six Cell House used bedsheets to tie walk doors closed in an attempt to prevent the E-Squad from entering.

The situation was deteriorating rapidly.

Sgt. Billy Baker, a member of E-Squad, climbed the ladder to enter Six Gun Tower and retrieve the Ruger Mini-14 rifle from Officer Geldback. He fired two shots toward the laundry area where Officer Smith was located, then fired three shots into the ground directly in front of the laundry. The inmates retreated to an area between the legal office and the recreation shop, which was out of Baker's line of sight in the tower.

E-Squad entered the yard through the sallyport under Six Wall Stand and formed a line facing the yard. Roughly ten rounds of CN and CS gas short-range projectiles were fired toward the inmates gathered under the water tower. E-Squad also fired shotguns to repel the inmates away from the officers locked in the yard office and laundry. Once E-Squad arrived, these officers were able to retreat to safety under Six Wall Stand.

Warden Scroggy and Sr. Capt. Hendricks watched all of this play out from the second floor of the administration building. As Scroggy barked orders from the window like a general in battle, Sgt. Roy Gill "accidentally" fired a canister round that sent a cloud of tear gas through the open window where Scroggy was staged. While it was treated as an "accident," everyone on the E-Squad knew differently. Scroggy learned the hard way that once E-Squad is deployed, the best thing for a warden or deputy warden to do is stay out of the way and let them handle the situation.

Lt. Pershing, one of the E-Squad commanders, used a bullhorn to order the rioters to lie face down on the ground or risk being shot. Fortunately, inmates began following orders as the E-Squad continued to fire round after round of shotgun shells and tear gas.

E-Squad finally made their way to Three Cell House after the yard was cleared and physically forced the inmates into a bullpen area to be restrained. One inmate tried to attack the squad formation, and Lt. Ezell hit him in the face with the stock of his shotgun. Nobody else stepped out of line after that.

Inmates continued to yell and scream after the violence subsided, but once locked in their cells, the riot was effectively over. Property damage was extensive. Miraculously, however, there were no fatalities. Only a few inmates suffered injuries.

The E-Squad efficiently and decisively stopped the riot as quickly as it had begun. This was yet another notch in the belt of one of the most effective emergency response teams in the entire Department of Corrections. As Lt. Pershing once observed, "We are the solution to the warden's problem." Indeed they were.

ELEVEN

NORTHPOINT TRAINING CENTER

My stint as the Deputy Warden of Security at Northpoint Training Center (NTC) began in 1984. Northpoint started receiving inmates just before I arrived, in 1983. The original prison structure was an old abandoned hospital, known as Kentucky State Hospital, with large dormitories, a mess hall, and recreational facilities. The property did not have an enclosure around it, and construction started almost immediately to build a secure double fence and gun towers. A control center was also designed to restrict access to the facility. Inmates began arriving just as the fence was being finished, and within six weeks, the prison was two-thirds full. NTC's projected capacity was seven hundred inmates. The biggest challenge we faced was the lack of a segregation unit, because that is a modern prison's primary method of punishing inmates for rule violations. The sixty-bed segregation unit now housed at NTC would not be built for a couple of years.

Dewey Sowders had served as warden at several other facilities, including the Kentucky State Reformatory, and he began recruiting staff from the reformatory and the nearby Blackburn Correctional Complex. He also hired many of the staff who worked at NTC when it was a mental hospital and juvenile facility. The Kentucky Department of Corrections was desperate for beds, and inmates started arriving well before the facility was secure. Staffing was way below the authorized level, but it opened anyway. As they did at KSP, wardens from other prisons began dumping their problem inmates at NTC, particularly those who had filed lawsuits and grievances. They were deliberately sending their "knuckleheads" to set up shop in the new prison on the block.

WHAT A RIOT

Just as Northpoint approached full capacity, a riot broke out primarily between white and black inmates. The prison was not ready to deal with a riot, so several E-Squads from other facilities were brought in to regain control—but not before three correctional officers were severely injured. There were many inmates injured as well, but thankfully no fatalities.

I was appointed deputy warden of security soon after the riot, and I assessed the security of NTC so that I could prioritize my to-do list. We already knew the most glaring deficiency was the lack of a segregation unit. The prison lacked holding cells. Housing was comprised entirely of open dormitories. There was no way to segregate inmates who got into fights or inmates who assaulted staff. There was no way to punish troublemakers. Despite these glaring shortcomings, we were still expected to institute some form of law and order. It was an almost insurmountable task. I met with the unit managers, and we devised a plan to convert broom closets into temporary holding cells. Unfortunately, the broom closets did not have commodes, so the inmates would need to be handcuffed and escorted to the restroom. It wasn't much, but it was better than nothing.

I also assessed the type of inmates who were being dumped at Northpoint. I recognized several who I knew to be troublemakers from KSP. I asked the classification managers to draw up a profile of the prison population. I wanted to know the racial balance and the security levels of our inmates. We discovered that our racial balance was out of line with the statewide average, and we had an unusually large number of close-security inmates. A close-security classification is between medium security and maximum security. Typically, close-security inmates are doing a lot of time and need closer supervision but are not considered maximum security. I brought this issue to Warden Sowders, highlighting the fact that we had over two hundred high-security inmates in a facility that didn't yet have a secure perimeter or segregation unit. It is common practice (and common sense) for medium-security inmates to be housed at a medium-security prison and high-risk inmates to be held at a maximum security prison. As far as we could tell, however, there had been no effort to sort out inmates according to their security level. The result was a prison riot soon after Northpoint opened its doors.

In retrospect, the prisoner classification system should never have permitted close-security inmates to be housed in a medium-security institution with open dormitories. With such glaring deficiencies, NTC was doomed to fail. It almost felt like the central office staff either didn't know or didn't care about Northpoint's problems.

Finally, mercifully, construction was completed on NTC's sixty-bed segregation unit in 1986, and this gave us the tools we needed to control the population. Northpoint would soon become accredited by the American Correctional Association—but getting there proved to be an uphill battle.

WARDEN DEWEY SOWDERS

The other problem handicapping Northpoint's early progress was bureaucratic red tape. Warden Sowders loved to play politics in his position. He would hire anyone who had been recommended by local or state politicians, and he promoted staff if they had political pull, no matter how incompetent they might be. This was Sowders' greatest weakness as a leader, in my opinion. I always recommended staff for promotion based solely on their ability and experience.

Though Sowders had his faults, he was a successful warden and was well liked by many in the Department of Corrections. He was a master with the budget, and he excelled at manipulating staff to get the job done. At the same time, Sowders showed me what not to do in a leadership position. Wardens should set an example for everyone else in the prison. That includes attending training seminars and acknowledging the hard work and skills of those around you. Sowders never learned these universal truths about his job.

After a number of years at Northpoint, I felt like I had a good grasp on my job as deputy warden. Now I had significant experience working in medium- and maximum security prisons. Confident I was ready for the next step in my career, I applied for warden positions in several states.

Ted Engle, the deputy director of corrections in Ohio, called soon after he received my application for warden. He wanted to meet. Ohio was building ten new prisons, and they needed experienced staff from other states. It was a golden opportunity. The only problem was that Ohio had an administrative regulation that prohibited hiring a warden who had not served in some other capacity in the state for at least six months. Deputy Director Engle asked if I would accept a position of deputy warden first, then he would assign me to the next open warden's position if I performed well as a deputy warden. I asked if I could have time to think about it. It would be a big deal to move my family to another state, but the challenge of learning a completely new way of doing things in another prison system appealed to me. Engle told me to take my time and call him when I was ready to make the move.

Little did I know fate was about to deal me a very different hand.

TWELVE

THE GREAT ESCAPE OF 1988

On June 16, 1988, inmates at KSP staged a mass escape in the middle of the night. I heard the news later that morning as I was getting ready to leave for work at Northpoint, some 200 miles from the Penitentiary. As the news spread, I breathed a sigh of relief that I wasn't there. I had worked through past escapes as a correctional officer at KSP, and I knew how stressful and dangerous the next few days (or more) would be. Very few details were known, except that eight inmates had escaped from the segregation unit. I didn't call any of my friends back at KSP because I didn't want to bother them. Besides, I doubted they would have time to chat with me.

At nine o'clock the morning of the escape, Warden Sowders called me into his office and asked if I knew about the situation. He told me what little he had found out and that Deputy Commissioner Mike Samburg wanted me to call him right away. Sowders already knew we would be sending our E-Squad team to the penitentiary, but I didn't think I would be asked to go. So I called Deputy Commissioner

Samburg and asked how I could help. I had worked for Samburg for a few years when he was a deputy warden under Al Parke. We were good friends, and I admired his leadership ability.

Samburg asked how quickly I could assemble a twelve- to fifteen-man team from my E-Squad at Northpoint. I told him it would take a couple of hours because they would have to go home and pack whatever they needed for an extended stay. But I told him that my team could be on the road by noon. Samburg said, "Phil, I want you to go and lead your team. You know the penitentiary inside and out."

I could tell Samburg was rattled. He sounded desperate, so I asked a few more questions. "Briefly tell me what happened and what it is my team is expected to do." I wanted to know whether we needed tear gas, riot gear, riot shields, etc..

Samburg said simply, "Bring it all." He went on to tell me who had escaped and where. Eight of the worst of the worst had escaped from Twelve Walk in Three Cell House. Not only was all available staff out of the institution on a manhunt, but inmates at KSP were lighting fires and creating disturbances throughout the complex, even though it had been locked down. There was hardly any staff left who could respond to riot conditions in almost every cellblock, and the inmates knew it. They were doing everything in their power to force staff to return from the manhunt to deal with problems at KSP. The goal, of course, was to buy the escapees more time to get away. "Hurry, Phil. It's getting worse every minute. Get here as quick as you can," said Samburg.

It took longer than expected to select the best team I could assemble, pack our gear, and get on the road. I briefed them as best I could. I told them we would run blue lights in the left lane as we raced towards Eddyville. In a separate vehicle, I took Lt. Larry Napier and drove ahead of the van carrying the others. Napier and I wanted to arrive early so we could assess the situation before my team got there. I think we probably averaged ninety miles per hour the entire length of the

Western Kentucky Parkway. Napier and I arrived about an hour before the others, but they were at KSP and ready to go by seven that evening.

Our first assignment was to shake down every inch of Three Cell House. Another team from KSR in LaGrange had arrived about the same time. Their team and mine searched inmates and cells for contraband, which was a massive job. We were finished by four thirty a.m. After a short rest so we could check ourselves into a local motel, we returned to KSP to help with the roadblocks and the manhunt.

The escape had occurred sometime between one fifty a.m. and two a.m. the previous night. Inmates had set a diversionary fire in another section of Three Cell House, and all available officers had left their posts to respond. This allowed enough time for nine inmates to break out of their cells, crawl through a heavily barred window, and down a thirty-foot wall using a power cord removed from a pedestal fan as a rope.

One prisoner, Jessie Brumly, was captured by Sgt. Blick as he made his rounds on the outside perimeter, but eight inmates managed to break free and disappear into the darkness.

THE ESCAPEES

You could not have handpicked eight more dangerous inmates to lead a prison escape. The gang included Bill Hall of Paducah, Kentucky, who was serving twenty-three years for burglary, wanton endangerment, assault, theft, and possession of a forged instrument; Derrick Quintero of Clarksville, Tennessee, serving thirty-seven years for robbery, kidnapping, theft, and two counts of escape; James Blanton of Farler, Kentucky, serving forty-eight years for receiving stolen property, burglary, wanton endangerment, escape, and for being a persistent felony offender; Leo Spurling of Louisville, Kentucky, serving life for manslaughter, murder, two counts of wanton endangerment, unlawful imprisonment, and being a persistent felony offender; Floyd Cook of

Gravel Switch, Kentucky, serving life for rape, assault, robbery, and being a persistent felony offender; Robert Sherman of Lilly, Kentucky, serving fifteen years for robbery, escape, promoting contraband, and wanton endangerment; Ronnie Hudson of Louisville, Kentucky, serving forty-two years for murder, assault, attempted escape, promoting contraband, theft, wanton endangerment, and being a persistent felony offender; and Joseph Montgomery of Louisville, Kentucky serving forty-two years for assault, attempted escape, murder, being a persistent felony offender, promoting contraband, and theft. This was like a who's who of bad guys. And they were suddenly free.

THE ESCAPE PLAN

The Great Escape had been weeks, maybe months, in the making. As I mentioned earlier, inmates had methodically hidden away hacksaw blades and smuggled them into Three Cell House. We never did find out where the blades came from or who had brought them into the cellblock. The maintenance shop kept their blades under lock and key, and they were counted at the end of each day. Investigators were confident the hacksaw blades didn't come from the maintenance shop. Informants told us that a dirty maintenance staff member had brought the blades in, and inmate legal aides smuggled them into Three Cell House. The informants didn't know enough to give names, but that is all we ever came up with.

Once the blades were in the unit, inmates used them to cut a small steel track that held the bottom of each cell door in place. They would hide their work by filling the cuts with toothpaste or shaving cream and black shoe polish. As previously described, once a door track had been manipulated, the bottom of the cell door could swing out even though the cell was locked. The door would still slide open and closed when the control center officer operated the switch, so nothing appeared out of the ordinary. The cell tracks were supposedly inspected every day by officers using a mirror attached to a stick, but detecting the inmates' handiwork was next to impossible if they had done a good job camouflaging the cuts.

Seventeen inmates had cut their tracks out of the forty cells on Eleven and Twelve Section of Three Cell House. Inmates could come and go as they pleased on the unit, provided the officer didn't see them. All it took was a diversion in another part of the cellblock to draw the officer's attention off the unit. Next, inmates had cut a metal screen over the escape window and then the heavy bars that more closely resembled solid steel slats. They were about three-eighths of an inch thick and two-and-a-half inches wide. It took a lot of time and effort to cut a hole large enough to crawl through that opening. There were two time periods when inmates could work on the window. One was during the daily exercise period, when at least ten inmates would come out together to mill about and block the view of the officers stationed at a desk behind a set of bars at the end of the walk. The other time was during the midnight shift.

The midnight shift officer would spend most of the shift away from his desk, visiting with other officers. In fact, it was later learned he only made his rounds and completed a count at the beginning of his shift, not every hour as policy dictated. The officer also failed to inspect cell bars and windows, as his post orders required. Another factor that benefited the inmates was the noise level of a nearby pedestal fan and three window fans, all of which drowned out the cutting sounds. At night, the lighting was also dimmed so inmates could sleep, enabling the culprits to work under cover of darkness. All of these elements contributed to conditions that facilitated the escape.

One final piece of the puzzle that surprised us in retrospect was the lack of information from informants. As a general rule, inmate informants would almost always send a note up front, or to a captain or unit manager, when something big was about to happen. Not this time. The inmates who had escaped were respected and feared by the rest of the prison population. They would kill a snitch, and everybody knew it.

THE ESCAPE

Even the most elaborate prison breaks, carried out by inmates who anticipate every escape contingency, rarely include a clear plan of attack once they find themselves on the opposite side of a prison wall. Unless there is help available on the outside, like a wife or girlfriend waiting with a getaway car, escapees will find themselves scrambling to get as far away from the prison as quickly as possible. These guys were no exception. After they scaled down the Castle walls, the escapees fled in different directions. One group of five followed the lakeshore, heading south. Another inmate ran down to the waterfront below a row of lakefront state houses. The last two inmates ran to a boat dock behind the warden's house and hid under the dock to wait until the coast was clear.

Of the seventeen suspects who cut the tracks on their cell doors, only a few snuck out of their cells at a time to minimize the risk they would be noticed. Despite this precaution, inmates found themselves lined up at the escape window, awaiting their turns. Tommy Crum was one of these individuals, but as fate would have it, he was too large to squeeze through the small escape hole in the window bars. His attempt to do so wasted quite a bit of time. Randall Young and Ernest Newton were waiting in line at the window when they heard Sgt. Blick's radio call that an escape was in progress and that he had apprehended Brumley. Officers stationed in Three Cell House ran to Twelve and Eleven Walk and saw Newton, Young, and Crum out on the walk. The inmates warned the responding officers that they would be taken hostage if they came on the walk. Warden Seabold was advised of this threat, and he instructed the officers not to enter until armed officers could respond. Seabold ordered Lt. Adams to put together a rapid response team, which included Lt. Mitchell, Sgt.

Prior, Officer Gray, Officer Choat, and Officer Jasis. They reported to the gun vault at One Walk Stand and were issued 12-gauge pump shotguns and .38 revolvers. Once the team had arrived in Three Cell House, they entered Eleven and Twelve Walk and quickly took control of the situation. All inmates were ordered to face the backs of their cells and place their hands on the wall. Crum, Newton, and Young were still out on the walk, but the sight of the armed guards encouraged them to race back to their cells the same way they had escaped. Lt. Adams warned that any inmate who failed to stand at the back of his cell with his hands on the wall would be shot. By this time, the inmates knew the officers meant business. It became deathly quiet for a moment, just as Officer Byron Jasis snapped the safety off his shotgun. You could hear the click of his safety up and down the cell block. The inmates were held at gunpoint until additional officers responded with handcuffs and leg shackles. The chief engineer, Jerry Merrick, also arrived with his maintenance team to secure each cell door with chains and padlocks, not just those that had been compromised.

Just prior to the escape, Sgt. Blick was making rounds outside the prison, looking for anything unusual and checking on inmate trustees who lived in a building next to Three Cell House. He took the count of trustees then walked into the boiler house to check on the boiler operator, Mr. Smith. After about fifteen minutes, he left the boiler house and entered Two Wall Stand to check on Officer Drollinger. They chatted for ten or fifteen minutes. Inmates used that window of opportunity to escape. Two Wall Stand is the gun tower next to Three Cell House. As Sgt. Blick was exiting the door to the gun tower, Officer Drollinger came out on the catwalk with her rifle and told Sgt. Blick she saw something. She wasn't sure, but she thought she saw a shadow going from Three Cell House past some vehicles parked alongside Three Cell House. Sgt. Blick looked around the parking lot and saw inmate Brumley exiting the window of Three Cell House. He was able to detain Brumley without incident. He radioed that an escape was in progress and escorted Brumley back to Three Cell House.

These events set into motion the largest manhunt in Kentucky history. Before long, there would be an army of correctional officers from four other institutions, state police from all areas around western Kentucky, as well as local police and water patrol officers. Approximately 150 officers were involved in the manhunt, as well as helicopters from the state police and National Guard. State police tracking dogs were brought in from other parts of the commonwealth. This was not only the largest manhunt in Kentucky history—it was also the largest mass prison escape in state history.

Blanton, Hall, Hudson, Montgomery, and Quintero were the first five to scale down the wall and escape. Once outside, they ran down a side street and crossed the main road in front of the prison before walking to the shore of Lake Barkley. At that time of night, there was no traffic and nothing moving. Once at the lakeshore, they made their way southwest. Within view of the prison, they walked through a neighborhood checking cars to see if any still had keys in the ignition. Many of the Old Eddyville residents had lived through an escape and manhunt before. Instead of locking their cars, some reasoned it would be better to leave the keys in the ignition, rather than to risk a desperate escapee breaking into a house and demanding a getaway car, money, guns, or whatever else was available. This was the case about a mile from the prison, where the inmates discovered a 1966 Chevrolet pickup truck in a driveway with the keys in the ignition. They stole the truck and made their getaway before roadblocks and a security perimeter had been established. Another ten minutes might have been too late. State police, city police, and prison guards soon poured into Old Eddyville to set up a perimeter, hoping they could contain the escapees who were believed to be on foot.

As the first group of inmates stole a truck, Sherman and Cook climbed down and took off in the direction of the lake behind the warden's house, diagonally across the street from the prison. They made it the short distance to the shore of an inlet and hid under a boat dock. Leo Spurling, the eighth escapee, ran down the side road in the same direction the first five had gone. By then, he could hear the commotion as KSP responded to the escape. So Spurling laid low in some weeds in the shallow water, hoping he would not be discovered until he could escape from the area. Spurling realized he had misjudged the intensity of the police response and manhunt. From Spurling's position, he could see and hear a state police tracking dog, prison guards reporting to work, and a state water patrol boat that had come within a few yards of his position. He was pinned down and would have to stay put. Shift change was at three p.m., and quite a few of the administrative staff as well as guards went off duty. They would be needed in the long days to come. By four p.m., it was quiet in the parking lots and the main road in front of the prison. Hungry and thirsty, he had to make a move. It would have been better if he had moved under the cover of darkness, but Spurling was desperate to put some distance between him and the prison. So he nonchalantly got up and casually walked across a parking lot and through the warden's yard. He noticed the boat dock ahead, but he had no way of knowing that Sherman and Cook were pinned down under the dock until they started calling out to him as he passed. Spurling joined them beneath the dock, and the three of them stayed there until later that night. They needed water and food, if nothing else. The escapees could hear police radio traffic being broadcast over a radio that somebody had left on in a nearby boat, and they soon learned the areas that were being searched.

As they listened silently from beneath the boat dock, Lt. Braden walked down to the dock armed with a .223 caliber Ruger mini-14. He was by himself. Braden walked up and down the dock, looking in the parked boats to determine if anything appeared out of place. The three escapees whispered to each other from below and decided they could take him. All they would have to do was to reach up on the walkway and pull him down into the water. Drowning him would be an easy move for three desperate men. Then they would have his rifle *and* his radio. It was almost too simple. Floyd Cook, however, hesitated to go through with the plan. He was afraid the noise would attract the attention of someone else patrolling the area. He managed to convince the other inmates to stay put for the time being.

Sometime around nine p.m., the three men swam across the shallow bay to an uninhabited wooded area. From there, they could travel over heavily wooded terrain, under the cover of darkness, to certain freedom. Or so they hoped.

THE MANHUNT

The next day, a National Guard Huey helicopter joined the search. The pilot and crew chief attended a briefing by Lt. Rick Pershing, the E-Squad commander for the penitentiary. He coordinated all law enforcement activity during the manhunt.

I knew Lt. Pershing well. We were old childhood friends and classmates at North Marshall High School. I happened to be in the command center for the briefing. The crew chief said he would need a prison staff person to ride along who could identify the escapees. I volunteered as one of the spotters. The crew chief made it clear we were not to fire at the escapees without his authority. We took our positions in the Huey. I was strapped in the door opening with my feet on the landing rail. I could lean out and observe directly under the helicopter. We began patrolling the area directly across the bay from the prison and worked our way several miles to Interstate 24. It was mostly wooded, with very few houses. What I didn't expect was the capability of the pilot and the Huey. He would lower the helicopter down to the top of the tree canopy. The wind created by the hovering Huey was like the hand of God, parting the thick trees so we could see the ground below. The pilot hovered so low at times that the helicopter blades popped the leaves of the trees. I was a little nervous about how low we were flying at first, but I got used to it. Eventually, we made a refueling trip to the airport at Kentucky Dam Village, but otherwise we completed our mission to search the wooded area all the way to the interstate. The whole effort took approximately ten hours. Unfortunately, we saw no trace of the escapees from the air.

The National Guard brought in several dozen sets of night vision goggles, which proved to be a tremendous help. By the second or third day, we knew at least some of the inmates had gotten away when the pickup truck was reported stolen, but we didn't know how many. The command center was fielding phone calls from concerned citizens who thought they saw something suspicious. Each call had to be checked out, which took time and manpower. We had also discovered that a vacation home near the lake had been broken into. Though we could tell things were missing from the cottage, including kitchen knives, we didn't have any way of knowing whether the escapees had found any guns.

BAD TO WORSE

As the manhunt continued, conditions inside the prison went from bad to worse. Agitated inmates continued to create disturbances in every cellblock. My team would often be called back to the prison to put out these literal and figurative fires. In one instance, we reported to Four Cell House to stop inmates from throwing rolls of toilet paper that had been set on fire. Their plan was to lure us into the cellblock so they could throw glass jars filled with feces and urine off the upper level of cells. (This was before fencing was added to each level to prevent inmates from pushing other inmates over the handrails to a certain death.) The glass jars were like bombs hitting the floor. If one of the jars struck an officer, it could have proved fatal. I entertained the idea of tear-gassing the entire unit but quickly decided against it because we did not have enough staff to deal with the aftermath. Instead, we took cover as best we could and methodically searched each cell to remove all the glass jars. Once the search was over, we left and the inmates settled down. Unfortunately, these pockets of unrest continued throughout KSP for days. We found ourselves spending an inordinate amount of time trying to maintain order at the prison when we should have been out hunting for the escapees.

ONE DOWN

On June 17, 1988, one day after the escape, several callers reported seeing an inmate near the perimeter we had set up between the lake and Interstate 24. At around three p.m., Sgt. Pryor called and reported that someone who was fishing near the interstate saw three people lying in the grass and weeds near the lakeshore. A team was sent to search the area, and Officer Richardville reported seeing two people run across I-24 and one person running down the westbound side of I-24. By three thirty p.m., E-Squad members Pershing, Galusha, McCarty, Ezell, and Richardville had returned from their hunt with inmate Bobby Sherman in custody. One down, seven to go.

A tracking dog was brought to the area by the interstate where Sherman had been captured. The dog could not pick up a scent, but a perimeter was set up around where two inmates were seen crossing the interstate. That night, at approximately twelve thirty a.m., I was patrolling in my state cruiser when I was flagged down by an officer on the side of the road who had just seen two men cross in front of him. The officer was wearing night vision goggles. It had happened just as I had pulled up to the scene. I asked the officer which way they went, and he replied, "They're right there!" as he gestured down an embankment. The area was at the edge of a woods and was thick with vegetation.

"Can you see them?" I asked incredulously.

"Yes!" he replied, once again pointing toward the vegetation at the edge of the woods. By then, there were about five of us searching the area with flashlights, but we didn't see anything. I decided to fire warning shots to pin them down. I positioned two officers with shotguns next to me and instructed them to fire on my signal. We each fired three shots. I aimed toward the area the officer had pointed to. The other officers fired into the woods. Not knowing if I had hit one or both, we searched the area but found nothing. Again, a tracking dog was brought in but could not pick up a scent. Since they had crossed our perimeter, we moved our perimeter about two miles further out.

As daylight broke, Officers Galusha, Ezell, McCarty, Agosto, Doles, Choat, Holland, and Richardville took inmates Spurling and Cook into custody. These were the two I had shot at several hours earlier. National Guard helicopter staff said they would fly the prisoners back to the prison. The inmates were cuffed and shackled, but the crew chief went a step further and tied a noose around their necks. He said, "I used to do this with prisoners in Vietnam. I always wanted to see what would happen if one of them jumped, so be my guest." The helicopter made a victory lap around the prison before landing in the parking lot.

Three down, five to go.

On June 20, 1988, the command center received a call that a stolen car with Tennessee tags was found near Lebanon, Kentucky. The vehicle was covered in Joe Montgomery's fingerprints.

Another report came in that positively identified inmate Billy Hall in Somerset, Kentucky. Local law enforcement was tracking him, waiting to see if he returned to the house where he had last been spotted. A few minutes later, a call came in that inmates Montgomery and Hudson had stolen a Jeep. These sightings were made over two hundred miles from the prison, however, so a decision was made to let local and state police take over the search in Somerset.

A small team was stationed in the E-Squad building at KSP to respond to any reported sightings. All the other E-Squads, including the Kentucky State Reformatory, Luther Luckett Correctional Complex, and Northpoint Training Center, were preoccupied with searching KSP cellblocks for contraband. Several knives were found in each cellblock. The inmates, meanwhile, were still highly agitated from the extended lockdown. Some refused to be cuffed, so E-Squad had to enter and forcibly remove anyone from their cells who failed to cooperate. These searches went on for what seemed like days.

At the same time, the E-Squads took turns patrolling local roads and responding to sightings. We were reasonably certain by this time that five of the inmates had escaped in the stolen pickup truck, but the public was still calling in suspicious sightings right around the lake we had to check out.

In fact, the escapees who stole the truck had made it to a lake resort area near Dover, Tennessee. There, they broke into several vacation homes to load up on supplies. Inmates Montgomery and Hudson then decided to split up from the rest of the group. They stole another car and drove to track down relatives of Hudson's in Taylor County, Kentucky.

SHOOTOUT AND CAPTURE

Kentucky State Police were working a lead that Hudson and Montgomery were on foot in Taylor County after abandoning the car they had stolen in Dover. Kentucky State Police set up a roadblock nearby and called Northpoint Training Center to ask for help conducting a search. Seven officers, including Capt. Sims and Capt. Napier, responded to assist. Soon after their arrival, a call came in that Hudson and Montgomery were spotted near a local church. Almost every available law enforcement officer descended on that area to flush the escapees out, which led to a foot chase through a cornfield behind the church. During the chase, inmate Hudson fired four shots from a .22-caliber pistol. Capt. Napier and Trooper Minks returned fire. Hudson tripped and fell in the hail of bullets. He threw his gun down and gave up. Montgomery quickly found himself surrounded and also gave up. Both inmates were captured and returned to KSP by the E-Squad.

Five down, three to go.

MURDER

Back in Dover, Tennessee, inmates Quintero, Blanton, and Hall drove to a house occupied by an elderly couple named Buford and Myrtle Vester. The Vesters were retired restaurant owners from Nashville. Quintero had done construction work in the region, so he was familiar with the resort area and many of its homes.

The three escapees had made plans to hightail it to Mexico as soon as they could. All they needed was another stolen vehicle, some food, cash, and guns. Many of the houses where the Vesters lived were only occupied on weekends. The remote, wooded area is located roughly sixty miles upstream from KSP, near the headwaters of Lake Barkley.

Their plan was to hide the discarded pickup truck as best they could and steal the Vesters' car. The Vesters did not have any close neighbors, making it less likely anyone would notice their suspicious activity.

After shooting the telephone connection box outside the house to prevent anybody from calling for help, the fugitives shot Mr. and Mrs. Vester through their bedroom windows. They then ransacked the house, stealing guns, food, and cash. Now fully armed and flush with money, the escapees were able to drive all the way to the U.S.–Mexico border, stopping only for gas. They crossed the border at El Paso, Texas, and holed up in a motel in Ciudad Juarez, Mexico, some ten miles south of the Rio Grande. At this point, they found themselves running out of money, but the fugitives were hesitant to commit another robbery in unfamiliar surroundings—or to risk drawing unwanted attention to themselves.

Hall made a phone call to a relative, who agreed to wire money to the group, but in order to obtain it, Hall would have to recross the border at El Paso to pick up the funds at a Western Union location. Texas authorities were alerted that the money transaction had taken place, and they arrested Hall in El Paso without incident on July 6, 1988. Three days later, Mexican authorities surrounded the motel and arrested Quintero and Blanton. They transported the convicts straight to the border and handed them over to FBI agents. There was no arrest warrant and no extradition order by the Mexican Federal Judicial Police —a move that actually violated Mexican law. From their jail cells in El Paso, the two inmates began arguing that their arrest and deportation had been illegal. Each prisoner was assigned a different attorney by the U.S. Magistrate, Scott Segall, who concluded that the legality of their arrests under Mexican law had no bearing on an extradition request by another country. Segall ordered the inmates held without bond and returned to Kentucky. The inmates' attorneys wanted time to appeal to the United States Court of Appeals for the Eighth Circuit, so the case would get caught up in legal proceedings. They argued this case had violated several international laws, including a longstanding extradition treaty between the U.S. and Mexico. The magistrate agreed with the district attorney, however, who argued that the Fourth Amendment stops at the Rio Grande and does not apply outside the territorial boundaries of the United States. The magistrate further concluded that even if he had found the arrests illegal, he couldn't ship them back to Mexico, and he couldn't give them a writ of protection to keep them from being arrested as soon as they stepped into Mexico.

Seventeen long months (and several appeals) later, the matter was finally put to rest when the Supreme Court refused to hear the case. The inmates were sent back to Kentucky to face new charges. They were then extradited to Tennessee to stand trial for the murders of the Vesters.

Inmates James Blanton, Derek Quintero, and Billy Hall each received the death penalty in Tennessee. Two of the three have since died of natural causes: Blanton in 1999 and Quintero in 2021. At this time of this writing, Hall is still awaiting execution.

All eight of the inmates involved were convicted of escape and other charges and were sentenced to an additional ten- to twenty-year prison term under Kentucky law.

As the events of that fateful summer lingered in the news for months, KSP tried to return to some sense of normalcy. In reality, prison staff felt even more demoralized as things slowly settled down. The deaths of two innocent people weighed heavily on the minds of everyone employed at the Castle.

THE INVESTIGATION

Following the escape of 1988, the Department of Corrections wanted answers. Garland Beyerly, Director of Security for the Department of Corrections, Warden Parke, and Warden Sowders were tasked with investigating the event and its aftermath. Their final report cited a number of factors that contributed to a breakdown in security at KSP. Overcrowding was a pervasive issue, made worse by a population of younger inmates serving longer sentences. In addition, the penitentiary had been built a century earlier, and had not been updated with modern lighting and security features that could have helped prevent escapes. And, equally problematic in my view, employees felt increasingly demoralized after years of federal court oversight that placed stringent demands on limited staff. The workload had increased dramatically in the 156-bed segregation unit, as employees struggled to comply with ACA standards and court-ordered changes. The review team determined that current staff simply did not have enough hours in a single workday to oversee responsibilities as varied as daily showers, meals, one hour of exercise outside the cell, attorney calls, and on and on. Among other recommendations, the panel suggested increasing the number of correctional officers by forty-seven positions. They called for security enhancements, including better lighting inside and out, solid steel cell doors instead of bars, increased oversight of inmate clothing and property, additional training for security, and some staff reassignments. They also recommended creating six new maintenance staff positions and halting all inmate labor in maintenance areas.

Warden Seabold had only been the warden for seven months when the escape occurred. For all practical purposes, he did not have enough time to learn the complexities of the prison with its 350 employees and 900 inmates. Had Seabold been in charge of KSP for a couple of years prior to the escape, he would have been fired—or at least moved to a different position. As it stood, Seabold received the full backing of Governor Wilkinson and the Department of Corrections.

PERSONNEL SHAKEUP

While Seabold managed to avoid any real accountability for the events of 1988, the Department of Corrections investigation concluded that the deputy warden of security should be replaced with a more aggressive person. They also recommended a change in the segregation unit manager.

After I returned to Northpoint with my E-Squad that July, things felt like they were slowly returning to normal. We welcomed the relative calm of NTC following the grueling and dangerous ordeal at KSP. I was more than ready to move on—but alas, the DOC had other ideas.

A few weeks later, Deputy Commissioner Mike Samburg called and asked me to meet with him in the Central Office of the Department of Corrections. He wanted to know if I had seen the investigative report on the escape at KSP. I hadn't read it, but Warden Sowders and I had discussed the findings over coffee. After spending almost two weeks back at KSP with E-Squad, I was intimately familiar with the circumstances that precipitated the greatest prison escape in Kentucky's history. Samburg explained that one of the DOC recommendations was to assign a more aggressive deputy warden of security. Samburg looked me in the eye. "Phil, you are that person."

"Oh, hell no," I replied. "I don't want to go back to the penitentiary. I've had enough of that place to last a lifetime."

Samburg ignored my protestations. "Phil, it has already been cleared by the governor on down. Even Federal Judge Johnstone has given his nod. Secretary Wigginton and his assistant Lyle want to meet with you."

"When?" I asked, slightly bemused.

"Now."

Samburg led me down the hall to Secretary Wigginton's office. Wigginton was seated with Lyle and Barbara Hickey, the human resource officer for the Corrections Cabinet. After ushering us in, Wigginton got straight to the point. "Phil, we need you to go down to the penitentiary and straighten that place out. Mike tells me you worked your way up from a guard."

I said, "I'm sorry, but I really don't want that assignment. I see it as a career killer. With all the lawsuits, consent decrees, and a federal judge watching every move, it is a no-win situation. What about the warden? Is he okay with this?"

Mike replied, "Phil, he will be."

"You mean he doesn't even know yet?"

"No, we wanted to talk to you first," Mike admitted.

I didn't know what to make of this. "If I agree, how long would you expect me to stay at Eddyville?"

Wigginton interjected, "Well, I don't know. Maybe six months to a year."

I thought for a moment. "How much of a pay raise?"

Wigginton turned to Hickey, who replied, "We can't give you a pay raise because it would be a lateral job change, not a promotion."

This was sounding worse by the second. I knew if I turned it down, my career would be over until a new governor and secretary were in office. On the other hand, I knew damn well that if I accepted the transfer, I would be stuck at KSP until something else catastrophic occurred. I asked if the Department of Corrections would pay for all my moving expenses. Lyle said yes, that they could do that. I clarified that I didn't mean a U-Haul. I meant an actual moving company that would pack and unpack everything. Lyle agreed. Wigginton went on to say that they needed my answer. He explained they had looked at all the other deputy wardens, and no one approached the experience or knowledge necessary to take on this job. I was their only choice.

Wigginton said he wanted to call Barbara Jones to join the meeting. Jones was the general counsel for the department. I knew and respected her from our time together fighting inmate litigation in federal court. She was a top-notch attorney, and I trusted her. Jones joined the meeting. Wigginton asked her to tell me about the conversation she had with Judge Johnstone. Jones conveyed that Judge Johnstone was very concerned about the situation at the penitentiary. He knew everything was very fragile and KSP was a powder keg. Johnstone advised DOC that they must do whatever was necessary to get things under control at the prison.

I asked for clarification. Was Johnstone implying that we did not have to follow every detail of the Consent Decree? Did this mean we could exercise martial law? Jones explained that regaining control of the KSP was more important. Once things returned to normal, we could once again prioritize our compliance with the Consent Decree and court orders.

Apparently, Governor Wilkinson wanted the KSP fiasco swept under the rug as quickly as possible. The mass escape had made national news, and it was a source of lingering embarrassment for the governor and the DOC. They wanted solutions that would fix this mess as quickly as possible.

I requested that I be able to bring my own unit manager to manage Three Cell House. They asked who I had in mind. I told them Brad Mitchell. I explained he was the best employee we had—tough as nails and relentless when he had a goal to achieve. Wigginton turned to Samburg and asked him to see if that could be worked out.

My next question was more pointed: "How much authority do I have to make changes? What if the warden doesn't go along with my proposals?"

Wigginton thought for a moment, then replied, "As far as I am concerned, you get that place under control no matter what you have to do. I don't think Warden Seabold is in a position to impede your progress."

It sounded like Wigginton was giving me the authority to override the warden. I hoped that wouldn't be necessary. "Okay, one last thing," I said. "After I've been there for six months, if I have met your expectations, what is next for me?"

He replied that DOC intended to make me a warden at one of the state prisons.

I wanted to be sure I had heard him correctly. "Six months and I will be promoted to warden if I can get the penitentiary under control?"

"Yes," Wigginton assured me. Stifling a smile, I stood up and reached out to shake hands with everyone in the room.

"When do I start?" I asked. Wigginton said that Samburg would work that out. As we left the room, I followed Samburg back to his office. We sat down and went back over everything I had just agreed to with a simple handshake. "Mike," I said forcefully, "I am going to hold him to it. I will go back to that hellhole, and I will restore order. But you will need to run interference for me when the warden doesn't like what I'm doing. I'm going to move fast and hard."

Samburg voiced his support. "Phil, thank you for stepping up. You will do fine."

"Okay, let's get started. Just remember I agreed to go for six months."

BACK TO THE CASTLE

By late July, all the arrangements were in place. A moving company was hired to coordinate the moves so that Deputy Warden Jim Morgan would be transferred to Northpoint and my family would be relocated to the deputy warden's house at KSP. In the meantime, I'd taken up residence at a local motel until my family could join me in Eddyville.

I wanted to learn everything I could about what went wrong at KSP. I also needed to gauge how bad the morale had gotten at the prison. I interviewed every lieutenant and captain. Most of these men had been my supervisors just a few short years ago. I knew all of them fairly well, and I hoped they would accept me as their supervisor. I made it very clear that I expected them to work together and to work with me to regain operational control of the penitentiary. I assured them that I would have their backs when the shit hit the fan, but I also needed them to be honest and straight with me when things went wrong. I explained that we were going to be more aggressive in our handing of problematic inmates. If a situation called for a heavy-handed approach, so be it—just don't lie about it, and don't cover it up. I told each of my officers, "We are going to restore order, and we are going to start today."

I knew that KSP supervisors were demoralized and embarrassed by the prisoner escape. Inmates were still setting fires, stopping up toilets to flood the cellblocks, and throwing feces and urine on officers they didn't like. I knew we needed to deal with this first. Assaulting officers with anything, let alone bodily fluids, was no longer going to be tolerated.

As I made the rounds in Three Cell House that summer, incidents arose in which a use-of-force team was assembled to do a cell extraction. I got the impression in those early days that the team was reluctant to use force because I was there observing the proceedings. After a cell extraction, I would call the team together and encourage them to be more forceful. I made it clear that a use-of-force team would need to hit hard and fast. Any inmate who resists authority exposes himself to the use of force until he complies with our orders. Put another way: inmates who posed a threat to the safety and security of the prison are fair game until they were restrained with cuffs. This was the only way we would get prisoners to fear and respect the use-of-force team. Line officers and supervisors were understandably surprised; they had never heard anyone from the administration explicitly encourage such forceful tactics before. Quite the opposite, in fact—they had been criticized for using force in the past, and they were reluctant to cross any line that would expose them to discipline or, worse, legal jeopardy. Many of these supervisors knew that I was one of the twelve officers who had been sued in federal court for brutality and harassment. Given my past experience, I think my team was surprised to hear me coaching officers to be more forceful. I reassured all of them that they would not face disciplinary action for use of reasonable force, so long as the inmate in question was resisting and would not submit to restraints.

NEW SHERIFF IN TOWN

I had been deputy warden of security at the penitentiary for about two weeks, and Three Cell House was still a mess. Staff assaults were up. Flooding and fires were still occurring. You could hear the constant sound of banging as inmates rattled cell doors and slammed their metal beds on the floor. Things were not getting better, at least not fast enough to suit me.

I made the rounds almost every day in the segregation unit, and it was clear that more had to be done to control the cell block. An early priority was to give each inmate a military burr haircut. One thing learned from the escape was that inmates could easily conceal hacksaw blades or handcuff keys in their long hair. The only way to detect contraband concealed in long hair is for an officer to run his hands all over the inmate's scalp then feel all through their hair. It was both time consuming and demeaning to the officers involved. So I issued a memo, delivered to each inmate, that from now on any inmate entering the segregation unit would be subjected to a military-style haircut. Furthermore, all inmates already housed in segregation would sit for a mandatory haircut immediately. It didn't go over well. Inmates told staff they would die first, daring officers to just try and cut their hair. Word got back to me and Sr. Capt. Hendricks about this, and I told Hendricks that I didn't know about him, but I wanted to be there when we did this. He grinned at me and said, "Me, too."

We selected the biggest, toughest inmate to go first. I led a squad of my best officers to extract him from his cell, and they held him in a makeshift barber chair while an officer cut his hair. What happened next was rather funny. Officer Rufus Diamond mentioned beforehand that he used to be a barber in the military, and I told him it was good enough for me. It wasn't good enough for the inmates. They threatened to sue us because Diamond didn't have a barber's license. My response was, "Fine. If you run out of ink and paper, let me know." I wasn't about to be intimidated by the threat of a frivolous lawsuit.

After fighting with the first inmate to get him seated, he kept moving his head back and forth to prevent Diamond from making contact with the shears. Our expert barber stopped and looked at me for guidance. I nodded and said, "Go ahead." Diamond found himself trying to manhandle the inmate's head with one hand and cut his hair with the other. Each time he made a pass, the clippers gouged his scalp. Now the inmate was bleeding, and I'm sure the scalp cuts hurt. I stopped Diamond for just a moment and told the inmate, "We are going to cut your hair the easy way or the hard way. Your choice, but I guaran-damn-tee you, we will not leave until it is done."

I motioned for Diamond to continue, and this time the inmate sat passively. He made another swipe with the shears, and the inmate yelled profanities. Diamond looked over at me and said, "Boss, this razor is too dull to cut hair."

I dispatched an officer to the inmates' barber shop to "borrow" an electric razor that we knew was in good shape. Fifteen minutes later, we finished the job and escorted the inmate back to his cell. I watched closely to gauge the reaction he got from other inmates. A few of them snickered, but almost immediately we had a volunteer. "Take me in next." Tellingly, there was little resistance from that point on. After watching the meanest and toughest guy go first—and walk away with a head full of nicks and scrapes—the other inmates did as they were told. We went on throughout the day cutting hair. I felt good about what we had done. We had regained control of the segregation unit, at least for a while. The officers saw that it was possible to do the impossible. Morale improved slightly, just because of this.

The other issue that continued to plague Three Cell House was violence directed at the staff. Inmates assaulted officers with food trays and bodily fluids, set fires, and flooded the floors with toilet water. We debated how to address this behavior in creative ways.

One idea was the use of a "food loaf" or "nutrition loaf." Each meal we served was approved by a registered dietician in the Central Office. While the dietician told us what to serve, we weren't told how to serve it.

I implemented a new policy. Any time an officer had food thrown on him, the inmate would be served a food loaf for a week or two. Simply put, the kitchen staff would take a food tray in the exact amounts prescribed by the dietitian, then put it in a blender and bake it in a loaf pan. No more liquid food. It was all blended and baked. Sure, inmates could still throw food on the officers, but they would be getting hit with a piece of dry bread instead of sloppy beans, soup, or whatever else was served for that meal. The inmates had no grounds to file a grievance and claim their food did not meet dietary guidelines. Prison rules and regulations did not say the food had to taste good—

and we took advantage of this oversight to curb inmate violence. Once the loaf policy was implemented, instances of food violence toward the staff ended almost overnight.

We also implemented a uniform policy to replace any street clothes worn by inmates in segregation. We only permitted one set of scrubs and one pair of shower shoes. This was another big change for the segregation unit. In the past, inmates had been allowed several pairs of blue jeans, T-shirts, a coat, and tennis shoes. They were also permitted all sorts of commissary items, including cigarettes. Our plan eliminated all commissary items for inmates in segregation. After all, this was a punitive unit. Why should they have privileges? Warden Seabold did not like this idea and reminded me that some of the inmates in segregation were not there for punitive reasons. He was right; we did have a large population of individuals in protective custody in Five Cell House. And there was a contingency of mentally ill inmates who did not fit in general population or protective custody. With this in mind, we reached a compromise. Commissary items would be permitted in segregation, but we would remove all lighters to discourage setting fires. To be clear, an inmate could still smoke, but he would have to ask an officer for a light. That newfound level of dependency forced inmates to treat officers with respect. If an inmate treated an officer poorly, he would just have to go without his nicotine fix.

My aim throughout all of this was to eliminate as many privileges as possible, thereby making conditions so uncomfortable that inmates would change their behavior to get out of segregation. To a large extent, the haircuts, food loafs, and loss of lighters alone served as a huge deterrent.

LIVING IN SEWAGE

I had been the deputy warden of security for about three or four weeks when I formulated another rather unpleasant response to inmate mischief. As I made rounds in Three Cell House one day, I got to Eleven and Twelve Walk and saw officers out on the walk sweeping up food and picking up trays that inmates had thrown out of their tray slot. Not only was the place trashed with food and food trays, but someone had flooded the walk by stopping up his commode. The culprit had also made spitballs out of toilet paper, and it was splattered all over the walls. It was humiliating for officers to have to clean up messes that a child would know better than to make. I called the officers over to the crash gate where I was standing and asked them what they were doing. "Well, sir, we have to clean this up because you said we could no longer use walk boys." A walk boy is an inmate volunteer who is calm enough to perform janitor duties or assist with serving meals. In fact, I had said we would no longer let walk boys out to distribute contraband and run errands for other inmates on the walk. I never suggested my officers had to clean up inmate messes.

The answer to this problem struck me like a lightning bolt. I said, "I tell you what. They made this mess, so let's let them live in it. Bring me a stack of towels and a case of toilet paper." The officers looked at me like I was crazy. I said, "Go ahead. I will stay here and take your duties," which was just to observe. A few minutes later, they came back with a stack of towels and a case of toilet paper. "Okay. Now let's build a dam across this walk at the crash gate to hold back the water when they feel like flooding the unit." We lined up rolls of toilet paper and covered that with towels to fashion about a six-inch dam. The dam worked. Water would seep under the dam, but it could easily be wiped up with a towel.

While I was standing at the officer's desk, I made a phone call to the business office and told the purchasing officer to go out and buy various sizes of rubber boots for my officers on Eleven and Twelve Walk. She asked, "How many pairs?" I said just buy all they have at the local farm store.

Then I told the officers their job duties said nothing about being a janitor or a babysitter. I said, "From now on, if an inmate throws something out of his cell, it stays right where he threw it. That includes food trays, toilet paper, feces, or whatever. Furthermore, it is not your job to mop up water. Get rid of the mops and buckets. You won't need them anymore. I'm going back to my office to cut new post orders that says exactly what I just told you."

The two officers didn't know what to think. They looked at each other and then me. One of them gave me a military salute and said, "Sir, yes, sir! Thank you, sir!" I just had to chuckle at this and returned the salute.

I went back and wrote the addition to the post orders and told Major Hendricks to communicate this order to each shift and the unit manager. At the end of the day, the warden went off duty before I could tell him what I had done. I don't think I ever told him, but I'm sure he knew. He never mentioned it.

Five days later, on a Sunday morning, I was home resting when there was a knock on my door. It was Lt. Billy Sewell, who was the Three Cell House supervisor on weekends. Billy was a year or two older than me, but we had been drinking buddies back in high school. I liked Billy. He was a big man just like many of the others who had made rank, but he was levelheaded and had a sense of fairness about him. I invited Sewell in. "What's going on, Billy?" I knew he was there for a reason; otherwise, he would not have bothered me on my only day off.

He said, "Mr. Parker, it's about your orders in Three Cell House. I think you need to come and see for yourself."

I responded, "Oh, you mean my orders not to clean up the inmates' messes?"

"Yes."

I said, "Okay, Billy. I know you wouldn't bother me if it wasn't important. I'll get dressed and be right over."

As I entered Three Cell House a half hour later, I thought to myself, *What the hell is that smell?* Then it dawned on me. The smell was Eleven and Twelve Walk. I went on up and stood and looked out over the walk. It was a hot August day, and the temperature was already ninety degrees. The officer on duty didn't say anything. He didn't have to.

Sewell walked up and said, "It's pretty bad."

I replied, "I'll go in and see if I have their attention. Remember, we didn't make this mess, they did." The floor appeared to be moving with maggots. Everything—the food, the urine, the feces, and whatever else —had turned septic. It was awful. In fact, words can't describe how horrible the smell was. I told the officer in the cage to let me in. I stepped over the dam I had built five days before, and immediately the water depth was over the top of my dress shoes. I should have worn the boots, but it was too late. Before I went in, I went over the inmate roster, looking for the toughest convict in the unit. I had a good idea that would be John Bennet. As I made rounds, you could not hear a peep from anyone. It was eerily silent in the unit.

Just as I expected, as I was passing Bennet's cell on Twelve Left, he said in a very low voice, "Mr. Parker, can I have a word with you?"

I said, "Sure, what's on your mind?"

He was standing in the same septic swamp water I was in. He sounded almost pitiful, then said, "Mr. Parker, if you will let me out of this cell with one other helper, we will clean all this up, and I give you my word it will not happen again."

I thought for a minute and said, "Okay, John, I'll give you one chance. Just remember, I didn't make this mess. If it happens again, tough shit. This is your home, and if you want to live like this, then just have at it."

John replied, "No, sir. You will not have any more problems." I considered this a huge victory, just like the haircuts. Inmates were starting to dance to my tune. In retrospect, it is hard to imagine five days of food trays, food scraps, feces, and who knows what else festering in August weather. I knew it was probably toxic and might even meet the criteria for cruel and unusual punishment, but I never so much as got a grievance over it. If I recall correctly, a few inmates may have written to the warden and newspapers, but I never heard any more about it. Everyone knew I would make good on my promise to let them lie in their own slop and filth if that's the way they wanted it.

SHIT DOWN

There was one other time toward the end of my stint as the new deputy warden when inmates threw feces on officers. Brad Mitchell, the unit manager I had brought with me from Northpoint, called and said, "Mr. Parker, they just shit down the Classification Committee."

I went right over to Three Cell House. It appeared as though one of the inmates outside in a recreation group had thrown a cup of feces at the area where the committee had been seeing inmates. It was the inmates' exercise period, so there were ten of them. The cup of feces had splattered on the table and paperwork, and some of it had splattered on committee members' clothes. No one saw who did it, but they had a good idea. I told the committee to clean up and call it a day. I was thinking of ways I could handle this, but there just weren't many good options except use of force. We were in the process of lobbying local politicians to legislate a new law to make assault with bodily fluids a felony, and we felt sure it would happen at the next legislative session.

I had one other trick up my sleeve, but I would need the right opportunity to make this work. The next day, I sent for Sgt. Holloway to report to my office. This was the same Holloway who I had gotten into a fight with the first day of E-Squad training, years before. I said, "Kenneth, I need your help, and I need to keep this quiet. I want you to go to town and buy a big roll of plastic like the kind you would put in your crawl space at home. While you're at it, I want two big rolls of duct tape. Bring these to my office as soon as possible. Next, I want four cans of CN tear gas grenades and a few 'mighty midgets.'" These were the smaller version of a tear gas grenade. "I don't want anyone else to know I have the tear gas. It will be safe in my office until I need it." He looked at me, and I knew he wanted to ask why, but he was a retired Navy veteran, and I knew he would do exactly as I asked without asking a question.

About a week went by after I had the tear gas and plastic. I put out orders in Three Cell House that I wanted to be called anytime any officer was "shit down."

I got a call from Brad Mitchell advising me that word was out the inmates were going to "shit down" me or the warden the next time either of us made rounds. I thought to myself, *Well, well. I guess I'm going to have to give them a target.* I told Brad I would be right over and asked him to keep everyone off of Fourteen Right until I got there.

Mitchell said, "I just came off the unit, and I heard it again from some of the snitches." He also said, "You can smell it."

I was wearing a business suit that day, which gave me plenty of pockets to conceal the tear gas. I grabbed the roll of plastic and duct tape and headed for Three Cell House. Mitchell was waiting for me, but he had no idea what I was up to.

I gathered up several officers along with Mitchell and said, "Okay, here's the deal. I'm going in by myself. I'm going to give them a target, but let me get this straight. There is a conspiracy among several inmates to shit down me or the warden. Is that what I understand?"

One of the officers spoke first. "Yes, sir. I wouldn't go in there if I was you. You can smell it."

I said, "Well, I'm not going to ask you to go in if I won't do it myself. I'm going in alone to make rounds. When you see someone throwing shit on me, start taping off this walk with plastic then go around the back of the walk and tape it off. You need to work fast because I'm going to gas the hell out of that place. But I don't want to gas the other walks that aren't involved." Again they looked at me like I was crazy, but they liked my plan.

They replied, "Yes, sir, boss, but be careful."

I said, "Okay, now gather the keys you will need to go around to the back of the walk. When you're ready, I'll go in."

Mitchell studied me for a minute and shook his head. "You're something else, boss. I never would have thought of that."

Time was up. I signaled for the cage operator to open the crash gate, and I leisurely strolled down the walk. Yep. I could smell it as I passed by a few of the cells. I turned around and went up the steps to Thirteen Right. No one had a word to say, not even the normal questions I got every time I make rounds. Complete silence. I made rounds on Fourteen Walk, this time stopping in front of each cell. No one even made eye contact or said a word. I figured one of them was getting his nerve up to attack me, then the others would probably start throwing shit. I continued slowly down Fourteen Walk. I took my time. I wanted to give them the target they were looking for. Nothing, not a peep. Back up to Thirteen Walk, and all the way back and then back to the steps and down. I was puzzled. Why wouldn't they take the shot? They didn't know I had tear gas. I hadn't told anyone, and I was sure Sgt. Holloway hadn't either. The only other people who knew what I was up to were at the gate, ready to seal it off when I launched the grenades. I couldn't figure it out.

I gathered up the officers after I exited the walk and told them to keep this quiet because I might try it again. I took Mitchell off to the side and said, "Brad, what do you think happened? I gave them a perfect target, and they didn't take the shot. Why not?"

Mitchell replied, "I can tell you why. You spooked them when you went in by yourself. Nobody does that. We escort nurses, caseworkers, the warden, you, and other deputy wardens. They are afraid of you. You are too unpredictable, and it spooked them."

I said, "Well, you may be right. I guess I should celebrate the fact that I didn't get shit down." I told him it was five o'clock somewhere, to come on over to the house, and we would have a drink.

He said, "Okay, boss. I've had a long day."

I never did get to deploy my plan to gas the unit, and it's probably just as well. That would have been a big lawsuit, I'm sure.

Although the inmates in Three Cell House didn't throw feces on me like they said they would, they continued to shit down staff. One of the worse cases I remember was the time an inmate threw feces on Officer Mike Laffoon. I had worked with Officer Laffoon at Northpoint before he transferred to KSP. He had a good sense of humor and was a lot of fun to be around. Laffoon was a good officer and did a great job. He had earned a spot on the E-Squad and worked in Three Cell House. It was roughly the same time period, during the fall of 1988, that Laffoon was assaulted with feces while he was making rounds on Fourteen Left. It was the worst case I had ever seen. As he walked down Fourteen Left making a count, an inmate threw a cup of shit right in his face. He didn't have time to duck, and he reactively opened his mouth in surprise. As bad as this sounds, he swallowed some of the feces. It was all over his face, in his eyes, and in his mouth. I had never seen an assault this bad. I was called by Mitchell, and I went right over to see if I could do anything for Laffoon. When I got on the scene, he was down on Fifteen Walk taking a long shower. He was given an inmate jumpsuit to wear while his officer's uniform was being washed.

I could only imagine how Laffoon felt. I think my reaction would have been to kill the inmate if I could get my hands on him. But we had developed a policy that required the victim to be separated from the location of the incident while the other officers four-pointed the inmate. We also required the cell extraction and use of four-point restraints to be filmed. Otherwise, it would have been too tempting for the officers to engage in vigilante justice. After Laffoon took a long shower and brushed his teeth, he vomited a few times. When he had finished vomiting, I tried to comfort him, but there just weren't any words that seemed appropriate, so I said, "Officer Laffoon, I want you to go on home. I don't think you need to be here right now."

He said, "I appreciate that, but I want to stay."

I said, "No, Mike, go on home and come back tomorrow."

He reluctantly agreed. I walked him out to the front gate. I felt so bad for him. It was awful beyond words.

After work, I went home and was still troubled by the assault. I called his home and asked his father how Officer Laffoon was doing.

He said, "Not good. He is out in the driveway puking." Apparently, Officer Laffoon was guzzling whiskey and then vomiting. I asked his father if he thought it would do any good if I came over to see him. His dad said, "No. Just let him drink and get it out of his system."

I told him, "Okay," but also said he should not hesitate to call me if there was anything I could do. I also asked him to please let Officer Laffoon know I had called to check on him. His father was upset just as much as I was, but there really wasn't anything else to do.

Officer Laffoon eventually recovered from the assault. He had a lot of good friends and drinking buddies for support, and as always, he continued to work and do a great job. I don't remember exactly, but a year or two later Mike Laffoon died of a sudden heart attack. He was only fifty years old. Most correctional officers die of one thing or another before they reach sixty. Some take their own lives. Some drink themselves to death. Most die young.

A few days after Officer Laffoon was assaulted with feces, another incident occurred. Staff assaults were still taking place in segregation, and as the deputy warden of security, I felt an obligation to try to prevent any threat to my staff. I had to react firmly, but I also had to make sure we didn't overreact. Maintaining the correct balance was always a difficult task. I left strict orders for staff to call me whenever there was a staff assault. For one thing, I would respond to the unit immediately if for no other reason than to show support. It would not be right to just sit back in my comfortable office while other staff suffered abuse at the hands of inmates.

Another staff member was assaulted with feces and urine, but not in his face. He was led off the walk to shower. Our priority was to remove an officer from the scene so he wouldn't take matters into his own hands. The officer in this case showered and waited on Fifteen Walk, knowing the move team would soon be down with the assaulting inmate to strap him to the bed. He patiently waited with a baton. As the move team passed by the location where he was hiding behind a door, the officer stepped out and struck the inmate with the baton. Unfortunately, the inmate was in restraints and could not cover or defend himself. He only hit the inmate one time before the move team stopped him from hitting him again. I'm sure he would have continued and possibly severely injured or even beaten the inmate to death.

I reviewed that case very closely because I knew that we would have to take disciplinary action against the officer for unjustified use of force. We might even have to fire him. After thinking about it overnight, I went to Warden Seabold's office and recommended a three-day suspension. I think Warden Seabold was ready to fire him, but I asked the warden to put himself in the place of the officer who just had feces and urine thrown on him for no reason. What would you do? What would I do? I can tell you that my first reaction would be to kill him if I could get my hands on him. If I could get a baton, I would beat him in a rage if no one stepped in to stop me.

We couldn't let the officer completely off the hook, but it would be an injustice to fire him. A lot was at stake. Everyone was watching to see what the administration would do. If we were to fire him, it would be another blow to staff morale. We could not condone the officer's retaliation, but I thought a three-day suspension would send a message that officers could not behave in this manner. Reluctantly, Warden

Seabold agreed with me. We issued the suspension, and the officer gladly accepted the disciplinary measure. He was sure we would fire him. Other staff were relieved as well.

Even though we showed empathy and compassion, the underlying problem was still not resolved. There would be more assaults. It was time to make a strong stand. If these assaults continued, I wasn't sure we could find good officers to work the unit. Our men and women rightfully expected the administration to protect staff from these threats. We considered placing all officers in protective jumpsuits, face shields, and latex gloves, but it just wasn't practical. It might even encourage inmates to assault the staff more. We needed a deterrent— but what? We never did find the answer to this.

There is one other story about Three Cell House when I was the deputy warden of security. I was making rounds as I usually did every few days. Mostly I made frequent rounds in Three Cell House to be seen by the officers, and I always tried to show support for what they had to do each day. After all, it wasn't that long ago that I was a guard in Three Cell House. I knew what it was like to have a bad day. And most days were bad.

BOOTY WARRIOR

The day in question was relatively normal, except for inmate Fleece Johnson, a.k.a. Booty Warrior, who was running his mouth and cussing all the officers. He had flooded his cell earlier in the day, and he was in four-point restraints for a few hours.

Brad Mitchell, Unit Manager, had moved him to the first cell on Fourteen Walk, which is the first cell you encountered when you walked in. From that vantage point, Fleece had a good view of every-thing and everybody who came into the unit. When he saw me come in, he mouthed something at me, but I didn't pay any attention. I went on up to the top of the cellblock and made rounds, then worked my way back down. It just happened that the only walk I had not been down was Fourteen Walk, where Fleece Johnson was housed.

When I got to the crash gate to go in, Mitchell came up grinning and said, "Fleece left you a present."

The other officers standing around were snickering, but I hadn't caught on yet. I said "What? What in the hell is going on?" They were all amused because I hadn't seen it yet.

Finally, Mitchell said, "Look out on the walk in front of Fleece's cell."

I glanced out and exclaimed, "Oh my God. I can't believe Fleece would do this knowing I was about to make rounds." Fleece had thrown a turd out of his cell, which had landed about six feet from his cell door. When I saw it, Fleece started laughing his ass off. He thought it was funny. I stood there for a moment, then I told the cage operator to hand me a riot baton. Mitchell and the other officers suddenly grew serious as I said, "I'm going to make him clean it up."

Brad said, "No, Mr. Parker, we will take care of it. Fleece was just being Fleece."

I didn't respond. I told the cage operator to open the crash gate to let me in, and I turned as I went in and said, "Everybody stay back. I'm going to handle this." When the crash gate closed behind me, I turned to the cage officer and said, "Open Cell 1. Fleece, get your ass out here and clean up your shit." I said it again: "Get a handful of toilet paper and come out here and clean up your shit." He realized I wasn't kidding, but he didn't refuse. He was grinning and laughing, but he came out and used the toilet paper to pick up most of it, and he returned to his cell and put it in his commode. Once again, I addressed him and said, "Fleece, come back out here and get the rest of it and then wipe the floor." He started to get belligerent, but I was standing there with a riot baton ready to bust his head. He knew from my tone and demeanor that I was serious. Fortunately, he did exactly as I instructed him. He put it in his commode, then sat down on his bed. I said, "Close Cell 1," and the cage operator secured his cell and opened the crash gate for me to exit. By then, most of the officers in the cell-block were standing outside the crash gate. They all wanted to see me make Fleece clean up his shit.

I had violated every policy I was trying to impart to the staff. For one thing, any time there is a planned use of force, the policy required it to be videotaped. Secondly, policy required a team suited up with helmet, padding, and shields. Fleece Johnson was a very dangerous inmate. He had attacked officers repeatedly. For whatever reason, Fleece feared me. He knew I would probably bust his head, and that day, I would have. I was sick and tired of inmates assaulting staff with feces. Rather than go back and try to explain to Mitchell and the officers and apologize, I figured the best thing to do was to never mention it again.

Years later, when I was warden, I heard this story recounted by someone who wasn't even employed when this happened. The story had gotten so embellished it was comical. Apparently I had dragged him out of his cell without a baton, kicked him in the head until he had had enough, then dragged him back into his cell. It had grown into a legend, and I just chuckled when I heard this story. I thought, *What the hell, let 'em think that.* I was ashamed of the truth, and the embellished version was better anyway.

SHOWDOWN WITH SECRETARY WIGGINTON

My six-month assignment at KSP was almost up. Anticipating my next move, I made a phone call to Ted Engle to see if the offer of a deputy warden position in Ohio was still good. He sounded glad to hear from me and said, "Yes. Are you ready?"

"Almost," I replied. "I got reassigned, and I'm about to fulfill my part of the agreement."

"You know George Wilson is our new director?" Engle asked.

"Yes, I know, but I'm not sure he remembers me."

"Sure he does," Engle assured me. "He said you were a good, solid employee, and you have a good reputation."

"Well, I appreciate that," I replied. "I will get back to you as soon as I finish up here."

I called Secretary Wigginton's office and told his assistant I wanted to meet with him to discuss reassignment from the penitentiary.

She put me on hold for a minute and came back on and said, "Can you see Mr. Lyle?"

I said, "No, I need to see the secretary."

She put me on hold again, came back on the line, and asked me to be there Monday at one p.m.

This was in February, and I had been at the penitentiary since August. Our agreement was that I would get a warden's job after six months, and there were witnesses to agreement. I was going to take the Ohio job anyway, but I wanted to see how this would play out. Meanwhile, Deputy Commissioner Mike Samburg had taken a warden's job in Virginia. I didn't have him to pull for me. It really didn't matter. I was resolved to resign and take the Ohio job, especially now that George Wilson was the director in Ohio. Mr. Wilson had been in the Kentucky system for years. He had been the Commissioner and then the Secretary of the Corrections Cabinet. I had never had a problem with him, but we had never worked closely. All my time was in prisons, and he was always in Central Office.

I arrived in Central Office thirty minutes before my appointment with Secretary Wigginton. Just before one p.m., I saw Barbara Hickey, the department's Human Resources Manager, go into his office. Five minutes later, Wigginton's secretary said, "Mr. Parker, you can go on in."

After the normal greetings and pleasantries, I opened the conversation. "Mr. Wigginton, I'm here for my new assignment." He looked as if he didn't know what I was talking about. I really don't think he remembered assigning me to the penitentiary. So I said, "If you will recall, you asked me to replace the deputy warden of security at the penitentiary, and we agreed on a six-month assignment. Then I was to be appointed as warden." Again, he looked as if he couldn't believe what he was hearing. He turned to his administrative assistant, Jim Lyle, who nodded his head confirming what I said was correct.

Mr. Lyle said, "Mr. Secretary, we did agree to reassign him as warden after six months."

Barbara Hickey didn't say anything. She probably thought I had a lot of balls to confront the secretary with this.

Mr. Wigginton looked at Hickey and Lyle and asked, "Do we have any warden vacancies coming up?"

Barbara said, "None that I know of."

Wigginton turned back to me and said, "Phil, you have done a good job, and we don't have anyone to replace you. Would you stay for a ten percent raise?"

I said, "No. I was told six months ago that it was not possible to give me a raise on a lateral transfer."

Hickey interjected, saying, "It is unusual, but it is possible."

"Well," I replied, "I have kept my part of the agreement to do my best for six months, and then I was to be reassigned."

Wigginton then asked Hickey, "Do we have any deputy warden vacancies?"

"Yes," she said. "We have a vacancy at KSR."

Wigginton turned back to me and said, "Phil, the best I can do is a deputy warden job at KSR and a ten percent raise."

I stood up and said, "I want to thank you for meeting with me, but I will be turning in my two-week notice effective today." No one in the room expected me to resign. I knew they knew I had been one of their best deputy wardens for four years.

As I was about to leave, he said, "Phil, do you have another job offer?"

I said, "Yes, I'm sorry, but I do."

He wanted to ask me where and what, but he didn't, and I didn't want to tell him. I figured it was best to let him wonder about it.

The next day, I called Ted Engle in Ohio and told him I had given my two-week notice and I was ready to come to Ohio.

He said, "Great! We have a deputy warden's position at the Corrections Reception Center (CRC) in Orient."

We set my start date for February 14, 1989.

THIRTEEN

OHIO BOUND

I reported to work at headquarters in Columbus, Ohio, and met with Ted Engle and George Wilson. It was just a meet and greet, but Engle informed me that I would need to attend the academy for three weeks before starting at (CRC) in Orient. That was fine with me, because it would be a great way to get to know Ohio Department of Corrections.

Once I finished the academy, I reported to CRC to start my new job as a deputy warden of operations. CRC was a new, large prison housing over two thousand inmates. It was a fascinating operation.

Sheriffs from all over the state would deliver inmates who had been sentenced to prison. We never knew what to expect. Some days we would receive thirty or forty inmates, and other days we would receive one hundred or more. It was run like a boot camp. Inmates would be stripped of all their clothing and dressed in prison coveralls. They would receive a burr haircut then wait to be screened by medical staff. Some were very sick with heart disease or cancer. We had a large medical wing for inmates with medical problems. Otherwise, inmates would go through orientation and would be given a handbook. There was a lot of down time until they would be classified and transferred to an appropriate facility.

Overcrowding was a huge problem in Ohio. There were several large prisons under construction, and several had just been activated. I wasn't used to seeing large prisons that could accommodate up to five thousand inmates in a single facility. Despite this, the prison system was way over capacity.

I was amazed at how they moved hundreds of inmates through the mess hall at CRC. A supervisor, usually a lieutenant, would stand on the sidewalk leading to the mess hall as inmates were released from one of the dormitories and made to form a straight line behind the lieutenant. During that time, talking or messing around was not permitted. The lieutenant didn't care how long it took; he wouldn't move the line forward until it was straight.

I watched this play out every day. The inmates weren't provided with raincoats or heavy coats. It didn't matter. If they wanted to eat, they had to fall out and form a straight line, even in pouring rain.

JOHNNY PAYCHECK

The medical wing was a different story. Many of the inmates were in wheelchairs, or they were confined to a bed. This is where I met Johnny Paycheck, a well-known country music singer and Grand Ole Opry member notable for recording the David Allan Coe song "Take This Job and Shove It." Paycheck had been convicted and sentenced to seven years for shooting a man in a local bar in Hillsboro, Ohio. The .22 bullet grazed the man's head, so he wasn't seriously hurt. Paycheck claimed self-defense. He spent several years fighting the charge, but he began serving his sentence at CRC in 1989.

When I met Paycheck, he was in the medical wing. He had severe

COPD from a lifetime of smoking and was on oxygen. Otherwise, Paycheck was fairly healthy for someone who smoked, drank, and used drugs. I went by his bed and chatted with him for a little while. He was in a good mood and assured me I wouldn't have any problem with him. Paycheck was rather philosophical about having to do time. He said, "I'll just have to make the best of it."

The upside of prison for alcoholics and drug users is they cannot indulge in their addictions, except on rare occasions when drugs are smuggled in or someone makes a batch of hooch. In the six months I was at CRC, however, I never saw or heard of a drug bust. It was a tight environment, where every moment was programmed.

As soon as Paycheck had been nursed back to health, we shipped him to Chillicothe, a large prison in southern Ohio. Paycheck was well-liked by staff and inmates. Art Tate was the warden at the time. Paycheck wanted to perform a concert for the inmate population. His real motivation was to stay involved in the music industry. He proposed this idea to Warden Tate, hoping the warden would go along with producing an album. The warden was all for it. Paycheck also asked his old friend, Merle Haggard, if he would help him. Not only did Haggard agree to help him produce new music, but he also agreed to perform with him on stage in Chillicothe. The warden had to clear this with the director in Columbus, but there was really no downside to allowing Paycheck to perform for the prison. The warden allowed a producer to come in and set everything up for a show at Chillicothe. Years earlier, Haggard had done time himself for robbing a roadhouse, and he and Paycheck were close friends. They cut an album, produced and recorded in its entirety of the concert at the Chillicothe prison. After serving twenty-two months in prison, Ohio Gov. Richard Celeste pardoned Paycheck.

GRAFTON CORRECTIONAL INSTITUTION

Following CRC, I was appointed warden at Grafton Correctional Institution (GCI) near the small town of Grafton, in northern Ohio. GCI is a medium-security prison and only a short drive to Cleveland. Because of its proximity to Cleveland, our inmate population preferred to do time at Grafton instead of one of the other prisons further south. This meant they would have more opportunities for family visits.

Designed to be one of Ohio's premiere prison complexes, Grafton was new and clean. No expense had been spared in construction. Grafton is where I met Ernie and Mindy Williams. Mindy was briefly employed at Grafton as the human resources manager, but she transferred across the street to a new prison called the Lorain Correctional Institute. Ernie remained at Grafton as the deputy warden of security. We became good friends almost immediately. He was a no-nonsense deputy warden who had started his career as a correctional officer at Marion Correctional Institution. Ernie was a captain when he was promoted to deputy warden. We both knew that we were on easy street, working in a state-of-the-art prison with well-behaved, medium-security inmates.

For the most part, my time as warden of GCI was uneventful. In addition to the new prison, we also operated a 1,200 acre farm with eighty dairy cows and a large pork operation. The housing for the farm inmates was an old dormitory with a kitchen and dining room. It was situated next to the dairy barn. There was an active railroad track running right through the farm property that led directly into Cleveland. Occasionally, we would have an inmate escape from the farm. They could follow the railroad tracks to the city, but more often than not an escapee would have a girlfriend or wife pick him up on the road. They never got very far.

Ohio's prisoner escape policy differed from Kentucky's. In Kentucky, the use of deadly force was authorized *as* an inmate was escaping. Once the inmate had escaped, use of deadly force was not authorized. In Ohio, the use of deadly force was authorized to stop an escape, and it was also authorized to capture an inmate if he refused to stop. I could not find a written policy on the use of deadly force to capture an inmate who had already escaped, so I called my boss, Tom Strickrath, who was the North Regional Director. He was also an attorney. Mr. Strickrath confirmed that deadly force was authorized to capture an inmate who had already escaped and would not comply with verbal orders to surrender. A recent example involved an inmate who had been shot and killed while running out of a house that was surrounded by correctional officers. It was a legal shooting, even though the inmate was unarmed as he fled. Wardens also had the authority to forcibly enter a residence if they were in hot pursuit of an escapee or had probable cause to believe the escapee was in the premises. A warrant was not necessary.

ESCAPE

On a warm spring day in 1990, we had an inmate walk away from the farm operation. When the workday was over, we took a close count of all inmates, inside and out. We were missing a gentleman named John Embry. He was about thirty-five years old, doing time for theft of a car. It wasn't his first crime, but he did not have a serious rap sheet. I didn't think of him as "armed and dangerous." We believed his girlfriend picked him up on a side road close to the dairy operation. The worst part was that this escape occurred on a Friday, which pissed me off because I knew it was going to mess up our weekend.

After calling in the escape to headquarters, I picked my best staff to go with me on the manhunt. In the past, we had used prison cars to stake out places where the inmate was likely to hole up, or we would stake out a crack house in the inmate's neighborhood. Using state vehicles was a dead giveaway that prison staff were on the hunt. This time I decided to wise up and use our personal cars. I think we had four cars in total, and about ten staff.

Once we had located his last known address before he entered prison, we staked it out most of the night. We did see people coming and going, but not him. I figured it was a matter of time. Lucky for us, we found out that his girlfriend had just gotten out of prison on parole. We got in touch with her parole officer and got her address and phone number. This was the house we were watching.

One thing I learned from stakeouts is that criminals like to party until about three in the morning. Then they go to bed and crash. You will be wasting time on a stakeout after three a.m. We returned the next afternoon about six p.m. Drug addicts, drug dealers, and prostitutes were just waking up and making plans for another night of partying. At least this is the way it plays out most of the time, especially on weekends.

One of the staff who I assigned to internal affairs was Eddie Young. Young had worked for the Lorain County Sheriff's Office for years as a detective. For most of his career, he worked undercover in narcotics. At one time, Young was assigned to work with the Drug Enforcement Administration (DEA) in Miami, FL. He was considered one of the best undercover narcotics officers in the country. Undercover narcotics officers often burn out quickly or they become targets. Some don't survive long. Making drug busts is dangerous work, and Young was good at it.

Young came up with the idea to place a phone call to the house we had staked out to try to flush the escapee out. He made a collect call to Embry's girlfriend, told her he was an inmate at Grafton, and said he wanted to warn Embry that prison staff were on their way to her house to search for him. Once he had made the call, we just sat back to see who left the house. We immediately saw several people running, but none of them was our man. When that didn't work, Deputy Ernie Williams called and told Embry's girlfriend that we were in her driveway and asked if she would come out and talk to us. We were still watching the house.

I showed her my identification and told her to get in my van for questioning. She was uncooperative at first, but Young reminded her that she was on parole and that his next phone call would be to her parole officer. Then I told her that because of my position, I could arrest her on the spot and take her to jail for a charge of harboring a fugitive. She kept denying, saying she didn't know anything, so I told Young to make the call, and I would hold her until the parole officer arrived. That was enough. She said, "I'll tell you where he is."

"Okay," I warned her, "but it had better be the truth." She gave us an address about five blocks away, but I wasn't about to let her go. I said, "I want you to take us to his location." She agreed and rode in my van.

THE CAPTURE

We pulled up and surrounded the house. It was a two-story apartment house with steps leading to the second-floor apartment. The girlfriend said he was on the second floor. I asked if he had any weapons. Her answer wasn't very convincing, but she said, "No." She also noted that he had been drinking since he had escaped and was probably asleep.

I made the decision to kick the door in and take our fugitive by surprise. I could have called the Cleveland Police Department to get backup, and maybe go in with a flash bang grenade, but I decided we would handle it.

As we were preparing to go in, the girlfriend started crying and implored us to let her talk him out so that no one would get hurt. We asked her to tell us who else was in the apartment, and we wanted to know whether Embry had access to any guns. She told us he didn't have a gun, but he did have a large kitchen knife lying next to the couch. She also said Embry was alone, and that she was supposed to come over and stay with him later.

We put her in another car and discussed how we were going to proceed. It was risky to go in forcibly, and it would be better if we could talk him out. We decided that he was probably drunk, and wouldn't cooperate, and he might have a gun. We finally decided to let her go in and talk him out. I told her, "You have five minutes. If he doesn't come out, we are going in."

She said, "That's fine. I can get him out." Young and I stayed at the bottom of the steps while she went in. Five minutes passed, then ten, and I started walking up the steps. They must have been watching because as Williams, Young, and I started up the stairs, the door opened. Embry stepped out with her in a headlock and a knife at her throat. We all had our guns drawn, ready to take him out. He started down the steps, and I was yelling at him to let her go, but he kept coming. I backed about five feet from the bottom step, still pointing my gun at his head. Now I could tell he was drunk. I said, "Let her go, or I will blow your fucking head off." I repeated this about three times, but he kept advancing, and I kept backing up. I must have convinced him at the last minute, because he shoved her away and then came at me.

I backed up until I felt a fence at my back. I couldn't back up anymore. He was then only about six feet from me and still coming fast. I screamed at him to drop the knife and lay down on the ground. Finally, I knew that I had to shoot him. I gave him one last warning as I squeezed the trigger of my .38 revolver. Suddenly, he disappeared from view.

Capt. Van Horn took Embry down from the side, but I never saw him approaching. I had tunnel vision, just like they told us about in training. All I could see in the final moment was my target, and I had been aiming at his chest.

That was a close call. One of my officers, John Blanset, had also come up behind Embry to grab him, and I was a millisecond from shooting Blanset when Embry was pushed to the side. If I had fired my weapon in that moment, I might have killed one of my officers.

In the end, we had Embry cuffed on the ground, and no one was hurt. We had to place him in the back of Ernie Williams' new conversion van to take him back to prison. I heard Williams tell him, "You had better not puke in my van. Do you understand me?" That kind of broke the tension, and I thought it was funny as hell, but I could tell Williams was serious. If he had puked in Williams' new van, there would have been an "ass whooping" on the side of the road. No doubt in my mind.

THE GHETTO ESCAPE

There was one other time that we were staking out an apartment in the worst ghetto in Cleveland. It was a large Section Eight housing complex and a hotbed of crack houses and prostitution. The Housing Authority gave us empty apartments to use for surveillance. We would set up by nine p.m. every night and leave after three a.m. Our focus was the apartment of an escapee's wife, and she was cooperating with us to some extent. She was also a prostitute, and there was steady foot traffic in and out of her apartment. The husband was smart enough to stay away from her place, but she also gave us his cell phone number to track him down.

When we called and asked him to surrender, he would talk to us, but he kept saying he had some things to do before he went back to prison. This went on for at least a week, and we grew tired of chasing him. Finally, we thought we had him cornered in an apartment that belonged to a relative. This was in the same bad neighborhood, and I decided it was time to get some backup from the Cleveland Police Department. It was eleven p.m. when Ernie and I walked into Precinct Five and asked to talk to the supervisor in charge. A short, stocky sergeant came out, and I told her we were closing in on an escapee and needed backup. She asked where he was, and I replied, "Garden Valley."

She studied me for a moment and said, "Have you been in Garden Valley?"

"Yes," I replied. "We've been working surveillance for the past few nights."

The sergeant looked like she was about to explode. "Mister, you are white. They will kill you in there. We don't even go near there this time of night."

I said, "Well, I'm going with or without your help."

"Okay," she said, exasperated. "Fine. You ride with me."

The sergeant called for three additional units. Together with our prison staff, we had roughly fifteen officers. I pointed out the apartment where we thought our suspect was hiding, and the sergeant drove across the sidewalk, through the grass, and right up to the door with her blue lights flashing. As I watched, she banged on the door and kicked it open. We went in and searched everywhere. Our inmate wasn't there.

As we left, I thanked the sergeant and said, "I'll let you know if we need you again." I'd had enough of that drama. She stood there looking at me as I walked back and got in the car with one of my officers. That was the last time I asked for assistance from Cleveland PD.

Soon after this misadventure, I was promoted to regional director over twelve prisons in the southern region of the state. I had a great job in Columbus, and I enjoyed working in Central Office. Something was missing, though. Faced with the daily monotony of regional administration work, I began to grow restless. I realized I needed more adrenaline in my life. Thankfully, I was about to get it.

FOURTEEN

BACK TO KENTUCKY

THE ADMINISTRATION IN KENTUCKY CHANGED AS IT ALWAYS DOES when a new governor takes office. The year was 1993. Sowders had accepted the job of deputy commissioner, and Jack Lewis was the new commissioner of the Department of Corrections. Bill Seabold was still the warden at Kentucky State Penitentiary, but they were looking for a replacement. To my surprise, Sowders called and offered me the job. I asked why Seabold was being replaced, and Sowders told me it was for his own good. Seabold had been in that position for over five years, and Sowders and Lewis thought it was time for a change. At first, I told Sowders I wasn't interested because I had just promoted to regional director in Ohio. I didn't feel it would be right to leave so soon. He understood, and I thanked him for asking. I thought that was the end of that.

A few months later, Sowders called again and said, "Phil, Jack wanted me to call you again to see if you were interested in the penitentiary." What he said next caught my attention: "They've just changed all positions to Hazardous Duty, which includes much better pay and a twenty-year retirement." Sowders added, "You can use your Ohio time and retire when you have twenty years." I realized I was almost at the twenty-year mark, but I would have to work another twenty-five years to earn a pension if I stayed in Ohio.

It was very appealing, if for no other reason than the possibility of an early retirement. I asked him what the job paid. He gave me a figure that was substantially less than I was currently making. I told him I couldn't work for what he was offering. Sowders said okay, and the conversation was over. I knew Sowders well. I thought I would never hear from him again. Another month went by, and Sowders called again. This time he asked how much salary it would take for me to make the move. Now I knew they were desperate. I told him that he would have to match what I was currently making. He said he didn't think so, but he would run it by Lewis. A few days later, Sowders called again and said he thought they could work out the money. He asked if I would come to Frankfort to discuss it with him. So I made an appointment and drove back to Kentucky for the meeting.

They agreed to the salary I was asking, but I had a few other demands before I accepted their offer. First, I did not want to have to call anyone to ask for permission to do my job effectively. I would make decisions based on my sound judgment and experience and what I thought was in the best interest of the prison. Second, I would bring a hardline approach to the wardenship at KSP. I wanted to run a tight ship, and that meant doing away with some of the more lenient (and risky) policies that previous administrations had allowed to continue for years. Sowders didn't like this. He was biting his lip. Lewis spoke up. "Phil, we need a strong leader who can hit the ground running, and we think you fit the bill."

I said, "I am confident I can manage the penitentiary, but you might not like some of the policies I bring with me. For example, one of my goals will be to implement inmate uniforms instead of street clothing. Another thing I would do right away is tighten down security wherever I find weaknesses, starting with death row."

As Sowders and Lewis knew, one of the previous wardens had tried to "normalize" death row by letting inmates have yard time with the general population and permitting them to hold down jobs in the kitchen. I told them I could go on and on about things I would tighten up. "If that's what you want, then I'm your man. If you want the status quo, then I probably should stay in Ohio."

Sowders was visibly agitated. He didn't like anything I was saying, but Lewis apparently did. "Phil, that's exactly what we want," he assured me. We discussed a start date and shook hands on the deal. As I walked out of the room, I knew that Sowders would be gunning for me if I ever crossed one of his imaginary lines.

Sowders had a habit of keeping close tabs on people he disliked or distrusted. I knew he was compiling information that was potentially detrimental to Warden Seabold. Sowders had also grown disdainful of Sr. Capt. Henderson, and he forced Seabold to demote Henderson back to captain while he was on probation. Seabold had selected Henderson for a senior captain position, but Sowders' informants hated Henderson because he tried to break up several unhealthy staff cliques. Sowders listened to disgruntled staff and forced Seabold to demote Henderson over Seabold's objections. This only served to undermine Seabold's authority and responsibility as warden. It was inappropriate and underhanded.

When I learned about Sowders' backhanded tactics, I almost changed my mind about accepting the job. Fortunately, I left Ohio in good standing. I was sure I could find another warden position there if this new Kentucky job didn't work out. I had developed a lot of close friends in Ohio.

My start date in Kentucky was February 1993. Commissioner Lewis wanted me to work one or two weeks in Central Office as my orientation back in Kentucky. This would give me an opportunity to meet some of the new staff and familiarize myself with some of the developments during my absence. I had been gone for four years, but not much had changed. I ended up only working a week in Central Office, which I thought was mostly a waste of time.

The first thing Sowders wanted me to do at KSP was to reassign Henderson to the midnight shift. I asked why he wanted Henderson moved. He didn't give me a good answer. He just responded, "I want him moved to the midnight shift."

I couldn't believe the deputy commissioner would get involved in the daily operations. I said, "Dewey, I will look at it, but I won't tell you I will do it. That's an operational decision that should be made by the deputy warden and warden." I made up my mind I would not play Sowders' games. Promotional decisions were mine to make, not his. Meanwhile I had just started, and Sowders and I were already butting heads.

Sowders had already given me marching orders to place Henderson on the midnight shift, and the demotion would have left an open position of major. But I resisted and did not place Henderson on the midnight shift. In fact, I later promoted him back to the position of major, but not without a showdown with Sowders. Capt. Henderson and I went way back to my days as a correctional officer. He was tough and had good leadership qualities. My only problem with him was he showed favoritism to some of his drinking buddies. I knew that I would have to watch for that, but it was not a big problem. We all tend to surround ourselves with people we trust and like. The deputy warden and warden have a duty to make sure that everyone has a fair shot at job assignments and promotions. With this in my mind, I knew Henderson would be my first choice to fill the position he had just been demoted from.

I interviewed the applicants for the major's position. I asked Henderson to interview as well. He wasn't going to reapply for the job. I insisted he at least go for the interview. Henderson reluctantly interviewed for the job he had just been demoted from. After the interviews, I met privately with Henderson and told him that I was submitting his name to fill the position, and it would have to be approved by Sowders, the deputy commissioner, and Jack Lewis, the commissioner. I told Henderson there was a good chance I would get fired for submitting his name. I also told Henderson I was going to try to make the promotion effective from the original date he was promoted, and I would try to get back pay for the time he was demoted. Henderson couldn't believe what he was hearing. Nobody had ever stood up to Sowders before.

SHOWDOWN IN THE COMMISSIONER'S CORRAL

I signed the personnel action requesting to place Henderson back in the major position. All promotions are reviewed by the deputy commissioner, so I knew it was just a matter of time before my request crossed Sowders' desk.

Sure enough, about two days later, Sandy Etheridge, Sowders' secretary, called and said, "Sowders wants to see you tomorrow morning at eight a.m."

I replied, "Sandy, that's a four-hour drive and you're in the Eastern Time zone. That's seven a.m. in my time. I'd have to leave home at three a.m."

Sandy put me on hold for a minute and came back and said, "Sowders wants to see you at eight a.m."

I said, "Okay. I'll be there." I hung up the phone, annoyed.

At three a.m., I hit the road driving the 220 miles to Central Office. I knew Sowders was pissed off, and I knew why. Now I was pissed too because he was playing a power game that had little time or patience for.

I was in a foul mood and began driving eighty to ninety miles per hour, but I had a new Crown Vic Police Interceptor. It was made for speed. I got to Frankfort about forty-five minutes earlier than I planned, so I stopped at a McDonald's for breakfast and to kill some time. I didn't want to be early.

After breakfast, I walked into the deputy commissioner's office and was greeted by his secretary, Sandy. I had known Sandy for several years and liked her. I said, "Hi, Sandy. I'm here for my appointment with Sowders."

She said, "Okay. I'll let him know you're here." She came back out of his office about five minutes later and said, "He'll be with you soon."

I knew that meant I would have to sit in his outer office for at least thirty minutes, maybe an hour. That was one of his passive-aggressive moves.

Finally, Sowders used the intercom to tell Sandy that he was ready for me. I had calmed down somewhat, but was determined to stand up to him. I walked into his office, and Commissioner Lewis was sitting off to the left side of his desk. They were both heavy smokers, and both were puffing away at cigarettes. Smoke was wafting up and hovering in a gray cloud over the room as I entered. I shook hands with the commissioner first, then Sowders, and sat down. Sowders got right to the point. "You're here to talk about your recommendation to promote Henderson."

I said, "Dewey, he is the best candidate, and that's who I want."

I could tell Sowders was livid. He was doing his best to hide his rage. "I want him on the midnight shift, and you have a lot of balls to put him back in for the promotion."

I replied, "Here's the deal. I don't know why you demoted him in the first place. You never told me what he did to deserve a demotion. In fact, I've heard the only reason he was demoted is because he pissed off some of the staff, who then complained to you."

Sowders didn't know what to say. He was holding back because Lewis was sitting there. You could cut the tension with a knife.

Lewis spoke next. "Phil, tell us why you want him as the security major."

"Bill Henderson was a captain when I hired in back in 1978," I explained. "I worked for him in Three Cell House, and I worked for him when he was the shift commander. We were on the E-Squad together. He knows more about the penitentiary and security than anyone else I know. He is a good leader and knows what he is doing. He is strong when he needs to be. He is the best choice, and he is who I need."

Lewis said, "Phil, we worry about his fraternizing with line staff."

"Commissioner," I replied, "I know that all too well. He and I have come to an understanding that I expect him to stop going to after-work parties and to keep his distance from line staff."

Lewis studied me as he lit another cigarette. He turned to Sowders and said, "Dewey, let's give him what he wants. If he says he needs Henderson in that job, let's let him have him."

Sowders looked at Lewis as he slowly put out his cigarette, then looked back at me and pointed his finger. "Okay, Parker. You can have your way on this, but if he fucks up, it's your ass. Are we clear?"

I said, "No, we are not clear. Let's get something straight right here and now. I told you I would run that penitentiary. I am responsible for everything that happens. If you don't like the way I am running it, you don't have to threaten to fire me. All you need to do is say the word and I will go back to Ohio. I have a job waiting for me if this doesn't work out."

Sowders narrowed his eyes and replied, "Parker, the honeymoon is over."

I stood up and said, "There was no honeymoon. If at any time you don't like the way I am running the penitentiary, just say so. If I disagree with you, I will resign." I was close to telling Sowders to go to hell. I wasn't going to back down.

Lewis was getting nervous that this exchange was about to explode, especially when I stood up. He tried to deescalate the situation. "Phil, sit back down and let's have a cup of coffee." I agreed. Lewis could see that I wasn't going to take any crap. He didn't want to lose control of the situation or lose me to another job in Ohio.

We engaged in small talk about the penitentiary and my preparations for an upcoming execution. Sowders just sat there at first, recovering from his angry spell. He finally asked about my wife and my son, Philip. This drama was all part of the power game, Sowders playing "bad cop" and Lewis playing "good cop." I went in ready for a showdown, however, and Lewis knew it.

After I finished my cigarette, I said, "Well, if you gentlemen will excuse me, I have a four-hour drive, and I have some things at work I have to get to. I appreciate the meeting, and I appreciate your approval of Henderson's promotion." I just had to rub salt in Sowders' wound.

I knew Sowders would try to retaliate. One little mistake and he would fire me if he could. Lewis knew I would do a good job, and I knew that as long as he was commissioner, Sowders couldn't touch me. I kept in touch with the movers and shakers in Ohio just to cover my bases, and they were ready to hire me back in a heartbeat. So as I returned to Kentucky to begin my new position at KSP, I felt ready to face anything—or anyone—that came my way.

FIFTEEN

HOME SWEET HOME

My first day as warden of the Kentucky State Penitentiary was March 1, 1993. I walked up the steps to the front gate, and it felt like home. I was greeted by a young correctional officer who appeared to recognize me, even though we had never met. I didn't have an I.D. yet, so I pulled out my Ohio driver's license, and he handed me a temporary pass. I paused in the hallway just to see if it felt any different this time. That all-too-familiar smell of one hundred–plus years of blood, smoke, and death suddenly hit my senses like a slapjack... the Castle Beast. With it came a rush of the memories and emotions I had experienced from my earliest days as a correctional officer at the Castle. I let the moment wash over me, and smiled to myself. Now I was running the whole show. As Humphrey Bogart said in the *Maltese Falcon*, this is the stuff that dreams are made of.

I knew I was home when I made my way upstairs to the staff canteen for a cup of coffee. My mind flashed back to the moment, some fifteen years earlier, when a nervous kid named Phil Parker walked up these same steps for the first time. The memory of Pat Ross's tragic death also came rushing back. I remembered that poor inmate bleeding out in front of me as I held his head in my lap. I thought about the incredible journey that got me to this point, the highs and the lows, as I took a sip of coffee and walked toward my new office. It was time to get to work.

Even though I had been away for four years, it felt as though I had never left. After all, I had started as a guard and had left as a deputy warden. Most of the senior staff knew me well. I hoped that many of the old-school guards and supervisors appreciated what I had accomplished as a deputy warden after the mass escape. If nothing else, I figured the staff was just happy that a complete stranger hadn't been appointed warden.

My first objective was to learn and analyze the new dynamics of the place. Why had Warden Seabold fallen out of grace with the commissioner and deputy commissioner? Who were the line staff that had a direct line of communication with the deputy commissioner? How were racial problems being addressed on the yard, and what was being done to control the flow of drugs and weapons? What were the inmates up to? Were they content, or were they going to test the new warden?

There are so many complexities to managing a maximum security prison. The 350 staff and 900 inmates create a multitude of issues that can have far-reaching implications. The warden must understand the nature of the beast, or it will devour him before he realizes anything is even amiss.

I had to make sure we were ready to respond to anything at a moment's notice. Our job was to anticipate and react immediately to any disturbance, stabbing, or assault, especially if these problems were racially motivated. For the safety of my staff and the inmates, I had to seek out ways to be proactive rather than reactive. In the world of correctional operations, it is essential to find and eliminate problems before they manifest. But how? For starters, I had a rack of riot batons installed near the entry between the administration building and the prison yard, so that officers could grab one on their way to a situation on the yard. As you probably know by now, a riot baton is my tool of choice when there is trouble. That was a small thing, but it was a start. What I really needed was a crystal ball so I could see into the future. It may sound silly, but many of the senior staff had developed an acute sense of when things weren't right. Almost like a sixth sense. They may not have known *what* was going to happen, but they knew *something* was going to happen. I had to find a way to tap into that sixth sense for the sake of everyone involved.

STAFF CORRUPTION

After a few months on the job, it became increasingly clear to me that staff corruption was a problem at KSP. I spent a lot of time with Lt. John Choat, who had been assigned as an internal affairs officer. Choat had a running list of staff members who he believed to be corrupt. He wasn't the only one. Capt. Henderson, Deputy Warden Patty Webb, Glenn Haeberlin, and Steve Bail all had their suspicions as well.

Corruption is like a cancer in any correctional facility. It can manifest itself in any number of ways. One of the most common is when staff work to undermine the administration by badmouthing their superiors to each other, calling headquarters as "whistleblowers," or even leaking sensitive information to the media. Even worse are employees who grow too close to the inmates and share information that inmates should never be privy to. Some even fall in love with prisoners. These scenarios often lead to employees smuggling in contraband such as hacksaw blades, handcuff keys, or drugs. This behavior isn't just corrupt and detrimental to the organization as a whole—it can also have lethal consequences. I knew that my time as warden would be a failure if I could not get a handle on the corruption and stomp it out.

To do this effectively would require a great deal of persistence...and a healthy dose of creativity.

I kept informal lists of individuals who I believed were corrupted by inmates, as well as those who I suspected had worked against Warden Seabold. The latter, I knew, would no doubt work against me. Some of the weaker staff always believed they would be protected by inmates if they found themselves caught in the middle of a disturbance or riot. During the riot of 1986, inmates had tried to enter the laundry and yard office to kill prison employees. Fortunately, the E-Squad moved in with shotguns and tear gas before the worst happened. The memory of that terrible incident still hung over the staff, however, and some were simply scared. Yet some of these folks believed, however naïvely, that they would be protected in a moment of chaos if they let the strong inmates skirt the rules and do what they pleased. I had to find a way to root out employees who approached their work with this dangerous mentality.

The first priority, however, was to terminate and arrest anyone who brought drugs and other contraband into the prison. It really wasn't that hard. Upstanding staff had their suspicions about who their "dirty" colleagues were. Inmate informants also were all too eager to share what they knew. It just took a little effort to work my sources. If necessary, I would assign additional staff to the internal affairs office to see this through.

It was somewhat harder to motivate the deputy wardens to get on board with my priorities. Deputy Warden Glenn Haeberlin had been moved from security to programs, and Deputy Warden Patty Webb had been reassigned from programs to security. Not surprisingly, these moves were made by Sowders in his role as deputy commissioner, not Warden Seabold. I already knew Sowders liked to improperly exert his influence in order to interfere with operational change. But why did he do so in this case? I soon discovered it was the same reason Sowders demoted Major Henderson to captain. Sowders was motivated by staff who went around Seabold and fed the deputy commissioner information behind the warden's back. This was just another way Sowders attempted to establish absolute authority. He was interfering with the daily operation of the prison, and there wasn't much Seabold could do to stop it. I was more determined than ever to stand up to Sowders and push back against his underhanded, counterproductive behavior.

In the meantime, however, I had my hands full trying to lead a number of deputy wardens who had become demoralized by Sowders' tactics. Faced with an administration that did not appear to have their backs, deputy wardens would often do little more than their eight hours of work before clocking out and heading home. Why should they go that extra mile if they felt unappreciated by their superiors? I had to find a way to motivate my staff. It would take time, but I was confident we would get there.

LOVE ON DEATH ROW

One of the more memorable problems I inherited as warden was the fallout from an illicit love affair between two female staff members and two death-row inmates, Benny Hodge and Roger Epperson. Donna Reimer had been an employee for over fifteen years. She was one of the first females employed as a correctional officer in the 1970s. Julia Nardino had only been an officer for about five years, but she was friendly and well-liked by staff. No one suspected these two employees could be corrupted. Both did their jobs well, and both took their duties seriously.

Benny Hodge and Roger Epperson had been sentenced to death for their part in the murder of Tammy Acker, the daughter of a small-town physician in eastern Kentucky. They had teamed up with a third criminal to rob Dr. Acker of over $2,000,000 in cash. During the home invasion, the suspects strangled Dr. Acker and murdered Dr. Acker's daughter, Tammy. Dr. Acker miraculously survived the attack, and his testimony led to the arrest and conviction of Hodge and Epperson.

I had only been the warden for three months when I received a phone call from Rod Kincaid, the FBI agent who worked the Acker murder. Kincaid informed me that Hodge had corrupted a correctional officer at Brushy Mountain by the name of Sherry Sheets. He said he wouldn't be surprised if Hodge attempted the same thing at KSP in an effort to escape custody. Kincaid also noted that as much as one million dollars had never been recovered from the robbery. He suspected that Hodge would try to get another female guard to fall in love with him, and he might use the prospect of a million in cash to sweeten the deal.

All of this lent credence to the rumor that Donna Reiner, my employee, was in love with Benny Hodge.

What amazed me was that Reiner was also Deputy Commissioner Sowders' source of information about Capt. Henderson. For reasons I could never quite figure out, there was no love lost between Reiner and Henderson. Reiner saved all of her love for Benny Hodge. The inmate received love letters and cards from someone on an almost daily basis, sent in envelopes with no return address and no signature. The more I looked into it, the more I became convinced these letters were coming from Reimer.

In the meantime, I notified Commissioner Lewis and Deputy Commissioner Sowders that I had begun an investigation into a potential escape plot from death row involving Hodge and Epperson. I now had the FBI warning me Hodge might be planning an escape. The FBI agreed to set up a meeting between me and an informant who had inside information.

DEATH THREATS

As this death-row investigation played out, I suddenly received multiple warnings that my life was in danger. A law enforcement source told

Commissioner Lewis I was "shaking the sugar tree" and I needed to watch my back at KSP. At the same time, a reliable informant sent word to me through Internal Affairs that a group of inmates were plotting to murder me on the yard. As if this wasn't enough, Governor Brereton Jones had someone from his office call me after he was briefed on the situation at the prison. They advised me to carry a weapon at all times and to stay off the yard unless I had a bodyguard. That last suggestion went in one ear and out the other. There was no way I would use a bodyguard, period.

These threats told me I was getting closer to the truth than I realized. I immediately set up a high-level meeting in Frankfort with Gen. Billy Wellman, the secretary of justice, the commissioner, the deputy commissioner, and a respected colonel in the Kentucky State Police.

I had asked for the meeting for two reasons. First, I wanted to brief them on what I suspected was major corruption involving up to twenty staff, death-row inmates, and the Aryan Brotherhood. The Brotherhood had somehow managed to corrupt KSP employees, and I was concerned this was compromising the safety and security of prison operations. Second, I wanted to launch a major investigation using one or more undercover state police agents.

My proposal was to use an undercover state trooper to infiltrate the circle of staff who I believed were controlling the flow of drugs and other vices into KSP. To my surprise, everyone in the meeting quickly agreed with my idea.

In addition to my request for an undercover investigator, I wanted to create a new position to coordinate these investigations in my office. Fortunately, a local state police detective named Jim Potter had just retired. Potter was one of the best detectives in the state. I had already interviewed him to see if he was interested in coming back to work as my new chief of internal affairs. Potter was agreeable, but first I had to get the position established—a process that required the approval of the commissioner and the secretary of justice. Commissioner Lewis was all for it, and Secretary Wellman agreed.

Before the meeting was over, Secretary Wellman told me he was sending a special state police officer to "debug" my office and home. He had reason to believe that my telephone was not secure. A few days later, a plainclothes state police detective showed up at my office with some sophisticated electronic equipment, swept my office for bugs, then checked my phone lines. He did the same thing in my house. Apparently, he didn't find anything, but he also didn't think my phone line was secure.

Commissioner Lewis called a few days later and said, "Phil, we need a secure phone line where you and I can talk and have one hundred percent confidence no one is tapped on to your phone." I agreed. Lewis kept going: "I want you to have the phone company come out and run a dedicated phone line to your office. I want you to be able to look out the window and see the phone line all the way to the telephone pole. It cannot go through the switchboard or anywhere else, not even to your secretary."

"No problem," I replied. "I'll get right on it."

I wondered what the commissioner knew that had prompted this call. Whatever spooked him, he never said, but he was adamant I should have a secure phone. Things were getting serious. I had the phone line installed as an unlisted number, and of course, I provided the number to the commissioner. He shared it with the deputy commissioner and the state police.

James Potter quietly reported for duty as my new investigator. The job was never posted, and there were no interviews. Potter simply showed up to work one day, and I called an executive staff meeting to introduce him. Nobody, not even my personnel officer, knew I had established the position ahead of time. To say my staff was surprised was an understatement, but they eagerly welcomed Potter to the team.

I put Potter in an office just around the corner from mine, and he immediately went to work screening phone calls and reading inmate mail. He was also able to obtain a search warrant for the phone records of Donna Riemer and Julia Nardino. The records revealed numerous calls from death row to both staff. I thought this was enough to fire both of them, but Deputy Commissioner Sowders and Commissioner Lewis disagreed. They decided they should be subjected to minor disciplinary action—the equivalent of a slap on the wrist. I was perplexed by this, but I didn't have time to question their reasoning. My team had too many balls in the air, and things were moving quickly.

Jim Potter was like a bird dog. He was a tireless and loyal investigator and a great guy to have in your corner. Potter's biggest flaw was that he could come across as curt and dismissive at times. He had no qualms about arguing with prosecutors or judges, and he didn't care who he pissed off. Most of the time Potter was calm, cool, and collected, but he could flip like a light switch.

As soon as Potter came aboard, the cards and letters increased. It was incredibly strange. Almost as though they were taunting us, saying, "You can't catch us, and there is nothing you can do about it."

Every few days, we collected a stack of correspondence and rushed it to a crime lab two hundred miles away to search for prints. We also hired a handwriting analyst to compare the letters to reports written by our officers. Incredibly, there was no match. Not only that, but the crime lab technician told us that whoever was writing the correspondence was wearing gloves. He wasn't able to recover a single usable print. We had been taking these letters to the crime lab for weeks, and I could tell they were growing tired of us. I didn't care. We continued to have the correspondence analyzed because I knew one of the culprits would slip up sooner or later.

Our undercover officer had hired in as a correctional officer. Nobody knew this was happening at KSP; I didn't even tell Potter about it. She had a control officer (supervisor) located in Bowling Green, Kentucky. This unit was comprised entirely of plainclothes detectives who worked white collar and organized crime, narcotics, and government corruption cases. They had the latest crime-fighting technology, and they were top-notch. I met with the undercover officer, her control officer, and a unit supervisor. Our undercover would report to the control officer, and he would pass information to me. If I needed to tell her something, I would call the control officer. Once every ten days or so, we would have a face-to-face meeting in a motel room in Owensboro or some other town where no one recognized me.

Our undercover's job was twofold: infiltrate the staff corruption ring and allow inmates to corrupt her. It was a tall order for a new hire. No one trusts the new kid on the block. It takes time and patience to earn the confidence of colleagues in a prison system, particularly if you are engaged in illicit behavior. So we set the plan in motion then let our undercover team work their magic.

In the meantime, I wasn't sure if I had a price on my head, but I was watching my back more than ever. I had been warned by the state police, the commissioner, and even the governor that my life was potentially in danger, and I didn't want to find out the hard way they were correct.

We continued to test the steady stream of correspondence in and out of death row until one day, out of the blue, BINGO! We recovered a thumbprint belonging to officer Julia Nardino on a card addressed to Roger Epperson. Now we were getting somewhere.

I was hoping we could get Nardino to flip on Reimer and tell us what she knew. She had already received minor disciplinary action for a number of death-row phone calls she accepted at home, but now I had her thumbprint on a card. We had her dead to rights, as the saying goes. Lt. Choat and I interviewed Nardino. She continued to deny any sort of romantic relationship with Epperson. Finally, I produced the card and asked if she had ever seen it before. Nardino looked at us, trying to hide the concern in her voice, and replied, "No, never."

"Then why would your thumbprint be on the card?" I asked.

Nardino looked down at the floor for a moment, then looked up at me and said, "You're going to fire me, aren't you?"

"Yes, I am going to fire you, but you need to be worried about being arrested. I have reason to believe you are an accessory to a planned escape."

I was using this to try to get her to roll over on Reimer. We read Nardino her Miranda rights. She continued to talk afterward, however, and admitted she had written all the cards and letters to Epperson. I asked if she loved him. She said, "No, not really. I was just going along with this because it was exciting. I'm really a good officer, and I like my job. Please don't fire me."

I kept pushing Nardino to tell me about Reimer, but she wouldn't share anything personal about the nature of their relationship. I still needed to know what Nardino knew about the escape plan. I also wanted her to confirm Reimer was sending in cards and letters to Benny Hodge. After she continued to stonewall us, I knew it was time to end the interrogation. We weren't going to get anything else out of her. I told Nardino my intent was to fire her, but in the meantime, she was on administrative leave and was not to come back onto prison grounds unless I called her. If she did try to enter the prison, she would be charged with criminal trespass. Nardino then asked, "What if I resign?"

"That's your decision," I replied. "It's up to you."

She said, "I want to resign."

We accepted her resignation then and there.

The next few days would be interesting. I was fairly sure we were getting close to nabbing the primary suspect in our investigation: Benny Hodge's girlfriend, Reimer. We knew it was just a matter of time before Nardino told Reimer everything that happened in my office.

AN UNEXPECTED LEAD

As luck would have it, a day or two later I got a call from Rod Kincaid, the FBI agent who had worked the Acker murder. He had Sherry Sheets in his office, and she wanted to talk to me. Sheets was the correctional officer at Brushy Mountain Prison who had fallen in love with Hodge before going on a crime spree.

I asked her why she wanted to talk. Sheets got right to the point: "Because Benny Hodge is going to escape. And when he does, he will find me to get his share of the money, and when he finds out that I don't have the money, he'll kill me." Now she had my full attention. I asked Sheets to tell me about the escape plan.

"First you need to understand he has one of your employees head over heels in love with him. She will do anything he asks."

"Do you know her name?" I asked.

"No, but I saw her in the visiting room. I can tell you what she looks like."

I thought for a moment. Sheets was telling me something that didn't make sense. "How were you allowed to visit him if you were part of his crime?"

She replied, "Yeah, I did five years in the federal prison. The warden before you agreed to let me visit, because I convinced him I turned over a new leaf."

Interesting move by my predecessor, I thought. "Okay. Tell me what she looks like."

Sheets described Donna Reimer exactly.

"How do you know she is in love with him?"

"Because Benny told me one day while we were at the visiting table," Sheets explained. "He said, 'See that correctional officer over there? She will do anything I ask.'" Hodge was bragging, but he reassured Sheets he was only using the officer to help him escape.

"That really doesn't make much sense to me," I replied. "Why would she help him escape?"

Sheets went on to say that Hodge was handsome and well-built. He could turn on the charm whenever he wanted. Women found him irresistible, and he used it to manipulate them. "That is exactly what happened to me at Brushy Mountain," Sheets explained. "Before I knew it, I was in love with him, and I would have done anything he asked."

I was still skeptical of her motives. "Okay, but I don't understand why you are telling me this."

"Warden, it's because Benny is planning an escape, and he will use her to do it. There's no question in my mind. She's part of it."

I asked about Roger Epperson. "Does he have a girlfriend here?"

"Yes," Sheets confirmed, "but I don't know anything about her. All I know is that they run together. They hang out after work, and they are good friends, but I can't tell you any more than that." Then she steered the conversation back to herself. "Benny thinks I have his share of the money. I was the banker holding everyone's money after we split it three ways."

"How much money are we talking about?" I asked her.

"We didn't stop [fleeing from the scene of our crime] until we got into Florida and rented a motel. We dumped all the money out and began counting it in piles. Most of it was in small bills, and it was old and moldy. It took a long time to count all the five-, ten-, and twenty-dollar bills, and there were a lot of one-dollar bills as well. We counted up to $1.6 million dollars before we had to stop because we were so exhausted from traveling all day. There was more left to count, but everyone agreed to just take their cut, and they didn't care about whatever was left."

To clarify, I asked, "Okay, was it over two million dollars total?"

"Yes. After everyone left the room, our share was lying on the bed, and Benny took what was left and dumped it on our pile of money."

"Okay," I said. "What happened next?"

I wasn't expecting her reply. "We made love on top of all that money."

I tried not to roll my eyes at the voice on the phone. What I really wanted to know was what happened to Hodge's and Epperson's share of the money. "Where is it now?" I asked her.

Sheets prevaricated. "That's why I'm calling you to stop the escape. Benny thinks I have all that money. When we were on the run from Florida, I was holding the money. As far as he knows, I still have it because I was the last one to have it when everyone was arrested."

I asked again if she still had the money. Sheets finally admitted that no, she had given it to a cop that she used to date back in Tennessee because she didn't have anyone else she could trust. I asked if the cop still had it. She said she didn't know. Something about her story bothered me, as I'm sure it did the FBI, but Sheets never wavered from her version of events. A large sum of money had been recovered by the FBI from the gang's attorney, Lester Burns. But it wasn't even close to the full amount that originally went missing. To this day, authorities believe there may be $1,000,000 or more still out there somewhere.

I could tell Sheets really believed an escape was imminent, so I pushed her to divulge their plan when the two of them were still plotting Hodge's escape. She explained that he wanted her to go to gun shows, pawn shops, Walmart, or any place that sold cheap handguns in order to buy as many as would fit into two pillowcases. They estimated that would be roughly a hundred guns. She was to make sure all the guns were loaded. Next, she was supposed to rent a getaway car and have it parked at the next exit on Interstate 24, heading south. The day of the escape, she was to go to Fort Campbell, which is about fifty or so miles south on I-24, and hire a sightseeing helicopter to go sightseeing. Once airborne, she would place a gun to the pilot's head and order him to fly over the penitentiary.

Hodge and Epperson would have their sweethearts escort them to the infirmary for a medical appointment, and from there they could easily scale the infirmary wall and wait. The helicopter would fly low over the yard, dump the pillowcases, and fly off for five or ten minutes. A hundred loaded guns on the yard would trigger an instant riot. Inmates would target the officers in the gun towers, and just about every correctional officer caught on the yard would be killed. In the midst of this chaos, the helicopter would fly back to pick up Hodge and Epperson waiting on top of the infirmary. Five miles down the interstate, they would land next to the waiting getaway car, kill the pilot, and haul ass out of there.

I couldn't believe what I was hearing. It could work. It was completely crazy, but it could work. The culprits just needed someone on the inside to make sure they were escorted to the infirmary at the right time.

I ended the conference call with Sheets and immediately called Rod Kincaid back to speak confidentially. I asked him if he thought Sheets was telling the truth. He believed she was. Kincaid said Sheets was worried that everyone believed she was hiding the money, and she was terrified that this made her a target. I thanked Kincaid for his help and hung up.

I didn't sleep well that night. I kept replaying the conversation in my head. It was a hell of a plan, and the more I thought about it, the more convinced I was that it would work.

I needed to move carefully. Reimer and Nardino now had a reason to kill me if I got in their way. Hodge would soon know that I knew what he was up to as well, and he could have me killed just for spite. I had to find a way to stop Reimer before things escalated any further, because she posed a threat to everyone at the prison as long as she remained employed there.

SHAKING THE SUGAR TREE

As warden, one of the tools I had at my disposal was the ability to lock up any inmate in segregation for any reason whatsoever—or no reason at all. I could also keep somebody in segregation for as long as I wanted. It was a privilege afforded solely to the warden, and I intended to use it.

After we found Nardino's fingerprint on a piece of correspondence, I called the captain's office and told the shift captain to lock up Benny Hodge in segregation. The captain asked, "What do I list as a reason on the detention form?"

I said, "Just put down *per warden.*"

This technique is what I called "shaking the sugar tree." I locked Hodge up just to see what fell out of the tree. Sure enough, something shook loose and fell out almost immediately. The next morning, Donna Reimer was waiting in my office. I could see she was really upset. I feigned ignorance. "Can I help you?"

"Yeah," she said, looking ashen. "I want to see you privately." I told her it would be just a minute.

I never meet one-on-one with an upset member of the opposite sex without somebody else present. They could say anything, and I wouldn't have a witness to back up my version of events. So I called Lt. Choat and asked him to come to my office for a minute. Once he was seated, I called Reimer in. She glanced at Choat, and I thought she was going to scream. She didn't like him, and didn't want him there. *Too bad*, I thought.

Reimer got straight to the point. "Why is Benny Hodge locked up? Is it anything I did?" She was fishing.

"I don't think so," I replied innocently. "Have you done anything that would give me reason to lock him up?"

"No, Parker," she said. "You know how this place is. People talk."

"What are they saying?"

She looked annoyed. "Never mind."

"Donna," I replied, "I'm the warden here, and I don't have to tell you why I lock up an inmate. Quite frankly, it's none of your damn business. Is there anything else?"

"No," Reimer muttered and stormed out of my office. I shot a glance at Choat, who was grinning from ear to ear. He knew I was just "shaking the sugar tree" to see what fell out.

A LUCKY BREAK

Benny Hodge stayed locked up in segregation for about two weeks, and I still hadn't given him a reason why. He contacted his attorneys in Frankfort, and they began calling me repeatedly, demanding to know why he was locked up. My response was simple: "I have him locked up for investigation, end of story." They didn't like that, and I didn't particularly care.

Reimer's role as a supervisor gave her access to almost anywhere on the yard and the prison. She tried to use this to her advantage when she suddenly showed up in Three Cell House one day to get Hodge out of his cell for a "legal call." This was highly unusual, but she had the authority to do it. One of the supervisors on duty that day was Sgt. Roy Gill. He was suspicious when she arrived to take Hodge out, but he went along with it.

As a rule, we were not allowed to listen or record calls between attorneys and inmates. Federal law permits inmates to speak confidentially with their attorneys, and Reimer was well aware of this. What she apparently overlooked was the fact we could monitor any call up to the point when a lawyer comes on the phone. Sgt. Gill delayed getting Hodge out long enough to set up a recorder on the phone in the private office Reimer and Hodge would meet in to take the call.

When Hodge finally came in, Reimer said, "Sit down, and I'll place the legal call for you."

Reimer picked up the phone, which immediately triggered the recording device. But instead of placing a call, she pretended to use the phone while they talked. After several minutes of this, she finally dialed the attorney's office. We'd caught everything on tape except for the conversation with the attorney. Five minutes later, Reimer stepped out of the office and told the officer he could take Hodge back.

Sgt. Gill hightailed it straight to my office and said, "You might want to hear this." I played the tape. To my disappointment, the quality was terrible. There was a tremendous amount of background noise. It just wasn't a good recording.

I passed the tape to Internal Affairs, and as I feared, they were unable to isolate the voices enough to find the evidence we needed to make our case. Then Choat had an idea. I could practically see the lightbulb go off over his head. "There's a lab in New York City that can clean up the audio enough for us to listen to the conversation. It'll cost upwards of $1,000. We won't know the final bill for sure until they examine the tape."

"What about the state police or FBI?" I wondered.

"If we could get them to do it," Choat explained, "it might take six months to a year to get it back. This is not a murder case we're talking about, so they're not going to treat it with the same urgency. The crime lab gave us this number to the company in New York. They have used them before."

At this point, I didn't care what it cost. A thousand dollars seemed like a lot of money to enhance a tape that was no more than a few minutes long, but I didn't have a better option.

"Okay," I replied. "Do a chain of custody, and overnight it to New York. I want it expedited as soon as possible."

This left me in a foul mood because I was hoping the recording would give us an ironclad case. We would know soon enough, I supposed, but I was getting damn tired of chasing my tail. I wanted to tie up the loose ends and solve this case.

A week later, Choat walked into my office unannounced. He was grinning like a possum. I knew it must be about the tape because he was carrying a tape recorder.

"Choat," I groused lightheartedly, "why don't you wipe that shit-eating grin off your face and play the damn tape?"

He set the tape player in front of me and pressed the play button. All the static and background noise was gone. It was like a completely different recording. We could hear numbers being pressed, then a dial tone, then more numbers, then a dial tone. Reimer pretended to use the phone while they talked. In between the sounds of her dialing, we heard voices utter things like, "I love you. Are you okay? Oh, I miss you so much. I can't wait until we are together." I was ecstatic.

"Damn!" I exclaimed. "We've got her!" Choat handed me a typed transcript. It was all the evidence we needed. "Let's get her in my office," I said. "I want you as a witness, and I want to secretly record everything that's said."

"Do you want her now?" Choat asked.

"Yes. I can't wait a minute longer. Just one thing, let me do all the questioning." Choat agreed and left to find Reimer.

While I waited, I found a place on the tape where Hodge mentioned something that had happened during his walk in segregation. I stopped the tape and rewound it again to that spot.

Choat knocked on the door and asked, "Are you ready for us?"

"Just you," I replied. "Tell her to wait." This is one of the tricks I learned from Sowders: never be in a hurry if you are about to question someone who's done something wrong. The longer Reimer sat in my outer office, the more nervous she would be. It might just soften her up a little.

I let ten minutes go by before I asked Choat to bring her in. I also had him start the recording device to capture our conversation. Reimer walked in, and I asked her to have a seat.

"Donna, do you have any idea why you are here?"

"No, I have no idea." I could tell she was nervous.

"I need your help in identifying a voice on this tape. It's part of an investigation we're doing." She scooted the chair closer. I pressed the play button and let it run for about five seconds. She said, "Yeah, that's Benny Hodge."

"Are you absolutely sure?"

"Yes," Reimer confirmed. "That's Benny."

"Are you one hundred percent sure?" I repeated.

"Yes."

"Okay," I said. "Let's see if you recognize the next voice." I let it play until Reimer's voice came up, and I stopped the tape.

"Parker," she snapped, "I don't know where you got that, but that's not me." I didn't say anything. I just looked at her. Reimer fidgeted in her chair and said, "That's not me, and you're not hanging that on me."

"Well, if that's not you, who is it?"

"I don't know, but it's not me."

"Okay," I replied. "Let's play the entire thing from the beginning."

About halfway through the tape, Reimer looked down and stared at the floor. I could tell she was defeated. She was ready to confess. Once the tape had played out, I said, "Donna, the game is up. There is no way you can deny what we just heard." I was hoping Reimer wouldn't resign, because I wanted to fire her. She was a tougher nut to crack than I expected, though, because she didn't resign. She also continued to deny any relationship with Hodge, even after admitting that the voice on the tape was hers. I finally placed her on administrative leave and told her I would call her back for a disciplinary hearing.

After I had written my report and summary of the investigation, I called the deputy commissioner's office and made an appointment. Sowders got on the phone and wanted to know what was going on. I told him about Julia Nardino resigning after I confronted her with the thumbprint on the card. I also told him I had a tape of Reimer and Hodge, and I had a report about the information I'd obtained from the

FBI. Sowders wanted me to meet him in Frankfort as quickly as possible.

CASE CLOSED

I have to say, I felt pretty good about this case. We proved that an employee was responsible for a serious security breach, and we had evidence that this same employee might be plotting to help a death-row inmate escape from prison. As far as security breaches go, it doesn't get much worse than this.

When I arrived in Frankfort for my meeting in the deputy commissioner's office, Commissioner Lewis was seated in his usual place next to Sowders' desk, puffing on a cigarette. They both knew I wouldn't be there unless I had a strong case. I handed each of them an executive summary of our findings. After they finished reading, I handed them copies of the audio transcript. Then a copy of my report detailing the information I'd obtained from the FBI.

We had worked on this case for over a year. I was proud of my team and what we had accomplished.

Sowders interrupted my train of thought. "Okay, Parker. We'll take it from here."

I stared at him in disbelief. I paused for a moment and said, "I want to fire her myself."

Sowders blew a puff of smoke off to the side and repeated, "Your work is done. We'll take it from here." Lewis didn't say a word. I got the feeling they had already decided what they were going to do, but for some reason they didn't want me to know.

"You *are* going to fire her, aren't you?" I asked.

Sowders wouldn't answer. He just said, "We'll let you know."

What a strange meeting. I finally got up to leave. There was no small talk, no pat on the back for a job well done. *Nothing.* I was dumbfounded.

Reimer knew she was facing termination, because I served her a letter laying out the evidence we had gathered. I also advised her she had a right to request a hearing with the commissioner, because my intent was to fire her. The commissioner would conduct the hearing, but I wasn't invited.

I had a four-hour drive home. I needed the time to process what had just happened. Were they going to cover this whole thing up? Why else would they cut me out of the disciplinary decision? *Something was rotten in the state of Denmark.* I knew that Reimer was Sowders' primary source of information when he decided to demote Henderson. She had a direct line of communication with the deputy commissioner and told him everything that was going on inside the prison. I suspected she was able to manipulate Sowders to get her pick of plum assignments and other perks during Seabold's tenure as warden. That all went out the window when I came aboard.

We had demonstrated beyond a doubt that Reimer was in love with a death-row inmate, and the evidence suggested she was conspiring to plan an escape. We had subpoenaed her home phone records, which proved she had accepted collect calls from death row. We had stacks of copies of love letters and cards, but no fingerprints. The thumbprint we previously found was on a card from Nardino, but we were never able to obtain Reimer's print on the cards or letters. We had her on tape telling Hodge how much she loved him. It was all there. As far as I was concerned, firing Reimer was the only acceptable course of action.

A day or two after the meeting in Frankfort, my personnel officer came into my office and said, "Warden, did you know they are transferring Donna to another agency, with a demotion?"

I wasn't pleased to hear that news, but I also wasn't particularly surprised. "That makes sense," I replied. "She handed me a form that I had to sign to make the move official."

I'd had enough of this whole sordid saga. Whatever reasons Sowders and Lewis had to protect Reimer, I would not be privy to them. Lewis did call me a few days later just to check on me and the institution. I wasn't going to bring up the case, but he finally said, "You know, Phil, Donna is close to retiring, and she is respected in the community. Sowders and I just felt that we could salvage her career by moving her to another agency."

I assured Lewis I could see where he was coming from. I really couldn't. Reimer had violated her sacred duty as a correctional officer and jeopardized the safety of everyone around her. I thanked the commissioner for calling, and I leaned back in my chair, lit a cigarette, and replayed the events of the past several months in my mind. In the end, I could only console myself with the fact that both correctional officers were gone, and I didn't have to worry about them. It was time to move on. I had plenty of other things to keep me busy.

PHOTOS

Judge Bill Cunningham and William "Snake" Woolum

Kentucky State Prison

Guard Badge Circa 1960

Knife Used by Aryan Brotherhood to Murder Ben Higgins

Left to Right: Dep. Warden Philip Parker, E-Squad Commander Larry Napier and Rodney Lawrence, Asst. E-Squad Commander, Great Escape of 1988

Kentucky State Penitentiary

1978 Emergency Squad

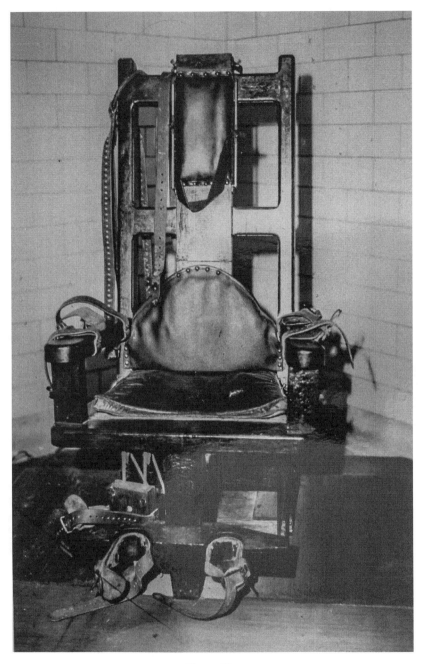

Electric Chair

Aerial View of Kentucky State Penitentiary on the Shore of Lake Barkley

Original Cell Block Two Constructed in 1880's

Warden Philip Parker

Whipping Stone/ Post in Cell House Two

Retired Sr. Captain Billy "Banging Billy" Adams with Warden Parker

Wardens Al C. Parke, Bill Seabold, and Philip Parker Walking the Yard

Command Center Hours Before McQueen Execution

Media Briefing Prior to McQueen Execution

Satellite Trucks Staged for McQueen Execution

Captain Kenny Holloway

Warden Parker Making Rounds in Cell House Three

Warden Parker Making Rounds on the Yard

SIXTEEN

TIGHTENING DOWN

One of my many priorities as warden was to limit the number of perks available to inmates in segregation. I told my executive staff early in my tenure we were implementing a new segregation policy, effective immediately. Our past practice was to release inmates who had been in segregation the longest if we needed access to a cell to house a new offender. Sometimes we would even reduce an inmate's time in segregation to mitigate capacity issues. For example, an inmate might have been sentenced to forty-five days, but he would be released in half that time if (1) his behavior was good, and (2) we needed his cell. "No more," I told my staff. "Forty-five days means forty-five days, and ninety days means ninety days. We're ending the practice of releasing inmates early, starting today." Everyone in the meeting said my plan would not work, because we simply did not have the space for it. I reminded them it was their job to find a solution. "When you need a bed and the cells are all occupied, throw a mattress on the floor and double cell." There was nothing wrong with double celling. It was done in almost every state. "Make it work," I said. "Meeting over."

Word got out on the yard almost immediately. I was always amazed at how fast news traveled in prison. When I made rounds later that day, some of the inmate legal aides came up and asked me if it was true that halftime was over. I confirmed their suspicions. "Warden," they griped, "that's a little harsh, don't you think?"

"Not really, no," I replied. "Just mind your p's and q's, and stay out of the hole if you don't like it."

Within two months of implementing this "harsh" new policy, there were about twenty empty beds in segregation. Inmate behavior improved significantly. Go figure.

I also stepped up drug testing, and I ordered the disciplinary board to mete out the maximum penalty for positive tests. My goal was to test roughly 25 percent of the population every month. The inmates jokingly accused me of running a Betty Ford Clinic instead of a penitentiary. Whatever they wanted to call it, the plan worked. The demand for drugs decreased over time, and we noticed a significant drop in the volume of narcotics smuggled into KSP. Betty Ford would have been proud.

As you might imagine, however, not everyone was pleased. Informants began telling staff that several inmates wanted to kill me—again. I was interfering with KSP's lucrative drug trafficking trade, and certain people wanted revenge. If that's how they wanted to handle this, so be it. I would just turn up the heat even more.

GETTING RESULTS

I was proud of the job Lt. Choat, Sgt. Dennis Yeager, Lt. Ronnie Youngblood, and others were doing to curb drugs and other criminal activity at KSP. We continued to deal with the occasional assault and stabbing, but they too had slowed down. For over a year, between 1993 and 1994, KSP did not have a single murder. No other warden could say that in the long and colorful history of the Kentucky State Penitentiary. We had no escapes during that period either. As 1994 drew to a close, it began to look like we had finally turned things around. The deputies were handling their responsibilities competently, and the lieutenants and captains were staying on top of problems. My unit managers and their staff seemed to be on board with the changes. All of this was great news, but I knew I couldn't grow complacent. The never-ending quest to find new ways to motivate my staff and keep the inmates in check was never far from my mind.

Then there was James Potter. The man was a perfect fit for Internal Affairs. He was a well-known state trooper and detective, but he had no real connections to the staff. He didn't attend our social functions, and as far as I knew, he didn't even drink. An island unto himself, Potter was the epitome of a no-nonsense, by-the-book law enforcement officer. His mere presence intimidated some of his colleagues to the point that they chose not to stick around.

When Potter came aboard in July of 1994, twenty-one (twenty-one!) employees at KSP tendered their resignations. I checked their names against the list of staff in my secret corruption file and realized most of these individuals were on my list. I assumed, incorrectly, that I would have twenty-three positions to fill with the best and brightest candidates I could find. Central Office had a different idea. They immediately cut twenty-three positions from KSP's budget, including three captain posts. The year before, Central Office cut over $1,000,000 from my budget. By my estimate, I found myself operating with almost forty fewer officers and a significant decrease in budgetary funds. We were expected to do more with less, which is never an ideal scenario in the world of corrections.

OTHER DIVERSIONS

Though drug activity and staff corruption cases had decreased precipitously by the end of 1994, our work neither slowed nor became more predictable. In January 1995, Walt Disney producers came calling to scout a prison location to film a Sharon Stone movie called *Last Dance*. They wanted to shoot scenes on the old death-row walk and throughout other parts of the prison. I resisted and discouraged the producers from selecting KSP because I didn't want the aggravation or the distraction. The last thing I needed was a movie production to complicate daily prison operations, even if it was Sharon Stone. My protestations fell on deaf ears.

Just as I predicted, the movie production was a pain in the ass. Movie producers, directors, and major stars tend to think the world revolves around them. And I'm sure in different venues it does. However, not in an operational maximum security prison. We were glad when they finally finished and things returned to normal.

As 1995 arrived and a new administration assumed power in Frankfort, the courts began advancing some of its backlogged death-row cases. We suspected the attorney general was tasked with pushing harder to move the cases along under Governor Paul E. Patton. I found myself fielding Supreme Court mandates and governor's orders to execute inmates on a regular basis, followed by repeated stays of execution. The more things changed, it seemed, the more they stayed the same.

Whenever I received an overnight package from the governor's office, I knew it was an executive order to execute one of the thirty-plus inmates on death row. I would always receive a courtesy call from the governor's general counsel advising me to expect the execution order, so it was never a surprise.

I believed it should be the warden's job to read the executive order to the condemned inmate and let him see the original order. I didn't like doing this, but I thought it was my responsibility. In retrospect, I don't know how many times I stood in front of a death-row inmate's cell and read the order over the twelve years that I served as warden. Seventy-five? A hundred times? It never got any easier.

Sometime in 1998 or 1999, I got a call from Assistant Attorney General David Smith. He opened the conversation with some small talk and said, "I really didn't have any official business today, but I thought you might be interested to know how many lawsuits you have pending. Any guesses?"

I thought for a minute. I knew we had a lot of lawsuits. I used to ask the officer in the legal office to keep a log of all new lawsuits, and we were averaging about five per week for a while. I finally said, "Hell, I give up. How many?"

He said, "Warden, you have one hundred fifty active lawsuits." I was expecting a ridiculous number, but even that took me by surprise. I don't remember what I said in response, but it was probably ugly.

I was reminded of a chance encounter I'd had with Judge Edward Johnstone on a Saturday at the local marina near KSP. Johnstone was the federal judge who presided over the litigation and Consent Decree. He was the last person I wanted to see on my day off, but there he was in the marina café, with some law clerks and office staff. He was taking them out on Lake Barkley for the day on a rented pontoon boat. As soon as I walked in, Johnstone spotted me. He always talked loudly, probably because he couldn't hear that well, even with hearing aids. "Hey!" Johnstone exclaimed. "There is the warden, the most sued man in the State of Kentucky."

The café was full of weekend boaters, and many of them looked up from their meals to stare. The last thing I needed was notoriety in this community. I always gravitated to the lake to get away from the stresses of my job; it was my escape. Annoyed at Johnstone's theatrics, I nevertheless made my way over to his table and introduced myself to his guests, and we chatted for a while. I came away from the conversation more eager than ever to leave my troubles behind while I spent some quality time on the lake.

The longer I stayed on as warden, the more lawsuits would pile up. They were terribly time-consuming for me, the attorneys, and the courts. Inmates could file lawsuits in *forma pauperis*, meaning they did not even have to pay the filing fees required of ordinary citizens. Eventually, the courts imposed new rules that required inmates to first file a grievance before they could file suit, and the courts began collected filing fees. This slowed the steady stream of lawsuits, but only slightly. I simply accepted that getting sued was a part of the job.

A SLICK CHECK SAVES THE DAY

September 20, 1995, was a routine day at the Castle. Internal Affairs was meeting with an inmate who had been locked up the day before and wanted to share information with us. We called this process a "slick check." Informants would occasionally violate a rule to get locked up in segregation instead of asking to be locked up for protective custody, prompting a slick check. This informant had slick checked the day before and sent word to Internal Affairs that he needed to talk. James Potter worked the case.

The inmate wanted to tell us about an escape attempt that was about to go down. It had been planned for a Monday, but the suspects had to postpone it to Friday because their connection on the outside wasn't ready. Scheduling conflicts, apparently. The informant met with us that Wednesday.

The escape plan was fairly straightforward. Inmates were going to highjack the trash truck and ram through the sallyport gate in prison industries. There were five suspects in on the plan. One of them had a girlfriend on the outside who was supposed to have a car and guns positioned just across the street from the sallyport. The reason it didn't go down Monday was because she had to buy two more guns. Now she apparently had the guns and the car, but the trash truck didn't run again in prison industries until Friday.

I called a meeting with Sr. Capt. Henderson, Deputy Wardens Haeberlin and Bail, Officer Yeager, and Lt. Youngblood. We went over the escape plan and decided it could work. The trash truck was a powerful, two-ton vehicle that normally picked up trash in the prison industry loading dock and the vocational school area. This spot was located in a cul-de-sac, out of the line of sight of the gun towers. After picking up trash in that area, the truck would back up the hill to the lunchroom and retrieve trash there. At this point, the vehicle would be pointing toward the sallyport about 150 yards downhill. We estimated the truck could easily get up enough speed to bust through both gates, because they were only locked with a chain and padlock. As soon as the truck blew through the sallyport, the inmates would only have to run a short distance to their getaway car.

They would hijack the truck at the garment plant loading dock, where most inmates took a smoke break. The garment plant produced prison uniforms, towels, sheets, and any other textiles that were needed throughout the prison system. Large scissors were issued at the beginning of the workday, then counted at lunch and again at the end of the day. Most of them were about ten inches long and easy to disassemble, in effect turning one pair of scissors into two knives. Two very deadly knives.

Armed with the separated scissors, the inmates would commandeer the truck from the driver and the escort officer. The only question was who would be assigned to truck duty that day. Lately, it had been Mike McCarty, a.k.a. Roho, and Anibal Agosto, a.k.a. Chico. These two officers were tough as nails. The inmates knew they couldn't fight them, so the only way they could make this plan work was attack with the scissors and kill them. Then they would commandeer the truck and make their getaway.

At our meeting, we discussed each of the inmates, and whether we believed they were able to attempt a daring escape. One of them was a biker, and the others were all considered dangerous convicts. We concluded they were very capable of pulling this off.

We decided to bide our time to see if the getaway car was staged across the street on Friday morning. Sure enough, we spotted the car in place just as our informant had predicted. I immediately sent a team to round up the five inmates who were getting ready to report to work. As they were being detained, one of the suspects had a guest appear at the front gate for an unscheduled visit. We later determined she was the one who staged the getaway car, but she cleverly reported to the visiting room to establish an alibi. Potter interrogated her. She confessed quickly to buying the guns and staging the car and eventually went to jail.

All the inmates involved in the plot were placed in segregation. It would be a long, long time before they were let out.

The entire episode reminded everyone how important it was to have a top-notch investigative team that cultivated relationships with prison informants. At least two lives had been saved, and likely more. It was a close call.

DANGEROUS CONTRABAND

As drug smuggling decreased toward the end of 1994, I started noticing some paranoia and resentment among KSP staff. A few incorrectly believed I had their offices and work posts bugged. Rumors also spread that we had hidden surveillance cameras in some locations. After giving it some thought, I concluded it was best to let them wonder about being under surveillance. Employees shouldn't have to worry unless they were doing something wrong. They already knew that we could obtain a warrant to review their home phone records, and we could secure warrants to search their cars if we had probable cause. It proved to be a fairly effective deterrent.

The inmates were getting tired of my hard line on drugs. We continued to drug test a large portion of the population each month, and we were imposing the maximum penalty on anyone who tested positive. In addition to this, we had arrested several inmate visitors and a few officers who were caught trying to smuggle drugs in to the penitentiary. Some of the female visitors would place drugs, either pills or marijuana, in small balloons or condoms and conceal them in a body cavity. Sometimes they would just place small balloons in their bras and hope the female officer didn't discover them during pat downs.

By far the most effective way to smuggle drugs in was vaginally. Once a visitor cleared the search, she could go to the restroom and retrieve the balloon. Next she would purchase potato chips or popcorn from one of the many vending machines and share her snack with the inmate. When the officers' heads were turned she would drop her balloon in the bag, and the inmate would eat the chips or popcorn along with the balloons.

Inmates had this down to a science. They knew they could vomit the balloons back up, but they would have to do so within thirty minutes of swallowing them. Otherwise they would have to pass the contraband out the other end. It really wasn't hard to smuggle small amounts of drugs in this way, and it usually worked.

Occasionally, informants would warn us that balloons were coming in on a certain date or by a certain visitor. In those cases, it was easy to obtain a warrant for a strip search of the visitor. It was more difficult, but not impossible, to obtain a warrant for a body-cavity search. This had to be conducted by a nurse, and the nurses understandably hated having to do it, so we usually tried to avoid cavity searches. It was better to try to bust the inmate after the fact, or if I had good reason, I could prohibit a visitor from ever returning to KSP. No warrant was necessary to bar visitors, and no warrant was necessary to search and drug test inmates. We could also place an inmate we suspected of smuggling in a cell with no commode. He would be forced to use a bucket for a bowel movement, and we could retrieve anything he passed. This was much easier than going through the hassle of securing a search warrant for a visitor.

For the first few years I was warden, I would conduct a surprise shakedown of the entire prison every couple of months. Sometimes I would hold over the midnight shift and keep the inmates locked in their cells while we searched. Other times I would schedule a training session for the E-Squad and have them target specific areas like death row and the yard. I would usually do this at the spur of the moment without telling anyone. Discussions of a shakedown had a way of leaking out to inmates, which gave them time to get rid of any contraband.

After months and years of this, even the threat of a surprise shake-down could have a desired effect. My staff liked to pretend that they were initiating a search just to see how many commodes we could hear flushing. It was fine with me if they flushed their drugs, because that saved twenty or thirty staff from having to conduct a shakedown on overtime. At least we got rid of contraband, and we always got a good laugh listening to the flushing throughout the cell blocks.

Not everyone appreciated our aggressive new efforts to curtail drug smuggling and drug use. Certain inmates hated it, and we started hearing rumors they were going to retaliate by taking hostages and killing staff. There was apparently also a price on my head. We took these threats seriously, but after meeting with my top security staff, I decided not to let up. Quite the opposite, in fact. I wanted to do more. I set up a drug intervention team to step up urinalysis and drug searches. We also worked our informants harder than ever. And through it all, rumors of retaliatory violence persisted.

I briefed the commissioner and deputy commissioner on the evidence that suggested inmates might try to take hostages or kill staff. I told them my plan to step up our efforts even more in the face of these threats. The commissioner wanted me to brief the secretary of justice, so I prepared a presentation and made the trip to Frankfort. I knew that once I briefed my superiors, they had a stake in this, too. I didn't seek their approval. My objective was to communicate the risks and possible consequences of our antidrug campaign at KSP. I got them all on board, which was like buying an insurance policy if things went south. This was also my way of testing the commissioner and deputy commissioner. If they weren't in my corner, I needed to know it now. Thankfully, they were.

One of my proposals did not gain traction, but it was worth a try. I wanted to purchase and train two attack dogs to patrol the yard. They could be unleashed to break up fights, especially if someone was being stabbed. They could also be used to protect staff during inmate assaults. And they might prove invaluable during cell extractions, particularly in cases where an inmate was armed with a knife. I made a compelling case for attack dogs, and the secretary was all for it. The commissioner and deputy commissioner, however, nipped it in the bud. We were still under the scrutiny of the federal court, and the commissioners were sure that general counsel would deny our request. They were probably right, but I regret we never ran it up the flagpole to know for sure.

One common misconception about prison guards is that they are always armed. We were not allowed to routinely carry batons, O.C. (pepper) spray, or tasers. Every chance I got at wardens' meetings or conferences, I would raise the subject of arming all staff members with O.C. spray. I also proposed to arm supervisors with tasers. Other wardens were all for it, but Central Office opposed my requests every time. The central staff was afraid officers would overreact and overuse weapons, even in instances when they were unnecessary. It ultimately came down to the threat of litigation. The Central Office feared that arming guards would lead to a flood of new and costly lawsuits. Whether that was true or not, it was clear to the rest of us that Central Office staff and attorneys had never worked in a prison. After you are forced to run into the middle of a fight or a stabbing without any kind of defensive weapon, you began to view the situation a little differently.

Sometimes I look back and am amazed at what we were able to accomplish with the tools we were given. The inmates we dealt with were often serving life sentences, they were angry, and they had nothing more to lose during a fight. The stakes are raised for all involved when self-preservation goes out the window. Thankfully, there were brave men and women who still showed up at work every day, without weapons or backup nearby, to patrol the yards and cell blocks of prisons. These were our forgotten cops. They enforced rules and maintained order and security without easy access to the tools they needed to accomplish their tasks. They deserved better.

Several years into my term as warden, I felt much better about the state of day-to-day operations at KSP. The more we reduced corruption at all levels, the more relaxed the inmates and staff became. Prison employees generally embrace law and order at the workplace. And, truth be told, most inmates want to live in a safe, clean environment. There were always going to be fights, stabbings, suicides, and escape attempts, but we had instituted policies that minimized these dangers, increased the quality of life for prisoners, and improved working conditions for prison staff. Things were looking up.

SEVENTEEN

A NEW DEPUTY

Patty Webb was deputy warden of security at KSP until July 1, 1994. She was transferred to Green River Correctional Complex, where she would eventually become warden. Everyone wondered who the next deputy warden of security would be at the penitentiary. I knew who I wanted, but there was no way I could select Bill Henderson as long as Dewey Sowders was the deputy commissioner. So, for the time being, I left the position vacant. About a year went by before Sowders asked me about the vacant position at a meeting. I told him I was performing the duties of both the deputy warden of security and the warden. After all, I had served as the deputy warden years ago.

I told him I would rather do without a deputy warden than to select the wrong person. He seemed okay with that answer, and I was surprised he didn't push me more on the subject. The position remained vacant. I think he eventually forgot about it.

I knew Sowders would retire once a new administration took over in Frankfort. In fact, he waited until Commissioner Lewis retired, then he followed suit on April 9, 1996. Doug Sapp was appointed commissioner and Tom Campbell took over as deputy commissioner. I liked both men. Lewis and Sowders had been career professionals, and it was a relief to finally have new leadership.

As soon as Sowders announced his retirement, I submitted paperwork to fill the empty deputy warden of security position. After interviewing several good candidates, I selected Bill Henderson for the job. His start date was August 26, 1996. I had fulfilled the duties of warden and deputy warden for over two years, and was glad to have somebody help ease the burden. My deputy was in charge of hiring new officers and recommending promotions among many other responsibilities, and there was a tremendous amount of paperwork to process on a weekly basis. It was not an easy job, and Bill Henderson hit the ground running. He had a lot of common sense, and he knew the penitentiary better than anyone, including myself. Most importantly, he had the respect of the staff and my complete trust and confidence in his ability. I knew I had hired an excellent deputy warden.

MAN ON THE RUN

On June 6, 1996, just before I announced Bill Henderson's promotion to deputy warden, we had an escape during a transportation trip. Inmate Kent Hill was being transferred by Officers Greg Stone and Bill McClure. About an hour into their trip on the Western Kentucky Parkway, inmate Hill started complaining he had to use the restroom. The officers decided to top off the gas tank and escort Hill to the restroom.

As soon as the car stopped, Officer McClure got out and opened the back door where Hill was sitting. When the door opened, Hill leaped out and took off running. He ran behind a building and kept going. McClure chased him for a short distance, but he was no match for the athletic inmate.

I was notified at seven a.m., and I dispatched four units to that area and called the state police. I told Stone and McClure to report back to KSP and to see me as soon as they arrived. We printed up escape handbills to pass out as the manhunt ensued, and Sr. Capt. Henderson and Deputy Warden Haeberlin quickly left to join the search.

I reported the escape to the commissioner. He requested that I notify Gen. Dan Cherry, the secretary of justice. The inmate was out of his leg shackles, but he still had handcuffs and a belly chain on. He would have to find a hacksaw to cut the lock off the black box cover that fit over the handcuffs.

Sure enough, Hill had broken into several outdoor sheds in a nearby subdivision looking for a hacksaw. Unfortunately for him, the state police and our units already had the subdivision covered up. He was caught at 9:50 a.m. by the state police and returned to KSP, just a few hours after his escape.

When Officers Stone and McClure were back at the prison, I had them come into my office one at a time. Stone was first. "Let me see your pistol," I asked. He handed it to me. I opened the cylinder of the revolver and counted six unfired shells.

"Did you reload?"

"No."

"You mean you didn't even fire your weapon?"

"No," Stone repeated.

"Why not?"

"I just didn't feel right about shooting a man in the back."

I explained to him that there was nothing in his post orders that prevented him from shooting a man in the back. "Your orders are to use deadly force to prevent or stop an escape."

"Yes, sir," Stone said. "I realize I should have shot him, but I just didn't."

I wanted to drive the point home. "In a situation like this, I expect you to return with an empty gun or a dead body. Do you understand?"

"Yes, sir," he repeated. I told him that would be all for now.

I brought in Officer McClure next and went through a similar line of questioning. I wanted to know why he didn't even bother to get out of the car and take a shot. The thought apparently never entered his mind. I pointed out that there was nothing in front of the fleeing inmate that could have been hit by gunfire. Even a warning shot might have scared him enough to stop running.

I'd heard enough. "Okay. That's all for now," I barked and motioned toward the door. I knew I had scared McClure, because he looked like he was about to cry. I was pretty sure he wasn't going to make the same mistake twice.

The next day, I had my usual seven a.m. meeting with my deputy wardens and senior captain. We discussed the previous day's events and what we could do to prevent this from happening again. I asked my team if anybody had searched the car when they got back.

Henderson looked at me and said, "Probably not. They got back and went straight to your office."

I told him to have someone search the car. Henderson got on his radio and gave the assignment to a lieutenant. Before the morning meeting was over, the lieutenant returned with a zip gun in his hand. A zip gun is prison vernacular for an improvised, single-shot weapon that is designed to fire a low-pressure cartridge. A zip gun could be made from a short section of pipe and some type of spring-loaded firing pin, as it was in this case.

The zip gun was found in the backseat where Hill was sitting. Guards learn early in their training to always search the seats of a car for contraband before placing an inmate in the back. The fact Stone and McClure didn't even bother to do that sealed their fate for me. I decided to fire both men.

Some people, I reminded myself, just aren't cut out to be corrections officers.

EIGHTEEN

FIRE IN THE OLD CANNERY

A FEW DAYS AFTER THE ZIP-GUN FIASCO, I DECIDED TO BLOW OFF steam by running my Jet Ski on Lake Barkley. I was in Kuttawa Harbor, about a mile northwest of KSP. As I bobbed in the water, I happened to notice a plume of thick, black smoke rising over the treetops in the direction of the prison.

I gunned the Jet Ski and got out in the main channel, where I could see more clearly. Just as I feared, something was on fire at the penitentiary. Several things raced through my mind. It could be arson, it could be a riot, or it could be a diversion for an escape. None of these scenarios put my mind at ease. I raced the Jet Ski back to the dock below my house as fast as I could and ran it up on the bank. As I sprinted in my house to change into something other than my swim trunks, I turned on my institutional radio. I could tell from the traffic that the old cannery was on fire. The old cannery had been converted into a case management office and recreation area for the inmates. The captain on duty had the yard locked down by the time I arrived, and Eddyville Fire Department was on the scene, trying to contain the conflagration. Unfortunately, there was not much they could do. The cannery burned to the ground.

Because the fire had occurred just before normal lockdown, I figured we were dealing with a case of arson. I called in James Potter, and he went right to work reviewing cameras and interviewing staff and inmates who were last spotted in the area. Potter had the case solved by the time I got to work the next morning.

We had just installed some security cameras in the recreation area. On one of the videos, we saw that as soon as an officer shut and locked the cannery door, he turned off the lights. Minutes later, in the darkness, you could see sparks fly from the plug where a window air conditioner was located. Then flames began shooting from the wall where the air conditioner was located. Soon the fire spread out of control. This wasn't arson; it was an electrical act of God.

We had to keep the institution locked down the next day because the surrounding utilities had been compromised, which meant repairs would be needed in the showers and other nearby areas.

Secretary Cherry and Commissioner Sapp wanted a briefing on the escape attempt and the fire, so I suggested I bring Henderson along to show them the video of the fire and go over the escape. They liked the idea of a face-to-face meeting, as did I. We got an early start the following morning, and were in Central Office before some of them even got to work. It was a good meeting, and I think Cherry was impressed with our response to both events. He understood that the penitentiary was a nonstop series of dangerous and deadly events. It was, but KSP was still far safer than it had been in the '70s and '80s.

ANOTHER DAY, ANOTHER FIRE

Prison fires are extremely dangerous. Hundreds of inmates can be locked in cells with no means of escape as flames and smoke spread out of control. They are completely dependent on an alert officer to let them out before tragedy strikes. Smoke is the more likely killer in these situations; the only things that could burn in KSP's segregation unit were sheets, towels, and maybe a fire-retardant mattress. More often than not, fires began when inmates lit up magazines or newspapers. As a guard, I responded to more conflagrations than I can count. A water fire extinguisher was usually all that was needed to get things under control. Occasionally, the smoke got bad enough that we would have to bring in fans to air the place out. Somehow we always managed to prevent catastrophic damage to the prison and a significant loss of life.

In the middle of an otherwise peaceful night in 1996, I jolted awake at the sound of the phone ringing. I hadn't smoked a cigarette in about three months, but I wasn't free of the nicotine monster yet. My wife also smoked, and there was always a carton or two lying around. Temptation was never far away. I rolled over in bed and picked up the phone, bracing myself for bad news. As the saying goes, nothing good ever happens after dark.

The control center officer greeted me and said, "Warden, we have a fire in Three Cell House. We're evacuating, and we have several staff down. Ambulances are on the way."

Oh no, I thought. My heart sank. Did I just hear correctly? Staff down and ambulances on the way? My wife was awake by then, and I repeated to her what I had heard while I threw on some clothes. I slipped my .38 snub nose pistol in my back pocket and asked, "Where are your cigarettes?" She brought me a brand-new carton. She probably thought I would grab one or two packs, but I took the whole carton and told her, "I don't know when I'll be back."

Running up the steps of the penitentiary, I tore open a pack of cigarettes and lit one as I approached the control center. I'd have to quit my nicotine habit another day.

"Where's the captain?" I asked.

"In Three Cell House," an officer replied.

"Okay. Call all the deputies, and then call the E-Squad."

"I started with you, and I've already called some of the others," she assured me. "They're on the way."

I went straight to Three Cell House to see if I could help. Roughly ten inmates had been released to the yard, and only a few of them were handcuffed. There wasn't time to cuff them. All told, about twenty inmates were being evacuated. It was completely chaotic.

The smoke was thick as molasses. Inmates were running for the exit, coughing and gagging. Most were wearing nothing but their underwear, but they wanted out. I couldn't blame them.

As I surveyed the scene, I spotted three injured officers sprawled on the floor. They were trying to stay low, beneath the suffocating smoke. Officer John Conley had been beaten up, and his arm was broken. His wife, Officer Susanne Conley, was holding her stomach, and she was bleeding from cuts on her face. Officer David Braden didn't say anything at all. He was alert but obviously in shock, and I could see a large gash on his head where a combative inmate had raked his cuffed hands across his face. Two other officers had been beaten up, but they would only need minor first aid.

Lt. Jimmy Lamb was the supervisor in charge. I asked him why the hell the inmates had set the fire. He gestured over to a figure hovering in the corner and replied, "They are trying to kill him." The "him" to which he referred was Brian Moore, a death-row inmate. "They set the fire to make us evacuate so they could kill that son of a bitch."

I turned to Lamb and said, "I'll take Brian Moore and hide him. You finish evacuating, and don't let them back in the cell house until the staff are taken out by ambulance."

"Okay, boss," Lamb confirmed.

I told Moore to follow me. I led him down a flight of steps to Fifteen Walk, which as a matter of coincidence used to be death row. When we were as far as we could go at the crash gate, I got in front of him and said, "Keep your damn mouth shut, and I'll try to keep you alive." Moore was scared and didn't say anything. I positioned myself where I could pull the pistol and shoot anyone who came down the steps. I thought the inmates would surely find us there. They had beaten up five officers who were trying to protect Moore, and even though the officers had managed to cuff their attackers and get them outside, I assumed there were others who still wanted Moore dead. I made up my mind I would kill the first son of a bitch who ran down those steps. Moore didn't know I had a gun or else he might have tried to grab it, and one of us would have gotten shot. I was pretty sure it would have been him, but you never know. He was a big, dangerous convict serving a death sentence, after all.

Moore was serving a sentence of death for the 1979 murder and robbery of an elderly man in Jefferson County, Kentucky. He had forced the man into his car at gunpoint and drove to a wooded area, where he marched him a short distance into the woods and shot him four times in the head with a .22-caliber pistol. The motive was robbery. Moore was arrested the following day and promptly admitted his guilt. He still had the murder weapon on him at the time of his arrest. It was an open-and-shut case.

Moore wasn't exactly popular with the other inmates on death row. An aggressive sociopath, he would often curse out staff and other inmates. Moore certainly wasn't liked by anyone in the segregation unit. In fact, I don't think I ever knew him to have a friend. He didn't even like himself.

All this ran through my mind as the two of us stood at the bottom of the stairwell, waiting for an attack that thankfully never came. I finally cuffed Moore and placed him in a cell on Fifteen Walk where he would be safe, and turned my attention back to the injured officers and the inmates who had escaped the fire.

Roughly twenty of the most dangerous inmates at KSP were now prowling the yard at night. Only a few of them were restrained with their hands cuffed in front of them. This wasn't an ideal situation, to put it mildly.

E-Squad members quickly began responding to the scene. I gathered up my officers and said, "Here's the deal. We're going to round up all the inmates and place them in the exercise pens. Let's get to it." The exercise pens were built to provide outdoor exercise space for Three Cell House. They were designed to hold roughly thirty inmates. I told the officers not to worry about who they locked up together; we just needed them secured as quickly and efficiently as possible.

The weather worked to our advantage. It was about forty degrees outside, and there was a light drizzle. Most of the inmates were barefoot and half-naked, and they had just run out of a toasty, warm cell block. This wasn't exactly their idea of a fun night out. Some of the inmates on the yard were uninvolved, but at this point we didn't know how many —or which—of them had attacked the officers trying to protect Moore.

The fires in Three Cell House had been started to create a distraction while the culprits targeted Moore. Typically, the inmates would pile up flammable materials like newspapers, books, magazines, bedsheets, and towels under their mattresses. If the fire grew hot enough, it could melt the mattress cover and ignite the flame-retardant mattress batting. It doesn't take much smoke to fill a cell block, especially if several fires are started at the same time. The inmates knew that a major fire and evacuation of the segregation unit would completely overwhelm everyone on duty during the night shift.

My officers had managed to fight off Moore's attackers, but the smoke had also worked in Moore's favor. He was able to run and hide during the chaos as everyone began coughing and struggling to breathe. I suspect that

Lt. Lamb's split-second decision to evacuate the area prevented multiple casualties. It doesn't take much smoke to overcome a person, and that section of the cell block was completely saturated. It got so bad, in fact, that smoke began spreading to some of the other walks. We were initially afraid we would have to evacuate all 150 inmates in the segregation unit, but the officers managed to get things under control before that became necessary.

It didn't take long to round up all the inmates and place them in what we called the bullpen. We opened all the windows and turned on the fans to clear the smoke from the cell block after we extinguished the fires. It wasn't necessary to call the fire department, but we needed at least two ambulances to transport our injured officers.

After the ambulances left, we were ready to bring the inmates in out of the drizzling rain. I walked out of the cell block to help the officers escort a few back in at a time. When the inmates saw me, they started yelling insults. It grew louder and louder, until the screaming sounded more like a riot than a bunch of freezing inmates standing around in their skivvies. I got on the radio and announced in a calm voice that we would not bring anybody in until they had quieted down and showed some respect. We would leave their asses out in the cold for as long as it took. I knew the inmates could hear my transmission, because the officers guarding the bullpen had their radio volumes cranked all the way up. I turned around and went back inside Three Cell House with several officers who didn't have on raincoats.

"How about we all take a break?" I asked as I lit a cigarette. "I think we earned it." We waited about fifteen minutes for the noise to die down outside. Any longer, and I risked having inmates die from exposure.

I stepped back out of Three Cell House and walked up to the bullpen. The inmates had grown as quiet as church mice.

I explained that we were going to cuff a few inmates at a time and take them back inside. The whole process only took about five minutes. Things were more or less finally back to normal.

As for the injured officers, they all recovered fully. The man who saved the day, Lt. Lamb, was eventually promoted to captain and then senior captain. Lamb had been an Airborne Ranger and was a good, solid supervisor who made sound decisions. Years later, after I retired from state government, I was appointed to run a local county jail. I made Lamb my chief deputy, where he once again proved himself time and time again. From my first day as warden to my last, I was fortunate to work with some of the best and brightest anywhere in the Department of Corrections, and I knew it.

NINETEEN

WILLIE THE COAL MINER

IT WAS NOT DIFFICULT TO FIND THE HUMOR IN SOME OF THE crazy situations inmates got themselves into. One of my favorite stories involved Willis "Willie" Davidson, a colorful gentleman who owned a wildcat coal mine in eastern Kentucky. He may have only finished eighth grade, but Davidson knew right from wrong. When he was riled up, he could be mean and treacherous. When he calmed down, he could be nice and polite. The people around him just never knew whether they were going to get Jekyll or Hyde on any given day.

Davidson found himself embroiled in a property dispute with a neighbor who owned land next to his coal mine. Property lines were often blurry around the mountains of Eastern Kentucky, and most of the land was not surveyed with any degree of precision. Disputes between landowners were often settled with a handshake... or a shootout.

Davidson's story was no different. His feud escalated for years, until one day, in a fit of rage, he and his neighbor shot at each other. As far as

I know, they both missed. But Davidson still ended up serving time at KSP for wanton endangerment.

Though he was already in his fifties when he reported to prison, Davidson made a good living mining coal and had access to more money than we were used to seeing in a penitentiary. In fact, he had about $60,000 in his inmate account at any given time, with access to a large bank account back home. Davidson tried to act like a big shot around the prison; he would give away canteen items just to impress other inmates. He also ended up paying well for protection, but he didn't mind. Lord knows he could afford it.

Whenever Davidson spotted me on the yard, he would strike up a conversation. It was always respectful, but he wanted me to know he was a big shot. "Hey, Warden," he'd say, "you need yourself a golf cart to get around on the yard. How 'bout I buy you one free and clear?"

"No thanks, Willie," I'd reply. "I need the exercise."

He wasn't done. "How 'bout I buy one for the nurses, so they can respond faster?"

"We have too many steps where a golf cart can't go, so I don't think that would work, Willie."

"Okay, Boss. I'm just trying to help."

"Thanks, Willie," I'd respond. "I appreciate you trying to help. Have a nice day."

It was always like that with Willie, until he would get angry at an officer and cuss him out over some petty matter. The officers had no choice but to write him up, which resulted in the captain placing Davidson in the hole. It was an endless cycle.

Once he was in segregation, Davidson could no longer smoke cigarettes. I had eliminated tobacco from segregation because of all the fires, and I was trying to make inmates in segregation as uncomfortable as possible.

During one of his stints in the hole, Davidson began experiencing severe nicotine withdrawal. He gradually spiraled out of control, behaving so poorly he got written up over and over again. Suddenly Davidson found himself facing six months in segregation, all because he couldn't smoke.

Thanks to the efforts of local Commonwealth Attorney G.L. Ovey, the Kentucky General Assembly amended a statute in 1990 that made it a felony for any inmate to assault prison staff with urine or feces. An inmate convicted of assault could be sentenced to an additional one to five years of prison time, to run consecutively with their current sentence.

Davidson racked up several five-year sentences for throwing feces on staff. We finally placed a plexiglass barrier in front of his cell so he could not assault anybody who walked by with his bodily fluids. This took care of the problem, but it didn't cure Davidson of his temper or meanness.

During one of my rounds, I stopped by his cell to try to reason with him. When Davidson saw me, he started crying and begged me to let him out of segregation so he could smoke. I thought for a moment and said, "Willie, I tell you what. Give me thirty days without a write-up, and I'll let you out and put the rest of your time on the shelf. But that time will be waiting for you if you come back in with a write-up." I thought I had given him an easy pass to get out of segregation. Thirty days of good conduct wasn't asking for much. All things considered, in fact, it was pretty lenient. Only Davidson didn't think so.

He glared at me. "Fuck you, Warden. Take your thirty days and get the fuck outta here!"

"Okay, Willie," I replied. "See you later."

He wasn't finished. As I walked away, he yelled at the top of his lungs, "$1,500 for anybody who shits down the warden!" He repeated his offer for good measure. "I'll pay anyone $1,500 for shitting down the warden!"

I turned around and strolled back to Willie's cell. "Willie, that ain't too smart. Why don't you stop making threats, and I'll come back to see you in a few days?"

"Fuck you, Warden. Hey, anybody that can hear me, I'll pay you $1,500 to shit down the warden!"

I looked at him amusedly. "Willie, are you serious?"

"Hell yeah, I'm serious!"

"You'll pay anybody?"

"Hell yes," he repeated.

"Okay, Willie. I'll throw shit on myself and you can pay me $1,500. Is that a deal?"

I thought it was pretty funny, but Davidson didn't. At least not until he decided to pull his Jekyll and Hyde act again. When I went back to check on him a couple of days later, Davidson was smiling as though nothing had happened. He admitted he thought my response was funny.

"Willie, I'm not your enemy," I told him. "I'll help you if you'll let me."

"Okay, Warden. I'm gonna be good, and then you'll let me out, right?"

"Thirty days, Willie."

"Okay, Boss," he promised me. "I'll be good."

The fact of the matter was that officers were getting tired of writing Davidson up several times a shift. He had more disciplinary time stacked up than he could ever serve. On top of that, he was facing at least two new felony convictions for assaulting staff with feces.

I finally let Davidson out of segregation, figuring he had made a good-faith effort to stay out of trouble. He was free to smoke on the yard as much as he wanted. And if my memory serves me right, I don't ever recall him being a problem after that.

Davidson finally made parole before I retired. He had been out about a year when he called me. Vicki Patton came into my office and said, "You'll never believe who's on the phone waiting to talk to you."

I knew it must be good, because she was laughing. "I give up. Who?"

"Willie Davidson."

Deputy Warden Henderson, Deputy Warden Haeberlin, and Byron Jasis were in my office at the time. I put Willie on speakerphone. "Hi, Warden," a familiar voice said. "Boy, I'm glad to be out of that place, but I want to come back and visit. I want to walk the yard with you."

"Willie, I can't let you do that, as much as I would like to see you. We just can't let an ex-con back in like that."

Willie wasn't going to give up that easily. "Well, okay. I didn't know. But hey, I bought me a camper! How about I bring it down and camp in your driveway?"

"No, Willie, I don't think that would be appropriate." I tried to change the subject. "Willie, I bet you're chain smoking out in the free world, aren't you?"

"You damn right! I'm sitting here looking at a carton of Camels. Hey, Warden, did you ever hear of a $6 hamburger?"

"Yeah. I think I saw where Hardee's had a $6 hamburger."

"They do," Davidson confirmed and then added for good measure, "I get one every day!"

"Well, that's nice, Willie. I have to go, but I hope you continue to enjoy those hamburgers and cigarettes."

"Okay, Warden. I'll see you later."

Davidson had made my day. He lightened the mood of an otherwise serious meeting, and everyone in my office had a good chuckle. I just hoped he wasn't going to show up in my driveway with his camper.

TWENTY

EXECUTION

THE MOST COMMON DEFINITION OF THE WORD "EXECUTE," according to Webster's Dictionary, is "to carry out." Within the context of the death penalty, then, the law directs the warden of the state penitentiary to *execute* a death sentence. When KSP opened its gates in the late 19th century, the most common method of execution was death by hanging. This changed in 1910, when the General Assembly passed a law establishing electrocution as the preferred method of carrying out death sentences.

Harold McQueen grew up in Berea, Kentucky, a quaint college town situated in the foothills of the Appalachian Mountains. Berea is best known for its local college, its art festivals, and the historic Boone Tavern Hotel and Restaurant. Local artisans dedicate their considerable skills to making rocking chairs, pottery, musical instruments, and quilts, among other goods. There is a certain charm to the place that, sadly, has grown increasingly rare in the hustle and bustle of modern America.

Despite his idyllic surroundings, McQueen didn't have a happy childhood. His parents divorced when he was two years old. When he turned ten, McQueen's father introduced him to alcohol. By age thirteen, he was drinking almost every day and committing petty crimes like breaking and entering. Child services came knocking at his door more than once. Then he quit school at the age of fourteen.

By his eighteenth birthday, McQueen was drinking an average of a case of beer a day. He joined the army to escape his troubled past, but before long he became addicted to heroin. McQueen eventually went AWOL from the army, was convicted of desertion, and received a dishonorable discharge. By the late '70s, his substance abuse problem had grown out of control. He was still drinking beer and whiskey every day, and chasing it all with heroin, cocaine, marijuana, or valium, whatever he could get his hands on.

Rebecca O'Hearn graduated from Eastern Kentucky University with a degree in agriculture around the time that McQueen was spiraling out of control. Those who knew O'Hearn remembered her as hardworking, honest, generous, and caring. She started working at a Minit Mart in Richmond to pay off student loans. O'Hearn hoped to attend graduate school, and she dreamed of starting her own landscaping business.

On the night of January 17, 1980, O'Hearn was alone at the Minit Mart getting ready to close up for the night. A Richmond police officer drove by to check on the store, and O'Hearn smiled and waved at the officer through the window. Harold McQueen and his cousin, William Keith Burnell, stood out front watching as the cop left, while McQueen's girlfriend, Linda Rose, sat waiting for them in a 1973 Ford Falcon. All three were drunk and high on valium. As soon as the patrol car disappeared down the road, McQueen and Burnell entered the store brandishing a .22 revolver.

In a matter of minutes, McQueen came running out carrying several small bags of money. Burnell followed closely behind with another bag that concealed a security camera he had yanked off the wall. They jumped into the Falcon and drove off.

After they made their getaway, a park ranger named Michael Rhodu pulled up to the Minit Mart for a soda. He discovered O'Hearn kneeling and slumped forward behind the counter, holding her bloody face in her hands. She had been shot once in the face and once in the neck at point-blank range.

Officer Larry Brock arrived at the scene almost immediately in response to Rhodu's call for assistance. Brock had just seen O'Hearn wave at him fifteen minutes earlier. He also recalled seeing two white males at the scene, one of whom he later identified as Harold McQueen.

Rebecca O'Hearn was barely alive when the paramedics arrived, and she died on the way to the hospital. The community was stunned. Deadly violence like this was rare in Richmond, and the randomness of the act left residents unsettled. There was a collective sigh of relief when authorities announced they had several suspects in custody. In fact, the killers were not hard to track down. Police arrested Burnell for driving with a revoked operator's license three days after the murder. The next day, police arrested McQueen and Rose on an unrelated theft charge when they went to the Madison County Jail to visit Burnell. A series of searches of the trailer where McQueen and Rose lived turned up a significant body of incriminating evidence, including a bundle of cash, a bag with two pistols, and a bundle of food stamps taken from the Minit Mart. Ballistics revealed that one of the firearms was the murder weapon. Finally, Rose led authorities to a local pond where police divers recovered the security camera that McQueen and Burnell dumped the night of the murder. It was an airtight case.

Prosecutors charged McQueen and Burnell with armed robbery and capital murder. After deliberating for less than four hours, a jury found both men guilty on March 29, 1981. Burnell was sentenced to two twenty-year terms for the robbery, and McQueen was sentenced to death for O'Hearn's murder.

I first crossed paths with McQueen after he was transferred to KSP in 1981. He never gave prison staff any trouble, and he was always polite and respectful to me. If McQueen was ever written up for a rule violation, I never knew it. After I was appointed warden in 1993, I made it my business to get to know all the men on death row. I would make rounds every week and stop and talk to any of the death-row inmates who wanted to chat. I wanted them to see me as a person, not as a warden who was out to execute them.

My orientation as KSP's new warden included a briefing on the status of death-row appeals and the likelihood of an execution during my tenure. I learned that McQueen's appeal was moving faster than others, and there was a strong possibility that he would be the first to be executed.

There had been 162 electrocutions and nine hangings in Kentucky since 1910. The commonwealth actually holds the unfortunate distinction of overseeing the greatest number of consecutive executions in American history, when seven inmates were put to death in one night in 1927. Though the last state execution had occurred over thirty years earlier in 1962, it was growing increasingly clear that McQueen's time was quickly running out. I knew I would likely be the warden tasked with overseeing his execution. I had a lot of preparation to do. I wanted to learn everything I could about the process by traveling to other states and witnessing their procedures.

I also spent a great deal of time examining my own ethical, moral, and religious beliefs as I came to terms with the realization I might have to oversee the execution of another human being. The magnitude and scope of this responsibility weighed heavily on my mind. I thought about the millions of soldiers who had reluctantly killed their enemies in battle. I thought about the Allied pilots who dropped millions of tons of bombs on Axis powers during the Second World War. How did they rationalize their roles after the fact? How did they process what they witnessed? Perhaps I would be scarred by the experience of putting someone to death, but I reasoned that if I chose not to do it, someone else would have to. It was a burden that I believed I must bear.

I further rationalized that my role in carrying out an execution was simply the final step in a long journey that led to a person's death. This was a responsibility that I shared with prosecutors, jurors, judges, the Kentucky attorney general, and the governor. We were all soldiers of justice, and we were in this together. Overseeing an execution was not something that I wanted to do, but I had accepted the responsibility when I accepted the job as warden. I was determined to carry out my duties with dignity and humanity.

PREPARATIONS

The electric chair in use at KSP throughout my career was the same chair first installed in 1910. Originally, the device and the electrical dynamo and switches that made it work were built by a man named Peter Wade Depp. If that surname sounds vaguely familiar, it should: Depp was the forebear of actor and Kentucky native, Johnny Depp.

In 1956, the old, original dynamo and switches were replaced with a modern switchboard. A single executioner was tasked with standing at the controls and waiting for the warden's nod. At the flip of a switch, two thousand volts of electricity would be applied for fifteen seconds then six hundred volts for the remainder of two minutes. A voltage and amperage meter could be monitored to ensure that everything was working properly. As McQueen's execution date drew near, we used a set of lightbulbs to test the system repeatedly. It appeared to work fine, but I wasn't satisfied. The equipment was just too old. I didn't want to risk a malfunction.

I called Commissioner Sapp and requested new controls. He understood why I thought it was necessary, but had to run it by the secretary of justice, General Dan Cherry, and the governor, Paul Patton. The changes would cost roughly $30,000—a figure I was familiar with, because I had been involved in replacing the electric chair controls at the Southern Ohio Correctional Facility at Lucasville during my stint as regional director. The price tag wasn't cheap, but it was necessary. Thankfully, Governor Patton and his subordinates agreed with my assessment. I had no problem getting their approval to upgrade KSP's equipment.

KSP started getting a lot of media attention as early as 1995. Just about every major newspaper and TV broadcast station began bombarding us with requests for interviews and tours of the death chamber. Most of them wanted file pictures ready to publish if and when an execution was carried out.

I was somewhat surprised to see so much attention suddenly directed toward Kentucky's death penalty. Other states were conducting executions on a regular basis, and most of the time they weren't front page news. Florida had just conducted a botched execution, however, and I suspected that might be the reason the media shifted its collective focus to KSP so quickly. I participated in quite a few interviews early on, because I wanted the media to get in and out before I had to tighten things up closer to an execution date. The press always wanted to talk to McQueen and the warden. McQueen's attorneys understandably didn't want him talking to anybody unless they were present. I always discouraged interviews with the inmates, but I would allow them if their attorneys approved it.

Another headache we faced was an influx of so-called "do-gooders" who came out of the woodwork wanting to minister to inmates on death row. This wasn't a problem unique to KSP: lay ministers often come knocking at maximum security prisons across the country, but their numbers grow exponentially whenever they catch wind of a possible execution. I always tried to protect death row from the constant stream of religious pontificators. Their true motive wasn't to help these men; they simply wanted bragging rights that they had ministered death-row inmates. It was sickening. I would usually point them in another direction and ask, "What about the men in general population or protective custody? Are you willing to minister to them?"

The answer was almost always, "No, I've been called to minister to death row." Whenever I heard this, I would politely tell them we had enough chaplains at the penitentiary, and we wouldn't be needing any more.

I was often reminded of a sage bit of advice my father gave me as I left for college: "Son, always watch out for the three P's and steer clear."

"The three P's?" I asked.

"Yeah. Preachers, prostitutes, and politicians."

In retrospect, I guess that was the best advice I ever got from my dad. To be sure, I don't mean to insult prison clergy, the good folks who do meaningful work every single day at correctional facilities across America. My disdain is reserved for the grifters who float from prison to prison, seeking opportunities for self-aggrandizement under the pretense of helping troubled souls.

Preparing for the first execution in thirty-five years was the hardest part of my job. I started by reading everything I could get my hands on that examined the procedures necessary to carry out an electrocution. I attended a conference in Colorado for wardens who managed death-row inmates across the country. I also planned to watch executions in Virginia and Alabama. I was somewhat ahead of the game, because I had already overseen preparations for Ohio's first execution in years. The knowledge I gained from that experience would prove invaluable in the months ahead.

People always want to know what it is like to witness an execution. In a sense, it's over almost as soon as it starts. Yes, it can be surreal to watch someone put to death, but there isn't anything overtly horrific or gruesome about the event aside from the fact that someone dies. I suppose the graphic nature of a firing squad or a hanging would be much different and probably more disturbing. I'm glad I didn't have to worry about that.

Once we had the new equipment in place and had rewritten all the relevant procedures, I felt we were close to being ready. I had to brief the commissioner, Secretary Cherry, and their staffs. We put on a demonstration at KSP and reviewed the procedures. Cherry, a retired Air Force brigadier general, was much more detail-oriented than I realized. He had several suggestions to amend the process, but saved his criticism until we were alone. He also asked me to completely redraft our procedures into a streamlined checklist and place it all in a manual. He explained he used to fly in the Air Force Thunderbirds, and they had a checklist for everything. Prior to any performance, they carefully follow a lengthy process of checking off every item. Only after each member had checked every box would they take off in a precise, well-rehearsed formation. It was an apt metaphor for my team as we prepared at KSP.

Taking Cherry's advice to heart, I set our previous procedures aside and started from scratch. Cherry drew up the format he thought would work best, and he said, "I want you to think about the very first thing that sets the preparations for an execution in motion."

I thought for a moment and replied, "The warden receives an executive order from the governor."

"Okay," Cherry said. "How much time do you need from that point until the actual execution?"

"Thirty days, if all goes according to plan."

Cherry nodded. "Okay. At x-minus thirty days, you check off that you received the order, and you record the completed date and time."

I saw where he was going with this. "Okay, I get it. We need this approach for everything we do, down to the last detail."

"You got it, Phil," Cherry replied. "Don't leave anything out."

The checklist required me to notify my executive staff and the execution team at x-minus thirty days. We had procedures to follow every day, up to and including x-minus one hour, x-minus thirty minutes, x-minus ten minutes, x-minus five minutes and, lastly, x hour.

I worked on these procedures for weeks. I would review every detail with my deputy wardens and add anything they came up with. Once we had our procedures where we thought they should be, Cherry wanted a briefing with his staff. If he didn't suggest any additional changes, we would schedule a dress rehearsal. But there were indeed changes to be made, and a lot of them. General counsel had to offer their input, as did attorneys from the secretary's office and the governor's office. The public information officer also had to review the procedures, and the commissioner and his staff would then review them all over again and suggest additional changes. This process went on for months.

Finally, we were ready for me to brief the governor's chief of staff, his public information officer, and his attorney, along with the secretary and the commissioner. All total, we had about twenty people at the briefing. Then we carried out a mock execution with the execution team, under the watchful eyes of everyone in attendance. I was under tremendous stress, but that was part of the plan. Cherry wanted to see how I would perform under the pressure of knowing the Governor's office and the secretary's office were hanging on every word I said and every move I made.

When the rehearsal was over, Cherry and Commissioner Sapp proudly congratulated me on a job well done. We were ready.

Throughout this process, my team was still being inundated with media requests. I started cutting back on my time with the press, and I asked Banister to handle all future requests. Still, the media onslaught was relentless. We even had a high-profile journalist reach out to my office. I returned from lunch one day and my secretary, Vicki Patton, said, "Tom Brokaw called."

"You're kidding," I replied.

"No, I'm not." Brokaw must have had a deadline, because I didn't hear back from him again. But his personal involvement speaks to the level of media attention we were getting.

I still found time to make rounds at KSP and handle all the usual paperwork, but I wasn't on the yard as much as I wanted to be. I had previously set aside time to eat an occasional meal in the inmate dining room, but not anymore. I was overwhelmed with attorneys, journalists, bosses, and routine things that demanded my attention. I still worried about stabbings, drugs, murders, and everyday fights inside the prison, but I had good deputy wardens, unit managers, and supervisors who knew what to do. As the x-hour drew ever closer, I had to devote all my time to preparing for the execution.

On June 11, 1997, I received word that Governor Patton had signed an executive order to execute McQueen. The attorneys faxed a copy to the penitentiary, and I received the original by overnight mail the following day. I began the notification process and went to death row to read the order to McQueen. I was as polite and respectful as I knew how to be, but it was an incredibly uncomfortable experience. McQueen was expecting the order, and he was very polite and respectful to me. I told him that if he had any questions at all to tell the officer on duty, and I would respond as soon as I could. I assured him I would be back in the coming weeks to discuss things like visitation, funeral arrangements, and so forth. He politely thanked me.

Gov. Patton ordered the execution to take place one minute after midnight on July 1, 1997. I didn't have the thirty days to prepare I had asked for, but nineteen days would be enough time. We were ready.

Media activity kicked into high gear after the announcement. I had to completely isolate myself from any press inquiries. At the same time, I turned over all my normal operation responsibilities to the deputy wardens. My secretary, Vicki, was excellent at running interference from nuisance calls and farming out correspondence and other matters to my deputies. My time was almost entirely consumed by calls from the governor's office and my bosses in the Justice Cabinet. I was also getting bombarded with calls from our attorneys, the attorney general's office, and the Department of Public Advocacy on behalf of McQueen. Most important of all, I had to go over the checklist and make sure we were on schedule as planned. I would usually try to review the checklist every morning with the deputy wardens, and they would brief me on the normal prison operations to make sure I had no surprises. I was so fortunate to have Bill Henderson in security, Glenn Haeberlin in programs, and Steve Bail in operations as my deputy wardens during this period. In many ways, they eased the burden during one of the most challenging experiences of my career.

DEATH WATCH

On June 19, we implemented the "Death Watch." This is a major step in any preparation for an execution. The inmate is moved to an area on Fifteen Walk in Three Cell House, close to where the execution would take place. No other inmates are housed on Fifteen Walk; it's reserved solely for the condemned. The individual is watched twenty-four hours a day by posted guards, and anything and everything that occurs is carefully logged. The primary purpose of a Death Watch is to make sure the individual doesn't hurt himself, but moving an inmate to Death Watch is also symbolic. It communicates to the condemned that his time is drawing closer. He is provided an opportunity to prepare mentally, without interference from other inmates. Just before we escorted McQueen to Death Watch, I told Sr. Captain Holt to let him walk around the cells and bid the other death-row inmates goodbye. It was the humane thing to do. I was told they really appreciated the opportunity to say their goodbyes to one another. We didn't rush McQueen. He was allowed to mingle as long as he wanted.

On June 24, McQueen received a stay from United States District Judge Thomas Russell. A decision was made in Governor Patton's office to continue the checklist and keep McQueen on Death Watch. There was a belief shared among the assistant attorneys general that the stay would be lifted. I didn't bother to follow the legal filings. I was too preoccupied with my own responsibilities.

On June 27, just three days from the execution, the stay was lifted by the United States Court of Appeals. I was advised by our general counsel it was very unlikely another stay would be issued, even though motions were pending in the U.S. Supreme Court.

I worked all weekend before the execution to brief staff at roll call and to address their questions or concerns. I wanted to make sure the officers knew they could not talk to the media and that our interaction with all the inmates should remain strictly professional.

On Sunday, June 29, the execution team arrived from the Green River Correctional Complex and the Western Kentucky Correctional Complex. They took over the Death Watch and assumed control of all non-administrative aspects of the execution. This procedure was designed to relieve my officers of the emotional burden associated with executing an individual some of them had known for almost twenty years. As for the warden's duties, they were mine and mine alone.

LAST MEAL AND FINAL ARRANGEMENTS

I met with McQueen on Sunday morning to offer a last meal. I told him he could order anything within reason. McQueen didn't hesitate. "Warden, all I want is cheesecake."

"That's it?"

"Yep, that's it."

Jokingly, I replied, "I was afraid you would order a T-bone steak or something."

"Cheesecake is my favorite food," McQueen said matter-of-factly. "That's all I want."

Next, we discussed his funeral arrangements. McQueen assured me that the Catholic Conference and his family would handle those details. We discussed the list of witnesses to the execution. Kentucky law allowed him three visitors of his choice, and he gave me their names. Lastly, we discussed his privilege of saying a few final words just prior to the execution. Fortunately, his best friend and volunteer chaplain, Paul Stevens, was present for our conversation. I suggested he and McQueen work out what he was going to say, if anything. Chaplain Stevens said, "Warden, I was hoping you would allow me to make the final walk with him, and I will read a statement from Harold."

"Paul," I replied, "I trust you, and I think that is an excellent idea. It's not in the procedure that you can accompany him to the chair, but I will allow it."

Chaplain Stevens thanked me and asked if I would join them in prayer. We held hands, and he offered a prayer for me and for McQueen. It was a moving moment for everyone present.

Afterward, I gently described the procedure we would follow in the minutes leading up to the execution. I told McQueen I would come to his cell and say, "It is time." I wanted to assure him that we would safeguard his dignity. "We will not cuff you or manhandle you in any way. You are man enough to walk in and sit down on your own."

"Yes, I will," McQueen agreed. "You will not have any problems from me."

Chaplain Stevens interjected, "Warden, you don't have to worry. He is ready."

I thanked them both and said I would be back frequently to check on things.

June 30, 1997, was the day before the execution. I knew I would have trouble sleeping. I needed a full night's rest, so I took a sleeping pill. I still woke up about four a.m., which was normal for me. My wife woke up, too, and asked what all the noise was. She said it sounded like generators were running just outside our door.

We had designated the large parking lot in front of the warden's house as a staging area for the media. We didn't know what to expect, but I assumed it would be busy. I had no idea.

I looked out the window, and my mouth dropped open. "Oh my god. Come here and look." We counted over twenty satellite trucks, parked virtually in our front yard. All told that day, my staff would count over 120 media and news organizations from all over the United States, including several foreign journalists.

The patrols had already started. Three hundred National Guard troops were on duty around the perimeter of KSP, just like we had planned. Their mission was to guard the power lines going to the prison, and they set up encrypted communications with the command center in Frankfort. The Kentucky State Police also set up roadblocks to keep demonstrators and tourists from interfering with prison operations.

I arrived at work at six thirty a.m. to start what would be one of the longest days of my career. The execution wouldn't be carried out until just after midnight, and the hours dragged on. At eight thirty a.m., I hosted designated agency commanders for a briefing in my office. The attorney general sent two attorneys ready to file motions with the local court if necessary. The National Guard sent an officer to communicate with the three hundred or so National Guardsmen who were on duty, and my boss, Deputy Commissioner Tom Campbell, was present. My office was the most crowded I had ever seen it. We had prepared for this, and everyone knew what to do.

"TOTALLY FRIED"

Sometimes you find humor in the most difficult of circumstances. In the weeks leading up to the execution, a radio talk show host out of one of the big stations in Louisville started a contest that he dubbed "Get Totally Fried at Kentucky State Penitentiary." The grand prize would include a limousine ride to Old Eddyville and a free overnight stay at a local hotel. The winner would also be issued a "press pass" so that they could get "totally fried." I didn't really appreciate the gallows humor, but the whole affair was about to provide a much-needed moment of levity during a difficult day.

During a break in the proceedings that afternoon, Capt. Vance, Deputy Commissioner Tom Campbell, and I took a break to watch the video monitors around the prison. We had security cameras all over the place. On one monitor, I noticed a black stretch limousine pull up to the roadblock, and we realized it must be the winners of that damn radio contest. I had Capt. Vance call down to tell the driver that they were not coming in as press, even with their "press pass," but we would permit them to go to a designated staging for demonstrators at the firing range. Vance looked at me and asked if I wanted the limousine searched. Not a bad idea. I instructed him to have the limo pull off the road onto our property and search the vehicle and its passengers.

It wasn't long before Vance got a radio call from a trooper who said, "We found a joint in the ashtray." By then, we were having a good chuckle. I ordered the troopers to detain the limo driver for promoting dangerous contraband, and we impounded the limo. We sent the two contest winners along to the firing range and watched as a wrecker came and hauled the limo away. I thought it was a hoot, and it passed the time for all of us.

Vance wanted to know what we were going to do with the two contest winners after the execution. I told him that wasn't our problem, and he just grinned. I never did find out whether the radio station sent a second ride to pick up their stranded comrades. I had other things to worry about.

THE FINAL FEW HOURS

Later in the day, McQueen's family and his girlfriend came for a final visit. That wasn't on the checklist, but I let his mother, aunt, girlfriend, cousin, and a baby visit for thirty minutes. They gathered on Fifteen Walk. I figured anything I could do to make this easier for McQueen was in everyone's best interests. The visit went well, but it was very emotional for everyone.

After they departed, I watched the cameras as McQueen was given his last meal of cheesecake. I had left it up to my foodservice manager, Ruth Byrd, to prepare the cake as she saw fit. She decided to buy a cheesecake from a store, and she also made two versions of her own. It was enough to feed the entire execution team. I watched until they were about done. I walked down to Fifteen Walk to ask McQueen if he liked his last meal. Chaplain Stevens was with him, and they said the cheesecake was outstanding. Out of the blue, Harold said, "Warden, sit down and have a piece of cake. It's so good." I wasn't prepared for that, and I really didn't know what to do. I was aware everyone in our command center was watching, and there was a live feed to the command center in Frankfort. My first thought was that this would look bizarre—the warden sharing a last meal with the condemned. But then I saw the earnestness in McQueen's face, and I sat down. He handed me a slice of his cheesecake, and I ate it appreciatively. I was somewhat overwhelmed that a man I was about to execute had offered to share his last meal. I was humbled. McQueen's gesture was about as Christian as it gets. I had shown him respect and compassion, and now he was returning the favor.

We sat and chatted for a while. "Harold," I asked, "how are you doing? I mean how are you really doing?"

He looked at me and said, "Warden, you don't have to worry about me. I know I'm going to be with the Lord in just a few hours. Now don't you worry about me. You are doing a fine job, and I couldn't ask for any more than you have done for me."

I had trouble holding back my emotions in that moment. I never figured I would share McQueen's last meal or he would console me. After a few more minutes of conversation, I stood up to leave and told him, "Harold, we are going to have to shave your head and let you take a shower in a few minutes. Then I will let you and Paul visit until I come for you. Your attorney, Randy Wheeler, wants to stay with you during that time. It's up to you if you want him here."

McQueen was too polite to turn anyone down. I was a little surprised his attorney wanted to spend these last few hours with him and take time away from McQueen and Chaplain Stevens, but he said it was okay. I wasn't going to let Wheeler stay all the way to the end, but I got an unexpected phone call from General Counsel Barbara Jones. "Justice Stevens has ordered you to let Randy Wheeler visit, with access to his cell phone, or he will stop the execution." Now the Kentucky Supreme Court Chief Justice was deciding who could visit, regardless of what McQueen wanted? I thought it was out of line, but the chief justice certainly had the power to halt the execution—and he probably would have.

We had set up a "ring down phone" for Wheeler at a phone bank to communicate with the Kentucky Supreme Court. A ring down phone enabled Wheeler to reach the justices en banc, just by picking up the receiver. He had apparently called the chief justice and demanded we let him keep his cell phone throughout the process. I didn't want any cell phones present, because they could be used to take pictures of the executioners. Wheeler's phone could have recorded everything—even the executioners as they entered the executioner's station. If nothing else, requesting to bring a phone inside struck me as incredibly insensitive. These were the solemn and private final moments of a condemned man. If McQueen had said no to Wheeler, I would have stopped him from visiting. And I probably would have resigned in protest or been fired before the day was over.

IT'S TIME

At about eleven forty-five p.m., I told everyone in the command center that the moment had arrived. Deputy Commissioner Campbell walked with me through One and Two Cell Houses, then down the steps to Fifteen Walk. I consulted with the team leader to confirm everything was ready, then I checked with the attorneys stationed at the phone bank. They gave me the nod to proceed. I made doubly sure that I had the key to activate the system in my pocket. I was just a few minutes early. We couldn't carry out the execution until after midnight, on July 1, 1997.

At precisely midnight, I walked up to McQueen's cell and said, "It's time, Harold." He had seen me coming and was already standing up when I arrived. McQueen's head had been shaved. His demeanor was sullen, but he had prepared himself for death. I opened the cell and walked beside McQueen and Chaplain Stevens. The execution team was all around to make sure McQueen didn't resist. I was confident that he wouldn't.

The mood was solemn as we walked the short distance to the death chamber. There, the electric chair waited, its open, wooden arms extending a deadly embrace to the condemned. Members of the execution team stood behind and beside the chair, just as we had rehearsed.

The electric chair itself is constructed of sturdy, heavy pieces of oak wood. It has just three legs: two in the back and a single leg in the front. The frame is bolted to the floor. Long, leather straps designed to secure the arms, legs, and chest are attached to the chair with large buckles. A metal strap electrode is fitted on the inmate's right leg. An electrode is attached to the head, and a brine-soaked sponge is secured to the scalp with a leather harness. (It is important to use a natural sponge, rather than a synthetic one, to ensure proper contact and reduce the chance of fire.) After the inmate is strapped into the chair, members of the execution team connect the electrodes using ordinary bolt nuts. Heavy-duty electrical cables run from the electrodes through a small hole in the bottom of the door to the execution equipment in the next room.

As McQueen entered the death chamber, one of the officers gestured nervously for him to be seated. McQueen undoubtedly knew what to do, but in the officer's defense, everyone in that room was nervous. He was quickly strapped to the chair.

I announced to the witnesses seated behind a large, glass partition that the execution would begin, and the curtain was pulled back to reveal the condemned.

FINAL WORDS

Deputy Warden Henderson turned on the microphone, and I said, "At this time we will proceed with the legal execution of Harold McQueen." I looked over at McQueen and asked, "Do you have any final words?" Chaplain Stevens stepped forward and read a statement he and McQueen had written together.

"I'd like to apologize one more time to the O'Hearn family. I'd like to apologize to my family, because they are victims as well. I'd like to thank everybody that sent me cards and letters and prayers. Everybody that sent me that, tell them to keep fighting the death penalty."

Then Chaplain Stevens turned to McQueen to say goodbye. Looking straight ahead, McQueen replied simply, "I love you, Father."

We closed the curtains before the team came in to finish securing the electrodes. I made sure Chaplain Stevens cleared the room as the wet sponge was strapped to McQueen's head. An assigned member of the team wiped away the saltwater that had dripped onto McQueen's brow. Finally, the team placed a black veil over his face. It was the last thing McQueen would ever see.

We opened the curtains again and left the room. I nodded to Deputy Warden Henderson, and he closed the door behind me. I looked over at the attorneys who were on the phone with the Supreme Court and Gov. Patton's office. They both gave me a nod, the prearranged signal that all was clear.

I walked around the corner into the adjacent control room. We had designed the new equipment so that three executioners would simultaneously press their buttons on my count of three, but first I had to insert my key to activate the system. The three-button system reduced the likelihood of an accident. It also minimized any psychological trauma associated with carrying out an execution, at least in theory.

"On my count of three," I said. "One, two, three."

The voltmeter surged past two thousand volts and the amp meter hovered around ten amps for fifteen seconds. McQueen's fingers clinched tightly.

I held my hand over the emergency stop button, just in case something went wrong. There was a possibility that the sponges, or McQueen's body, could catch fire. From my vantage point, as the execution was in progress, I could see blue arcing all around the sponge on top of his head. Steam rose from the headpiece, but nothing more. Deputy Warden Henderson was standing at the door with two officers holding fire extinguishers. Had it been necessary to use them, Henderson would not open the door until he knew I had the key in my hand, ensuring the electricity was off. We had rehearsed this carefully.

People who ask me to describe an electrocution are often surprised when I tell them the process isn't particularly graphic or violent. The Hollywood version, as depicted in movies such as *The Green Mile*, simply does not happen during a real electrocution. If the prisoner has been securely strapped to the chair, there are no body convulsions. Loss of consciousness is instantaneous.

After two minutes, it was over. I brought in the prison physician, Dr. Steve Hiland, who used a stethoscope to listen for heart activity. When he was satisfied, he turned to me and said, "Warden, this man has expired."

At that moment, I turned to the witnesses and said, "The legal execution of Harold McQueen was carried out at 12:10 a.m. in accordance with the laws of Kentucky."

The witnesses were escorted out of the room. Several of them went to the media staging area to relate what they had seen to the press. Others just left the premises. I stayed in the execution chamber until the coroner and medical examiner came in, took pictures, and examined the body. McQueen's remains were then removed from the chair and placed in a body bag on a gurney. Two men from a local funeral home rolled the gurney out of the death chamber and through the prison. Since we were in lockdown, other inmates did not see the gurney as it was being rolled out. They placed the body into a hearse and drove it to the medical examiner's office. Following an autopsy, McQueen's family took care of the burial.

When I finally went home that night, I had difficulty sleeping. It was hard not to replay the events of the day over and over in my mind. It took time to process it all—and it would take time to heal.

I reported to work the next morning at eight thirty a.m. and went straight to the captain's office to check on things. We had already decided to return to normal operations. Most of the prison population kept up with the news on a local TV station, but there had been no protests or rioting among the inmates. Aside from a number of supportive calls from Frankfort commending a job well done, it was back to business as usual at KSP.

Two days later, July 3, we had the annual warden's cookout for the inmate population. The deputy wardens, other department heads, and I cooked hamburgers and hot dogs on a large BBQ grill we had borrowed. We also served baked beans, potato salad, and watermelon for dessert. A band came in to perform for the inmates. It was a rare treat to have charcoal-grilled hamburgers and hot dogs, and we let the inmates enjoy all they could eat. This was the closest thing we could have to a Fourth of July picnic in the penitentiary, and the inmates appreciated it. No fights broke out that holiday weekend. Nobody threatened each other. Nobody even talked back. For one brief, shining moment during the summer of 1997, everybody actually got along.

TWENTY-ONE

ON CAPITAL PUNISHMENT

Wrest once the law to your authority: To do a great right, do a little wrong.
- Shakespeare

I have been fortunate to call Kentucky Supreme Court Justice Bill Cunningham a friend for many years. An Old Eddyville native, Cunningham was born in a home overlooking the Cumberland River, right across the street from KSP. He spent much of his youth in the shadow of the old Castle, exploring the riverbanks and backwoods of the storied little town that would eventually be flooded to create Lake Barkley.

Justice Cunningham and I developed a special bond as a judge and a prison warden. He would visit the prison often and always wanted to go out on the yard to mingle with the inmates and staff. Everyone knew him, and to a person they liked him. It was not unusual to see Cunningham joking and kidding around with an inmate he had known all his life during one of his visits. He has always demonstrated an extraordinary amount of patience and compassion for those who struggle in life—and he goes out of his way to help those in need. Judge Cunningham's selflessness is one of his greatest gifts.

Throughout our long friendship, Kentucky Supreme Court Justice Bill Cunningham and I have written one another to share our personal reflections on a wide range of subjects, including capital punishment. We both agree that the death penalty, while imperfect, is a necessary component of any fair and balanced criminal justice system.

Justice Cunningham once wrote me the following about death row:

SOME JUDGES BELABOR TO THE CONDEMNED THE HORRIBLE prospects of their future life behind bars. I find it unbecoming and tacky for a judge to do so. Never humiliate a person when they are helpless. It's a good way to get yourself killed.

Death. It speaks for itself. Clean, dignified, simple, and just. Everyone gets the message. A human life is important. It will not be taken without consequences. Consequences as severe as the crime, and as old as the scripture.

I believe in the death penalty because I believe in justice. A democratic society has decided it is a just punishment through its elected representatives. A democratic society has decided that in this case, through a rigorous maze of due process restrictions, twelve law abiding, decent and well-meaning Americans have unanimously decided that it fits this particular crime. I agree. Makes no difference as to color of the offender or whether it serves as a deterrent. In this particular case, this particular defendant, for this particular crime, on this particular day, deserves to die by lethal injection. God have mercy upon his soul.

. . .

AFTER READING CUNNINGHAM'S THOUGHTS, I ADOPTED TWO axioms that would guide me from that day forward. First, "Never humiliate a person when they are helpless." Cunningham was speaking about sentencing a man to death, but I treated this as a Golden Rule that would inform the rest of my career as warden. When men are in handcuffs or behind bars, some will yell profanities and insults at you in a fruitless attempt at self-preservation. These are human beings at their lowest point. They are helpless. The only thing that humiliating a restrained individual does is demonstrate you are the weaker person. And it implies that you are in the wrong line of work. If you cannot show patience and compassion for all people, despite their trespasses, then you are not qualified to hold any position of authority over them. At least that's the way I look at it.

The second axiom I adopted is: "Death. It speaks for itself." In all their dealings and encounters with the men on death row, officers and administrators would do well to remember this universal truth. Our personal views about the death penalty do not matter within the context of our work. Capital punishment is, and always has been, a matter of law that is debated, adopted, and sometimes rejected by elected representatives in state legislative bodies. As a warden (or any member of corrections), I must remain professional, dignified, and detached. Our duty is to administer justice as it is written. Full stop. No reason to explain your personal views on the matter, no reason to apologize, no reason to engage with others who may disagree with you. In the end, death speaks for itself.

A NEW DIRECTION

McQueen's execution gave everyone pause to reexamine their own attitudes toward the death penalty.

The ensuing debate led to a general consensus throughout state government that electrocution was an abhorrent method of capital punishment. A bipartisan movement quickly grew to replace electrocution with lethal injection as the state's primary method of execution. While I would argue that electrocution brings about an instantaneous and painless death, I do not believe the same is true for lethal injection. The condemned feels some level of discomfort as the intravenous needles are inserted into his arms. He can feel the drugs enter his veins, often accompanied by a burning sensation, before they render him unconscious. Medical experts acknowledge that the drug cocktail can take several minutes to work, and botched executions have taken as long as two hours. The process is certainly not as instantaneous as electrocution.

Facts aside, it became clear Kentucky was ready to abandon the electric chair in favor of lethal injection. I prepared to draft a new prison policy and procedural checklist for lethal injection, but I couldn't begin until I saw how the new law was written. Commissioner Sapp worked with legislators to craft the new death penalty statute, and Sapp gave me every opportunity to weigh in with personal insights and suggestions during the process.

The first thing that came to mind was perhaps the most obvious: I insisted we change the time of execution from midnight to a more reasonable hour. Sapp was receptive to my concerns, but he was afraid they would fall on deaf ears in Frankfort. The reasoning behind midnight hour executions is a little convoluted. A death warrant is often good for just one day. If an execution is not carried out during that twenty-four-hour period, the state must re-petition the court for another death sentence. The midnight timeframe also provides a full twenty-four hours to work through any potential temporary stays of execution before time runs out on the sentence. At least that's the theory.

Whatever the rationale, I thought it was absurd to stay up all night in order to carry out a death sentence. Sapp was all ears. "Okay, then, what time do you want it?" he asked. I told him that the seven p.m. hour would be best for us, after the inmates' daily activities and their evening meal. We could all be home by midnight, and the following day wouldn't be as physically exhausting for everyone involved. Sapp agreed with my reasoning. He got on board with the idea, presented it to legislators, and the Kentucky General Assembly added language to allow the warden to set the execution time. Sapp and I were pleasantly surprised at this result.

Once the bill was drafted, I was afforded every opportunity to review the language and object if anything presented a problem from an operational standpoint. At least I was consulted before the law passed, and for that I was grateful. Now with law in hand, I could write our policy and procedural checklist for lethal injections.

TWENTY-TWO

LETHAL INJECTION

Kentucky's lethal injection procedure utilized a three-drug cocktail, identical to the system used in every other death penalty state. These three chemicals are each separated by an injection of saline to clear the IV lines. This minimizes the chance that two drugs might obstruct the tubing after coming in contact with one another and congealing.

First, sodium pentothal is injected to render the inmate unconscious. This drug is a barbiturate that in therapeutic doses works as a rapid-onset, short-acting anesthetic. In large amounts, sodium pentothal can stop respiration. The dose administered during an execution is designed to do the latter.

Second, a flush of saline is followed by an injection of pancuronium bromide. In therapeutic doses, this works as a muscle relaxant during anesthesia. In lethal amounts, pancuronium bromide will paralyze the lungs.

Following another saline flush, the third chemical is an injection of potassium chloride. In therapeutic doses, potassium chloride is a treat-ment for low blood levels of potassium. In lethal amounts, it stops the heart.

At the time of Kentucky's first lethal injection in 1999, every state we studied was using this three-drug cocktail. The drug combination was an attempt to mitigate any medical complications that might arise through the use of just one drug at a lethal dose. Some medical experts believed that these medications, administered together, would minimize the condemned's pain and suffering.

In addition to this lethal drug cocktail, we offered the recipient a therapeutic dose of valium to calm jittery nerves. This was optional and entirely up to the inmate.

Throughout my research, I traveled to observe lethal injections in other states. While some jurisdictions followed a slightly different procedure prior to the execution, this three-drug cocktail and the doses administered were the same in every case. I discovered that the most challenging step in any lethal injection is locating a suitable vein and getting a saline drip. Once the needles are place, the drugs are injected into a port on the IV line by a single executioner. The executioner usually stands behind a curtain, or in our case behind a one-way glass partition in the same room as the electrocution equipment. Their iden-tity remains confidential to everyone but those who are present to carry out the execution.

The executioner has to push eight large syringes through the lines quickly and efficiently, but not with enough force to rupture the IV. If the tube breaks, the executioner would immediately switch to a backup IV. Simply put, the execution team prepares a primary IV site and a secondary IV site to circumvent any unforeseen complications during the procedure. A vein failure without a backup site might be considered a "botched execution," which is the worst possible scenario for all involved.

Wardens have nightmares about supervising botched executions. I was going to do everything in my power to ensure this didn't happen under my watch.

TWENTY-THREE

DUE DILIGENCE

The autumn before Kentucky's new lethal injection statute was signed into law, I found out that former KSP Warden Al Parke had overseen several recent lethal injections as warden of the Indiana State Penitentiary. Warden Parke invited a Kentucky delegation to observe how they conducted their lethal injections. I contacted Deputy Commissioner Tom Campbell to suggest that we send a small team to Michigan City, Indiana, for the next execution scheduled on November 20, 1997. The group included Deputy Commissioner Campbell, Public Information Officer Mike Bradley, Deputy Warden Bill Henderson, and me.

Parke took me under his wing, as he always did, and allowed me to observe the execution from a side room where an attending physician was staged. I could see and hear everything that transpired, even though I was not an official witness.

The execution went more or less just as I anticipated, save for the fact the inmate, Gary Burris, vomited as the first drug was administered. Parke explained it was not unusual for an inmate to vomit if he had a large meal just before the execution. I suppose that is why you cannot have anything to eat prior to surgery.

Burris appeared to stop breathing almost as soon as Parke gave the order to proceed. Within minutes, the physician seated next to me entered the execution chamber to listen for a heartbeat. "Warden," he confirmed, "this man has expired."

After observing a number of lethal injections in other jurisdictions, and drafting our own procedures at KSP, my team felt ready to move forward the moment Kentucky's bill became law. We wouldn't have to wait long.

On March 31, 1998, Gov. Patton signed the lethal injection bill. To avoid legal challenges, the new law allowed condemned inmates to choose between lethal injection and electrocution if their sentencing predated the bill's passage. Everyone sentenced after that date would be executed by lethal injection. KSP had roughly thirty inmates on death row who could now choose either method of execution. This made our job slightly more challenging, but we were fully prepared for either eventuality.

The commissioner gave me a sixty-day deadline to have the necessary drugs, IV lines, and other medical equipment in stock and ready to use. I assured him we would be prepared.

EDDIE HARPER

Eddie Harper was sentenced to death for murdering his adopted parents, Alice and Edward Lee Harper Sr., after sneaking into their home in the dead of night and shooting them while they were fast asleep. Harper, who had been laid off from his job as a machinist the year before, stood to inherit an $86,541 insurance policy on his father's life. Harper testified at his 1982 trial that his father had implored him to shoot him and his wife because she was mentally ill, and the elder

Harper couldn't bear to put her in an institution. The jury quickly found him guilty of two counts of capital murder. He was sentenced to death and spent the next seventeen years on death row at KSP.

I had a feeling that Harper would be one of the earliest inmates to face execution under Kentucky's new lethal injection bill. I knew Harper from his many years at KSP. He would always greet me when I made rounds, though most of the time we did not engage in any meaningful conversation.

One day after the new law passed, Harper intercepted me to say that he was stopping his appeals. I asked him why. "I'm on my last appeal anyway," he explained, "and I want to get it over with."

Somewhat taken aback by his dismissiveness, I asked, "Have you thought this over?"

"I have," he replied. "I don't want to live on death row any longer, but I also don't want life without parole if my appeal is granted. This is no way to live."

"Well, Eddie, as far as I am concerned, that is your business."

"Yeah, I know, but I wanted you to know."

"Eddie," I replied, "I don't know what to say. I just hope you've thought this through."

"I have," he assured me.

When I got back to my office, I called Commissioner Sapp and told him I thought we might have a "volunteer" to be the first to be executed by lethal injection. He said he had heard the rumor that Harper was considering dropping his appeals. "I think he's serious," I replied. "We'll just have to wait and see."

Nothing moves quickly through the court system, and capital punishment cases may be the slowest of all. Many death-row inmates welcome the glacial appeals process for obvious reasons. Harper was an exception; his attorneys were not moving fast enough for him. Everyone in Harper's orbit—legal counsel, inmates, friends—tried to talk him out of dropping his appeals, to no avail. His mind was made up.

It did not take long for the media to get wind of Harper's request to be put to death. Within weeks, it was being sensationalized as front-page news. This was uncharted territory; in the long and colorful history of Kentucky corrections, nobody had ever voluntarily been executed. His request naturally raised questions of competency that had to be litigated. Namely, whether Harper was capable of rationally deciding to waive further appeals and whether he was competent enough for the execution to proceed.

Harper began talking to the media, making it clear he wanted to die as quickly as possible. He did not want to spend another day on death row. He also did not want his appeal to be granted, because this would undoubtedly lead to life in prison without the possibility of parole.

I tried to put myself in Harper's place. I agreed that death would probably be better than living out my life in prison. It wasn't an easy decision either way, but I respected his choice to stop the appeals process.

After roughly a year in legal limbo, Harper was finally granted his wish. Gov. Patton signed his death warrant, setting the execution date for May 25, 1999. With a copy in hand, I walked to Harper's cell on death row and read the order to him. I wouldn't say he was ecstatic, but he sounded relieved to hear the news. Harper asked me if I thought it would be stopped. "Eddie, I have no idea," I replied. "I think you can halt the execution at any time by restarting your appeals, but that is your decision. I'm just here to officially notify you there is a date. As we get closer, I'll be back to talk to you about witnesses, funeral arrange-ments, and so forth, but now is not the time."

"Okay, Warden," Harper said simply. "Thanks for coming over. I'll see you later."

The clock was ticking. His execution was less than three weeks away.

SOUNDNESS OF MIND

On May 18, 1999, a hearing was held in the United States District Court in Louisville to determine whether Harper was competent to stop appealing his death sentence. The judge was U.S. District Judge Joseph McKinley. The attorneys representing Harper were Randall Wheeler and Suzanne Martin from the Department of Public Advocacy. Harper's decision placed Wheeler and Martin in somewhat of a difficult situation, because he had technically fired them. Given the questions of Harper's competency, however, they felt an obligation to be relieved by the court rather than their client.

Before the hearing started, my officers brought Harper in, dressed in his red prison uniform. His attorneys were not yet seated. Harper came over to the table where I was sitting with the attorneys from the attorney general's office and asked, "Warden, can I sit with you?"

I looked at him, surprised. "Why?"

"Because I'm on your side. I don't want to sit with the public defenders."

"I don't think so, Eddie," I replied. "You'll have to sit over there, or I suppose you could ask the judge, but I don't think he'd allow it."

"You're probably right," Harper agreed, looking sightly disappointed. He shuffled back to his table, still wearing leg shackles, and took his seat.

The hearing began. Judge McKinley allowed Harper to represent himself, though Wheeler and Martin continued to argue against Harper's competency.

There was little doubt in my mind that Harper was competent enough to make his own decisions, and I explained this during my testimony. McKinley also heard from Joe Stuart, the unit manager on death row, and our prison psychologist, Ken Thomas. Other mental health experts also testified Harper was competent.

Attorneys Wheeler and Martin asked for a stay of execution over

Harper's objections, citing trial errors and Harper's mental state. They did their best to advocate on behalf of their former client, but it was an uphill battle. Throughout the proceedings, McKinley listened very carefully to everything Harper said as his own counsel. In the end, the inmate's rational arguments convinced the judge as much as, if not more than, anything the rest of us had to say. McKinley ruled that Harper was indeed capable of making the decision to halt his appeals, and he removed Wheeler and Martin from the case. Harper was granted his wish; the execution could move forward.

After the hearing ended, Harper shuffled over to where I was standing and asked, "Warden, can I be moved to the Death Watch as soon as I get back?"

"Yes, Eddie," I replied. "I think I can arrange that."

Harper was relieved the hearing went his way. Watching Harper depart the courtroom, it struck me that this was the first time I had ever seen a person of sound mind and body so eager to end his life. It was surreal and very poignant.

DEATH WATCH

The Death Watch began on May 20, just five days before the execution date. I was present at the infirmary on May 14 when Harper was checked by medical staff as part of our execution protocol. Harper struck up a conversation and told me about his love for Tammy Brown, an investigator in the Department of Public Advocacy. Brown was a frequent visitor at KSP as part of the team that defended death-row inmates. She knew Harper had developed an infatuation for her. I think Brown believed his infatuation would provide him with the motivation to continue appealing his case. It didn't work.

The execution was scheduled for seven p.m. on May 25, 1999. We had scaled down our request for National Guard troops and the Kentucky State Police at KSP, but they were still included in our planning. Media engagement had diminished to some degree after the circus surrounding McQueen's execution, but this still drew a fair amount of media interest as our first lethal injection. I was just glad I had the foresight to push for future executions to be conducted at a time of my choosing, instead of one minute after midnight.

FAITH AND FORGIVENESS

Harper converted to Catholicism during his time on death row, just like McQueen. Chaplain Stevens was also his spiritual advisor. In the waning days of Harper's legal fight, Catholic advocates had counseled the inmate that his decision to forego the appeals process could be considered a form of suicide. This really bothered Harper, but Chaplain Stevens continued to minister to him without questioning his decision. Stevens was the real deal. He had been a volunteer chaplain at KSP for as long as I could remember and chose to continue his work well into retirement.

Stevens suffered a terrible and tragic event decades earlier when he returned home from work one day to discover his twenty-year-old daughter, Cindy, had been murdered by a man for whom she was babysitting. Cindy was lying in a pool of blood on the floor of their home, and the killer was passed out nearby. Rather than lash out violently as many fathers might have done in the moment, Stevens called the police. He then turned to his faith and eventually found forgiveness for his daughter's killer.

The inmates on death row knew about Chaplain Stevens' tragedy, and the heartbreaking story gave them hope for forgiveness. Stevens carried a faded black-and-white picture of Cindy he sometimes showed to inmates. Her rosary beads remained at the prison where they were passed among the prisoners, gaining iconic status for men seeking solace. They believed he was a saint, and perhaps he was. Stevens expressed love for each and every one of the inmates, and he accepted them regardless of how terrible their crimes were. He was a better man than most. Chaplain Stevens had my trust and admiration, and I was always grateful that KSP benefitted from his good deeds.

PREPARATIONS

I allowed Harper to spend the majority of his last day with his son, George Harper, and his wife and grandchild. Harper had never been close to his son. He'd spent almost the entirety of his son's life behind bars, and the boy grew up never really knowing the man who had fathered him. George called me a few days before the execution and asked me if he had to attend. I assured him he had no legal obligation to be present, and it was entirely up to him. George wanted no part of it, but he felt it was the right thing to do because his father had asked him to be there. Harper had tried desperately to make up for lost time after his son was grown, and George did his best to show compassion for the man who had killed his grandparents and cheated him out of a normal childhood. I don't know how George managed this, but I admired him immensely for it.

I had to end their visit at two p.m. so we could finalize preparations for the seven p.m. execution. As is often the case, several last-minute developments made this process more complicated than my team had anticipated.

Barbara Jones, General Counsel for the Department of Corrections, had called me the previous week during a meeting with Secretary Cherry. Jones wanted to know what I would do if Harper decided to restart his appeals at the last minute, even after we had the IV line sited and ready. I really hadn't thought about it, but I replied I would proceed because I had an order from the governor. That was the wrong answer. "Phil, you have to stop the execution if he wants to stop it, even at the last minute."

My mind raced through several scenarios. "How do we handle this if we are past the point of no return?" I asked. "Say we have started pushing the sodium pentothal. It might not be possible to keep it from killing him. What if he mumbles something as he is losing consciousness? Do I interpret that as a possible attempt to halt the execution and restart his appeals?"

Jones was unequivocal. "The answer is yes. You have to do your best to revive him to make sure he didn't change his mind."

"That would look like a botched execution," I replied, "especially if we try to revive him and fail. The fallout for the DOC could be disastrous."

We continued to review every possible scenario that crossed our minds, and we came up with two or three solutions. First, I would have an ambulance and paramedics standing by, or at the very least our doctor and a nurse with a crash cart ready to apply an Automated External Defibrillator. Second, we would stock whatever antidote was necessary to counteract the effects of the lethal drug cocktail. Third, I would plan to position myself next to Harper's head so I could hear any declaration he might make during the execution. Four, we would install a valve or petcock on the IV line in the event we needed to instantly stop the flow of drugs.

My team clearly had some additional preparation to do in the days leading up to the execution. I assured Jones I would work all this out and keep her informed of our progress.

Before we hung up, I thought of something else. "One other thing, Barbara. When I attended the execution in Indiana, the inmate vomited as soon as the first drug began to take effect. I want everyone to know that I have a weak stomach, and I would no doubt puke, too."

I said this to add a little levity to the conversation, but I was also serious. "I don't do puke! Deputy Warden Henderson is my backup in case I can't continue for any reason, but he has a weak stomach, too. In fact, he would probably puke as well."

I was really worried about it. I didn't think Harper would change his mind at the last second, but I still had to stand next to his head so that I could hear him clearly and turn the IV valve. The thought of getting sick in that moment was enough to turn my stomach even now.

"If he pukes, I puke," I repeated to Jones. "Let's just hope he doesn't." I wasn't kidding that time.

My team worked hard to ensure that all these contingencies were in place as the execution date rapidly approached. I had them check and double check every last detail. Finally, I felt we were ready.

Harper asked Chaplain Stevens to be present as his spiritual advisor. Father Drury would normally be called upon to perform the last rites, but this presented another problem. Drury came to my office and informed me he didn't think he could perform the last rites because he viewed Harper's decision to stop his appeals as an act of suicide. This really bothered me. I wanted Harper to face death with every assurance that he would go to Heaven. I implored Drury to reconsider. "Why don't you think about it and maybe ask the bishop or other scholars to see what they say?"

As soon as Drury left my office, I called Father Frank Roof, a prison chaplain and close friend from Paducah.

"I will come down and work it out with Father Drury," Roof reassured me. "Don't worry about it." I was relieved. I wanted to put Harper's mind at ease during his final hours.

Father Roof arrived early on the day of the execution. He and Drury met with me before they walked over to Three Cell House to check on Harper. Seated in my office, I listened as the two priests engaged in a theological debate about the last rites. Drury maintained it was not proper to perform the rites on somebody who had chosen to end his own life. Father Roof insisted it was. He quoted several passages to make his point, including an excerpt from the Catechism of the Catholic Church: "We should not despair of the eternal salvation of persons who have taken their own lives. By ways known to him alone,

God can provide the opportunity for salutary repentance. The Church prays for persons who have taken their own lives."

After some back and forth, Drury agreed. The matter was settled right there in my office. As the two stood up to leave, Father Roof came over with a big smile and said, "Don't worry, Warden. It'll be taken care of." I was grateful for my friend's spiritual guidance. Now Harper would have Chaplain Stevens and Father Drury to lean on for support. I knew he was in good hands.

And yes, Harper received last rites just prior to the execution.

THE FINAL HOURS

Harper was served his final meal around three thirty p.m. His request included three BLT sandwiches, potato chips, an RC Cola, and a pecan pie with vanilla ice cream. Actually, Harper had asked for a cold beer with his last meal. I told him we would give him a non-alcoholic beer, but when I ran this by my bosses, they didn't like the idea. We had to replace the O'Doul's with a cola. There was plenty of food to share with Chaplain Stevens and our prison psychologist, Ken Thomas. It was clear from the security footage they were enjoying the meal and the fellowship, so I decided to stay away. Part of me also feared I might be put in a position to join them for dinner if I arrived too early, as I'd done with Harold McQueen. I gave them as much time as I could before walking over to make final arrangements.

After his son left, Harper and I sat down to discuss his personal possessions and funeral arrangements. He asked me to give his son a chain and cross, a book, photographs, and a written prayer. His other belongings, including a television and radio, were to be given to three of his friends on death row. Harper's son did not want to handle the funeral arrangements or burial, so these details were left up to me. I explained that the state would only pay for cremation and suggested we could bury his cremains at an inmate cemetery on the grounds of the

Western Kentucky Correctional Complex. Harper was fine with that and thanked me. I assured him I would take care of everything.

The day of the execution had been uneventful. We were locked down, and there was nothing going on. I asked Program Director Patti Treat to rent extra movies to play on the institution's TV channel to entertain the inmates. We also served three good meals that day, which the inmates always appreciated. With full bellies and movies to distract them, the inmates didn't have any reason to complain. It was quiet throughout the prison. Thankfully.

Beyond KSP's walls, we had reduced the need for state troopers and the National Guard, but there was a small contingency just in case. Those who were on duty coordinated with E-Squad to cover the road-blocks leading to the prison. Only a few protesters showed up this time, and media coverage was relatively small compared to the McQueen execution. I estimated roughly thirty-five state troopers and thirty National Guardsmen on site, and they far outnumbered those who showed up outside the prison.

THE EXECUTION

A few minutes before seven p.m., Deputy Commissioner Tom Campbell and I arrived at the execution chamber. I checked with the team to confirm that everything was ready. Two sets of eight syringes were lined up in a tray at the executioner's station, including backups in the event that the first drug cocktail failed to work. We had prepared an electrocardiogram for the attending physician to monitor Harper's heart activity throughout the execution. Everything appeared to be in order.

At my cue, the official witnesses were led into the witness room. The curtain obstructing their view of the execution chamber would remain closed until the IV team had successfully started an IV drip in each arm. Once we were ready, I checked to see that all witnesses were seated.

Harper entered the chamber and quietly laid down on the gurney. His face appeared expressionless as the team strapped him down and affixed heart monitor pads to his chest. After some difficulty finding a suitable vein in his left arm, the physician finally inserted one of the IVs into his left hand. During this process, Harper suddenly spoke out to me.

"Warden, come here!"

I was standing a few feet away to give the team room to work. "Warden, come here," Harper repeated. "I want to ask you something."

I approached him and replied softly, "What, Eddie?" Whatever it was, it was taking his mind off the needles being jabbed into his skin.

Harper looked up at me. "Warden, tell Tammy I love her. Promise me, Warden. Tell Tammy I love her." I knew he was talking about Tammy Brown, the mitigation specialist from the Department of Advocacy. This was the last thing I expected him to say.

"Eddie, please don't do that," I replied. "She is a married woman." Harper repeated his request, only this time he was pleading with me.

"Please, promise me. Please."

How could I refuse a request to deliver a message from a man we were about to execute? "Okay, Eddie," I assured him reluctantly. "I'll tell her." A look of relief spread across Harper's face, and he smiled at me.

I wondered why Harper wanted me to relay his message instead of Chaplain Stevens or Father Drury. I supposed he couldn't ask the attorneys he fired. Why didn't he do it himself? I really didn't want to deliver the message, but how could I not after giving my word? The thought of calling her to share Harper's words weighed heavily on me, because I didn't want to interject myself into what appeared to be an inappropriate relationship between an inmate and a married woman. I was planning a short vacation with my wife the moment this was over, but I knew I would have to deliver the message before we left. I wouldn't be able to relax and recuperate otherwise.

Once everything was ready, I took my position next to Harper's head and signaled to Deputy Warden Henderson to open the curtains. I looked over and saw George Harper, Harper's son, seated in the front row. I'd hoped he would decide against attending the execution, but there he was, staring at his father strapped to the gurney with IV lines in his arms. I couldn't imagine what George must be feeling. How heartbreaking and bizarre, to watch your father's voluntary execution. The scene resembled a Shakespearean tragedy.

Deputy Warden Henderson switched on the microphone. I looked over at the attorneys seated by the phone bank just outside the execution chamber. It was their job to stop me if they received word of a last-minute stay from a court or the governor. They nodded to continue.

I addressed the witnesses through the glass. "At this time, we will proceed with the legal execution of Edward Harper." Looking at Harper, I asked if he had any final words.

He apologized for killing his adoptive parents. "I want to say to my mom's side of the family that I am sorry for what I've done. I'm sorry about the pain I caused them. I loved my parents with all my heart, even though I committed a terrible crime against them.

"To my son, I want you to know that I'll always be with you in spirit. George, I love you, and I'll be on the other side waiting for you, boy. That's all I have to say."

When Harper finished, I told the executioner to proceed. In my earpiece, I could hear a voice say, "Beginning step one," followed by, "Beginning step two," and so on, as each of the eight syringes were injected into the IV line.

I glanced at the audience and saw Chaplain Stevens seated next to Harper's son, his hand resting on George's shoulder. I will never forget the expression on George's face. He looked like a young child watching a horror movie. As Stevens attempted to comfort him, George shifted uncomfortably in his chair and wiped the tears streaming down his face. It's a scene that will haunt me for the rest of my life.

Harper stopped breathing moments after the first drug entered his system. After the eight syringes were emptied, the disembodied voice in my earpiece stated simply, "All steps complete." The executioner asked the physician to enter the chamber and check Harper's vitals. "Warden," the executioner finally said, "the doctor has declared this man expired at 7:28 p.m."

I turned to the witnesses and announced, "At approximately 7:28 p.m., the execution of Eddie Harper was carried out in accordance with the laws of the Commonwealth of Kentucky." It was over.

We closed the curtains, literally and figuratively, on Kentucky's first lethal injection. To my relief, Harper passed quickly and peacefully. Everything had gone as planned. I thanked my team for their professionalism and told them we had done our best for Harper. I was proud of them, as always.

AFTERMATH

I waited a few days before reaching out to Tammy Brown to relay Harper's message. I dreaded making that call, but I'd given Harper my word. My secretary, Vicki, tracked Brown down and got her on the line. I stared at the blinking light on my desk phone and realized I still didn't know how I was going to convey the message. I reluctantly picked up the receiver.

"Is this Tammy?"

"Yes."

"Tammy, it's Phil Parker. I'm calling because Eddie Harper asked me to pass a message along to you."

"Oh?" Brown replied. I could sense a mix of curiosity and trepidation in her voice.

"Eddie wanted me to tell you that he loved you." There was silence on the other end. I waited to see if Brown had any questions. I couldn't be sure, but it sounded like she was crying. Finally, I said, "That's all I have. Goodbye, Tammy." I honored Harper's dying wish and repeated what he asked me to. No more, and no less. It wasn't my responsibility to comfort Tammy Brown, and I had no intention of doing so.

There was one more phone call I needed to make. Several weeks after the execution, I reached out to George Harper to check on him. George's wife answered the phone, and I introduced myself. When she replied he was at work, I asked how he was holding up. Her answer was terse. "Not good. George is struggling right now."

I could hear that I had upset her. "Just tell him I'm available if he has any questions or ever wants to visit the cemetery. Please tell him I'll be glad to help him."

I apologized for bothering her and tried to explain I wanted George to know I was thinking about him. Her tone softened a little as she replied, "Okay. That's considerate of you. We appreciate it." She thanked me, and we hung up. That was it.

My heart ached for George. He was truly a victim of his father's crime.

The final task was to bury Harper's cremains. Several weeks after the execution, Vicki came into my office carrying a shoebox-size package. "Here," she said.

Vicki set the parcel on the edge of my desk. Looking up from my work, I could tell she was upset. I examined the box and realized it was from the crematorium. "Oh," I replied, "that's Eddie." I'm not sure Vicki was entirely amused by my gallows humor, and I don't blame her. She left the box on the edge of my desk. That afternoon I made arrangements for Harper's burial at the Western Kentucky Correctional Complex prison farm cemetery, and I called Father Drury, my prison chaplain Joe O'Cull, and my director of programs, Patti Treat, to help me arrange a funeral service.

During my call to WKCC, however, I neglected to mention that we were burying cremains rather than a full-sized casket. My fishing buddy, Perry Jones, used a backhoe to dig a perfect, six-foot-deep grave.

Looking down into that hole during the funeral, I felt badly that they'd done all that work for nothing.

After Father Drury conducted a beautiful service, I realized that I had no way to lower the box six feet into the ground. If I dropped it, the container might burst open. And if I reached too far over the edge, I risked falling in and joining Harper myself. Neither scenario was very appealing.

As I looked around, I spotted Jones and an inmate crew waiting nearby to close the grave. I told Father Drury I would be back in a moment. Dressed in my dark suit and tie, I jogged roughly the length of a football field to ask the farm crew if they had something we could use to lower the box into the ground. To my relief, they produced a small rope that was perfect for the job. I turned around and jogged another hundred yards back to the gravesite, suit jacket flapping in the breeze, and ceremoniously lowered Harper's cremains into his final resting place. That was the day I convinced myself I might've missed my calling as an NFL running back.

Several weeks later, Vicki stepped into my office and gestured toward my phone. "You need to take that call."

"Who is it?" I asked.

"The crematorium."

Oh no, I thought. There must have been a mix-up. Maybe we buried the wrong person. Why else would the crematorium be calling now? Vicki mentioned that the gentleman on the other end of the line sounded slightly upset. "Shit, that's all I need," I said to no one in particular. I picked up the phone.

"Warden Parker. May I help you?"

The caller introduced himself and then got right to the point. "Warden, when are you going to pay the bill?"

Somewhat surprised, I asked, "Are you talking about Eddie Harper's cremation?"

"Yes," the crematorium owner confirmed.

"Well, as soon as you send me a bill, I will process it for payment."

"I did send you a bill," he replied. "It was in the box."

I almost laughed out loud. "Well, hell, I didn't even open the shipping box because I knew what was in it. Just send me another bill and I'll pay it as soon as possible."

I could tell the owner was relieved he wouldn't have to strongarm a prison warden to pick up the tab. "That'll be fine," he replied, chuckling.

It was finally over. I paid the bill, and Harper went to his eternal rest.

TWENTY-FOUR

PASHA VS. THE JUDGE

Roughly a year before I started my career as a prison guard, Circuit Judge Ed Johnstone established a courtroom in the basement of KSP's administration building to hold hearings, pretrial motions, and other non-jury proceedings. It was a brilliant idea: hosting court proceedings at KSP helped to mitigate the risk of transporting dangerous inmates to the courthouse in Eddyville. It also saved the significant costs associated with paying extra guards for transportation. By the time Judge Cunningham took over, these so-called "rule days" had become routine at KSP on the first Friday of the month.

On January 7, 2000, Judge Cunningham arrived at the prison to hold hearings for several troublemaker inmates who had committed crimes inside the prison. One of these individuals was Uriah Pasha, an African-American inmate who had repeatedly assaulted prison staff. His birth name was Kenneth Uriah Ross, but a judge had granted him a legal name change to Uriah Marquis Pasha. (He would later change his name yet again, to Jacta Est Alea. The Latin phrase *jacta est alea,* attributed to Julius Caesar, translates to "the die is cast.")

Pasha likely suffered from mental illness, but he went undiagnosed because he refused to cooperate with mental health professionals. He was assaultive and dangerous and appeared to be angry at everything and everyone he encountered. Pasha disliked Judge Cunningham because he believed Cunningham was unsympathetic toward inmates. He wanted a new judge to hear his case. And he figured the best way to secure a different jurist on the bench was to attack Judge Cunningham in open court.

On that midwinter morning in early 2000, Judge Cunningham asked the correctional officers to remove Pasha's handcuffs prior to the court proceeding. The judge usually ordered cuffs removed during a hearing so the inmate could sign documents and raise his hand to take an oath. The move also extended a certain degree of respect to defendants in a difficult situation.

Once the court was ready to proceed, Pasha shuffled over to the podium in his leg shackles to provide his defense. He positioned himself only a few feet away from the elevated bench where Judge Cunningham was seated. Commonwealth Attorney G. L. Ovey stood at the prosecution podium, less than ten feet away from Pasha.

The moment Judge Cunningham opened the hearing, Pasha took a few well-timed steps and leaped over the bench to attack the judge. Cunningham was faster than Pasha, however, and used his feet to kick the inmate away. Thankfully, Pasha did not land a single punch, but he came close. Judge Cunningham's bench flipped over, and correctional officers tackled Pasha in what looked like an NFL pile on after a QB sneak. The guards struck Pasha several times during the melee, and one of them, Harry Whisman, suffered a broken finger. Pasha was quickly cuffed and dragged out of the courtroom, back to the hole.

I heard the commotion from my office just as Vicki exclaimed, "Phil, something is going on in the courtroom."

I ran down the steps as quickly as I could. By the time I entered the courtroom, the correctional officers covering Pasha were beginning to pick themselves up. Pasha had been cuffed and was under control. I quickly went over to Judge Cunningham and asked if he was okay.

He had more composure than most people would in the immediate aftermath of a vicious attack. "I'm all right," Cunningham assured me as he began to help us straighten the chairs and place the bench back where it belonged.

If he was frightened, he didn't show it. In hindsight, I was amazed he didn't even appear to have a surge of adrenaline. I certainly did as I ran down the steps.

Fortunately, we had several cameras in the courtroom that caught the incident on tape. Pasha admitted during an interrogation that he believed he could change venues, and perhaps even secure a transfer to a different prison, if he were to attack Judge Cunningham. His plan backfired spectacularly. We piled disciplinary reports on Pasha, which essentially guaranteed he wouldn't see the light of day for quite a while.

In the years that followed, footage of the courtroom attack aired on several television shows, including *Court TV* and *Big House*. The incident was also used to train court bailiffs and enhance courtroom security across the state and beyond. In the end, were incredibly fortunate that no one suffered injuries, aside from Harry Whisman's broken finger.

Whether reporting for duty as a guard or a warden at KSP, I never knew what to expect from one day to the next. This sense of uncertainty, of peril, never wavered throughout my entire career behind the walls of the old Castle.

TWENTY-FIVE

LUMPKINS' MURDER

One of the most dangerous events I experienced as warden occurred on an otherwise normal summer day in 2001. As inmates were being let out for the evening meal, a young man named Steven Felleny lay in wait outside the Six Cell House door. Felleny was armed with a large, prison-made knife. He had been released from segregation in Three Cell House earlier that same day. Inmate Timothy Lumpkins was also released from segregation at the same time. Both had been interviewed by Internal Affairs and cleared prior to being released back to general population.

Lumpkins was a member of an all-black prison gang called Gangster Disciples. Felleny, a physically imposing white inmate, was a suspected member of the Aryan Brotherhood. There was no love lost between the two men.

Throughout their time in segregation, both inmates were housed only a few cells apart on the same walk in Three Cell House. In the days leading up to their release from the hole, they began trading racial insults and threatening each other. The situation deteriorated to the point that they vowed to kill one another on the yard. Well aware of the feud, Internal Affairs attempted to defuse the simmering racial tension by interviewing each of them separately and warning of further consequences if the fight escalated beyond Three Cell House. Both inmates gave their word not to retaliate in response to the other's disrespect and insults. Satisfied that the war of words had blown over, Internal Affairs decided to release both inmates from segregation at the same time. It was a tragic mistake.

Hours after they were freed, Felleny ambushed Lumpkins as he exited Six Cell House for the evening meal. Lumpkins suffered multiple stab wounds before bleeding out on the sidewalk. He died in a matter of minutes. Lumpkins' friend, inmate Perry Bell, tried in vain to defend him during the attack. Felleny also stabbed Bell several times, and the latter was rushed to the local hospital in critical condition. Felleny escaped the altercation without so much as a scratch.

Realizing that the racial nature of the murder presented us with a serious problem, I locked the prison down immediately. We knew that the minority population, particularly the black gang members, would seek revenge. White supremacist inmates would now be armed in anticipation of a retaliation. I knew we couldn't release anybody from lockdown until this was resolved. Locking things down was one way to cool things off. It also bought us time to scrutinize the simmering tension so we could make appropriate decisions to try to resolve the conflict.

After eight years as warden, I knew all the gang leaders at KSP. I also knew they held a certain level of respect for me as the man in charge. I made rounds and talked with both black gang leaders and members of the Aryan Brotherhood. Members of the Aryan Brotherhood promised this conflict was over unless the black inmates retaliated. Of course, they knew and I knew that their enemies wouldn't let this go. It was only a matter of time before somebody avenged Lumpkins' murder. The black inmates assured me that this thing was far from over. How could I expect them to sit back and let this happen without a fight? I knew that would be their answer, but I had to try.

The autopsy report came back a few days later while KSP was still in lockdown. As I studied the autopsy and photographs, I spotted a prison-made knife taped to Lumpkins' leg near his groin. The knife was discovered by the medical examiner after his clothes were removed. Despite Lumpkins' access to a weapon, Felleny enjoyed the element of surprise and struck before Lumpkins had a chance to pull his knife. The fact he had been armed and ready for Felleny was significant. I decided to use that piece of information in an effort to negotiate a peaceful resolution to the crisis.

I also had one other trick up my sleeve. A few years earlier, I had met a widely respected civil rights activist and minister from Louisville named Bishop Dennis Lyons. Bishop Lyons had protested my decision to ban minority inmates from wearing Malcom X T-shirts. I had also banned confederate flag and swastika T-shirts from the white population. This move made front-page news, and the editors of two major newspapers published articles in support of my decision. Bishop Lyons, however, told the press he feared I was going to start a race war. I assured him that I was trying to prevent a race war. We obviously didn't see eye to eye at the time.

In the wake of Lumpkins' murder, I placed a call to Bishop Lyons. I could tell he was surprised to hear from me. After exchanging pleasantries, I got to the point. "Bishop, I need your help. I'm dealing with the aftermath of a racially motivated murder, and the prison has been in lockdown for days. I'm afraid that if I try to return to normal operations, we'll have a bloodbath on our hands. The racial tension is so thick, you can cut it with a knife."

To my surprise, Bishop Lyons knew Lumpkins from his days living in Bishop Lyons' Louisville neighborhood. "How can I help?" he asked.

"Bishop, I would like for you to come down and make rounds with me and talk to the brothers. Maybe you can help me negotiate a peace settlement."

To my relief, Lyons was willing to help. "Sure, Warden. Give me until tomorrow, and I'll plan to meet you at the prison." The next day, Lyons arrived with two other local civil rights activists whose names unfortunately escape me now.

We made the rounds in the cell blocks and returned to my office for a meeting. During our walk, I tried to give Bishop Lyons and his guests privacy while they talked to several of the black inmates. Afterward, Lyons confirmed my worst fears.

"Warden, you have a serious problem. If you release inmates from the lockdown, you will have a war."

"I know," I replied. "I was hoping you could help."

"I'll try. What do you have in mind?"

I showed the men the autopsy pictures and explained, "I think we should set up a meeting with all the black gang leaders and their lieutenants in my conference room. I'll show them the picture of the knife taped to Lumpkins' leg. We need to convince them that this was a fair fight, not an ambush. Lumpkins was prepared for the attack. He just couldn't get to his knife in time."

Bishop Lyons studied me as he thought about my suggestion. Finally, he spoke. "I'm not entirely sure that'll work, Warden, but it may be the only way out of this. Let's give it a try."

"Okay," I told my guests. "I'll set up the meeting, and I'm counting on your support and encouragement."

Lyons assured me he was in my corner. "I'll help however I can."

As everybody gathered for the meeting, I had my staff serve coffee and other refreshments. We removed the cuffs from the inmates as they entered the conference room in an attempt to establish trust and foster a constructive dialogue. There were armed security guards posted just outside the door, and the inmates still had leg shackles on, but I wanted to treat them with the respect necessary to encourage a successful meeting. As we sat across from each other, I sympathized openly with their situation.

"I understand your anger. I realize the position you've been put in. And to be honest, I expect you to plan to retaliate. But I can't let that happen. So here's the deal: if we can't settle this thing peacefully, then I'll be forced to convert this prison into a place that is locked down permanently. Everybody will be in segregation from now on. There will be no school, no work, no prison industry, and no recreation or yard time. Nothing."

The inmates looked at each other in disbelief as I spoke. Charles Morton, aka Baby Ray, was the most powerful Black gang leader. He spoke on behalf of the group. "Warden, I don't think you can do that. We will sue the pants off you."

"Well, we'll see about that," I replied. "Have you ever heard of the federal prison not far from here in Marion, Illinois?" A few nodded their heads. "They had a similar problem," I explained. "Now that place is in a permanent state of lockdown. I don't want to do this. I really don't. But I can, and I will, if you force my hand." I could tell I had their attention.

"I want you to look at this picture," I continued, passing around the autopsy picture of the knife strapped to Lumpkins' leg. "Fellows, it was a fair fight. Lumpkins was armed just like Felleny. He was probably on his way to attack Felleny, but Felleny jumped him first, and he didn't have time to pull his knife."

Baby Ray spoke up: "We didn't know he was armed." I could tell the inmates were reassessing the situation.

"He was. That picture is proof. I'm hoping you can see your way clear to agree it was a fair fight and just let this thing go."

To my relief, Bishop Lyons made a point to agree. "Brothers, you all know me from the 'hood.' The warden is trying to help you save face and get this prison back to normal. This is your only way out. You need to go back and tell the other brothers what you heard here today."

I brought the discussion full circle: "I need your word that you will control the others. I already have an agreement from the white inmates that this mess is over unless you retaliate. So what's it going to be? Peace or lockdown?"

Baby Ray looked at his friends and then at me. "Warden, I'll give you peace, but I can't guarantee you it'll last if one of us is attacked on the yard again."

"That's good enough," I replied. "Are we all in agreement?" Everyone in the room nodded their heads. I looked over at Bishop Lyons. "Bishop, we have a peace settlement. Are you in agreement?"

"Yes, Warden. I do agree, but before we depart, I'd like to offer a prayer." Everyone in the room bowed their heads as Lyons prayed for peace and wisdom. It was a nice touch. I was grateful to have Bishop Lyons by my side that day.

The meeting was over. As promised, I gave the order to return KSP to normal operations the next day.

That was a close call. Too close. I realized as I went home that evening that my nerves were completely shot. This had been building for a while, but the threat of a race riot almost sent me over the edge. I was exhausted to the point where I wasn't sure how much more of the prison I could take. Unbeknownst to anyone else but my wife, I started contemplating retirement. My time at the old Castle had just about run its course.

A few days after the meeting with the inmates, I woke up early and went into the office to get some work done before anyone else arrived for the day. As somebody who rarely sleeps in, this wasn't out of the ordinary for me. What happened next, however, was anything but ordinary. At around nine a.m., I started experiencing debilitating chest pains. As I sat in my office signing papers, I felt a sharp pain shoot down my left arm. My jaw started hurting. I couldn't catch my breath, and I suddenly felt like I was going to pass out. I called my secretary, Jeri Parish, into my office and told her I was having a heart attack. I must have been white as a ghost because Jeri looked terrified. Between labored breaths, I asked her not to call an ambulance and said I would drive myself to the doctor. Jeri tried to insist we call an ambulance. Stubbornly, I told her, "No, I'm not going out of here that way."

I was so weak that I could barely walk. As I stood up, I realized I had to hold on to the wall as I made my way out to the front desk. With Jeri watching in silent protest, I mustered the strength to look relatively normal as I walked down the steep front steps of the prison to my car. (I'm sure I looked anything but normal, but I tried my best not to draw too much attention to myself.) I put the car in gear and slowly drove up the steep, winding road out of Old Eddyville. Somehow I traveled the six miles to my doctor's office without running off the road, though it was touch and go the whole way. I felt like I was going to pass out at any moment.

I walked into Dr. Steve Hiland's office. The receptionist told me to have a seat. "No," I gasped. "I'm having a heart attack. I need help right now." Jackie Bail, the nurse practitioner, met me in the hallway and held on to me until I could lay down on the exam table. She quickly connected me to the EKG.

After Jackie reviewed the EKG results and listened to my heart, she said, "Warden, you're not having a heart attack. You're having a panic attack."

I was in so much discomfort I actually argued with her. "No, I'm having a heart attack. You better call an ambulance."

"Phil, I listened to your heart. It sounds normal, and the EKG readings are normal, too," Jackie assured me. "This is an anxiety attack. You've been under tremendous stress for too long. I won't know until we do bloodwork, but I suspect you've used up all your hormones and adrenaline. You probably have nothing left."

I stared at her in disbelief. An anxiety attack? I didn't feel anxious or nervous, so how could I be having an anxiety attack? I was still convinced it was my heart.

"Do you have someone to drive you home?" Jackie asked.

"Yes, my wife is on the way."

"Okay," Jackie replied. "When she gets here, I'll give you a shot that will knock you out. You need to go home and rest for at least a week."

Rest sounded good to me. After sleeping in a haze for several days, I woke up suddenly feeling much better. Rather than follow the expert advice of my doctor, I returned to work the very next morning. I should have stayed in bed and continued to heal, but I felt like I had to get back before the next crisis hit.

I soon realized this need to prioritize the prison over my own health and well-being was part of the underlying problem. This job was consuming me.

I called Commissioner Vert Taylor and told him I was giving my two weeks' notice. He was clearly not expecting this. "Phil, you've thrown me for a loop. Who're we going to get to replace you?" Taylor sounded slightly frantic.

I was ready for this. "Easy, Commissioner. Deputy Warden Haeberlin has been here for years. He can handle the job."

Commissioner Taylor thanked me for everything, and we wished each other well.

I RETIRED IN AUGUST OF 2002, LOOKING FORWARD TO MANY years of rest and relaxation. I was done with the old Castle. Or so I thought.

I didn't know it then, but the Castle wasn't quite done with me.

TWENTY-SIX

ONCE MORE UNTO THE BREACH

In the spring of 2009, I learned that my old mentor, Al Parke, had come out of retirement to accept the position of deputy commissioner under Commissioner LaDonna Thompson. I also received word that Tom Simpson had retired as warden at KSP.

I called Parke to congratulate my old friend on his return to DOC. The department was lucky to have him back, and they knew it. Parke had more executive experience at the time than anyone working in Kentucky corrections. During our call, I asked him about Warden Simpson's retirement and replacement. Parke explained that his replacement would probably have to come from out of state. There were no current wardens who wanted the job, and they weren't about to promote a deputy warden to manage the state's only maximum security prison. I replied that I would hate to see an outsider take the job. It had been done in the past, when Warden Bordenkircher and Warden Scroggy were hired from out of state to take over at KSP. They were both good wardens, but neither stayed on the job longer than three years. Following the twelve months it typically takes for a new warden to learn the ropes at KSP, a three-year term is simply not long enough.

When I called Parke, I had no intention of resuming my duties as warden anywhere, let alone at KSP. After he said that DOC didn't have a good candidate waiting in the wings, however, the thought of a limited return to KSP began to appeal to me. I reasoned it might be easier to tackle the work at this stage, knowing that this would be a shorter term. I also wanted to help my friend in his new position. "You know," I told Parke, "I *might* be interested in coming back for a few years while you're deputy commissioner."

He jumped at my tentative offer. "Phil, I didn't think you'd be interested, but you're the only one I know who can handle the job. If you're serious, I'll run it by the commissioner."

"I have to run this by my wife before I can agree to it," I told him. "Why don't you and the commissioner discuss it, and I'll talk it over with my wife?"

That evening, Katie gave the idea her blessing if that was what I wanted to do. Several days later, I accepted the appointment in a meeting with Parke and Commissioner Thompson. And just like that, I found myself walking back up the front steps to the old Castle. As I walked through the front gate, the first thing that entered my mind was the antiquated, musty smell I always used to notice on the inside. Had I exaggerated that in my memory? Did it still smell the same? I paused and inhaled the still, prison air. Yep, there it was. The beast of the Castle. I smiled and headed for my office.

Once I was back in the saddle, it felt like I had never left. I knew every crack and crevice of KSP and still knew a number of staff and most of the inmates. There was no adjustment period for me this time around.

My first order of business was finding a new deputy warden. The position had opened up when Deputy Warden Greg Howard was promoted to warden at Luther Luckett Correctional Complex in LaGrange, Kentucky.

I placed a call to Ernie Williams, my old deputy warden during my term as warden in Grafton, Ohio. Williams was immediately interested, especially if the position came with a lovely state house on Lake Barkley. He was in luck; I told him he could live in the warden's residence, since I wouldn't be needing it.

I was pleased to discover that everything at KSP was running smoothly when I took over. This was a credit to the two wardens, Glenn Haeberlin and Tom Simpson, who filled in after I retired.

There were only three events during my second term I considered significant. The first was a riot that seemed to manifest out of thin air.

RIOTOUS BEHAVIOR

The race riot of October 2010 broke out on the yard after a white inmate disrespected a black inmate in the gym one afternoon. That incident ended without any physical altercation, but during the evening meal, the white agitator returned to the gym and viciously attacked his black counterpart. The fight spilled out of the gym and onto the yard. As Deputy Wardens Williams and Dunlap quickly intervened to escort the injured black inmate to the prison hospital for first aid, Williams instructed a new officer, Jim Ward, to patrol the recreation area behind the laundry and yard office. Ward discovered a large number of inmates gathering there to see what the commotion was about.

The sight of Williams and Dunlap walking by with the injured black inmate antagonized black gang members on the yard. One of them got into an altercation with white inmates near the gym entrance. Other black inmates ran over to join in, and the violence quickly spread throughout the large group standing near Officer Ward. In the blink of an eye, 150 inmates began fighting each other across the yard. The Aryan Brotherhood quietly dug up the knives they had buried under nearby picnic tables as the chaos erupted, but they waited to see whether the black gangs had armed themselves before joining the melee.

Williams and Dunlap returned from the hospital just as the riot started and positioned themselves near Officer Ward in the middle of the pandemonium. No one attacked Officer Ward or the deputies.

Williams quickly radioed for all available officers to report to the scene just as the bell for lockup began to sound. Uninvolved inmates left the yard for lockup, and staff arrived to separate the fighters on the yard, in the stairways of Five Cell House, and inside the door to Six Cell House. It was an uphill battle, but order was eventually restored to KSP.

I was on my way home for the day when the call went out over the radio. I turned around and raced the fifteen miles back to KSP, just in time to catch the tail end of the riot. I knew we had a long night ahead of us trying to sort things out.

In the end, neither the Brotherhood nor the black gangs used their weapons. When my team studied the security footage, they were able to identify most of the fighters. We also saw the Aryan Brotherhood arm themselves with shanks and subsequently confiscated the weapons they had buried under the picnic tables.

The video of the incident was spectacular, to say the least. I had never seen 150 inmates fighting at the same time; the footage looked like something out of a Hollywood movie. We concluded that the presence of the deputy wardens on the yard, and the speed of the officers' response, probably prevented a number of deaths during the riot. All available staff ran to the scene and started separating and cuffing rioters almost immediately. Another minute or two, and the armed inmates would have joined in. The loss of life would have been significant. We were lucky this time.

Central Office advised me to call the incident an "altercation" instead of a riot when I submitted an Extraordinary Occurrence Report the following week. This terminology minimized any chance the media would pick up the story and run with it. Fair enough. It was one hell of an altercation.

After the dust settled, I met with my deputies and told them how I wanted this handled in-house. "We're going to send a message that this is totally unacceptable," I explained. "The lockdown will remain in effect for the foreseeable future." I wasn't done. "A lockdown means a lockdown. Inmates won't be escorted to the dining room for meals. They won't be allowed out of their cells for showers. All visitation is cancelled. All recreation is cancelled. All phone calls are cancelled. We're going to nip this in the bud."

I turned to Deputy Warden Dunlap. "Make sure the food service staff has plenty of peanut butter and jelly and some bologna. We won't be serving tea or Kool-Aid, and no ice. They can drink water from their sinks. If the inmates don't like this, we'll shut off the cable TV and air-conditioning. If that doesn't work, we'll go in and confiscate their commissary items." My goal was to make the inmate population miserable, just short of violating their civil rights. I wasn't going to have another riot on my watch if I could help it.

I wanted the gangs on both sides to forget their petty grievances and redirect their attention and hostility toward me. I knew it would just be a matter of time before the inmates bent over backward to end lockdown and restore their privileges.

"One last thing," I told my top staff. "Let's not be in any hurry to resolve this. A couple of weeks without showers, ice, visitation, and phone calls, and I think they'll be sorry this ever happened."

I made rounds on the third day of lockdown. Almost to a man, the inmates' biggest gripe was they couldn't shower. When they stopped me to complain, I pointed to their sinks and replied, "You have water and you have soap. That's all you are getting."

A few days later, they started asking about the food. "Warden, aren't we supposed to have hot meals?"

"Right now, I can't trust you all to go to the dining room," I told them, "because all you all want to do is fight."

One of the legal aids argued that they had a constitutional right to be fed hot meals.

"Show me in the Constitution where I am required to provide you with a hot meal," I replied. The silence was deafening. I walked away slowly, trying not to smile.

Over the next week, most of the inmates grew so tired of the lockdown they began to promise my staff that they wouldn't fight again. It wasn't enough. I wanted them to be so sick of this situation that they would feel like it was Christmas to get a hot shower. It's funny how the little things we take for granted become the most important things in the world when they're suddenly denied.

After several weeks in lockdown, we decided to escort a few inmates at a time for a hot meal. This was a test to see whether any physical altercations broke out between the black and white populations. Nobody fought, and everyone got a hot meal.

Next, Deputy Warden Williams had all the inmates form lines outside of their respective cell blocks. When the lines were straight, he would move the inmates to the mess hall. Armed E-Squad officers were dispatched throughout the yard and the dining room during this experiment. There were no problems.

The final step was to resume showers. We didn't open the main shower house on the yard, but we allowed a few inmates out at a time to take hot showers in the cell block. Still no problems.

Finally, after a long and protracted lockdown, we returned to normal operations.

Throughout this ordeal, I sent a clear signal that my administration would handle things a little differently than my predecessors. The inmates knew that we would make their lives miserable if they ever dared to riot again.

HUNGER STRIKE

The next major incident that posed a challenge was the death of Charles Blakey. Blakey was a young, African-American inmate who had landed in our supermax unit, Cell Block Seven. He committed several rule violations that resulted in a lengthy stay in segregation, including assaulting staff and throwing urine and feces on officers. As a result, Blakey was stripped of most items in his cell, including his mattress and most of his clothing. Angry over his punishment, Blakey went on a prolonged hunger strike.

I had our medical personnel monitor Blakey's weight and vital signs daily. Days stretched into a week. A week stretched into two. His vitals appeared normal throughout that period. Then suddenly, over the course of twenty-four hours, it became clear that Blakey's condition had deteriorated rapidly. Nurse Practitioner Chanin Hiland ordered the supervisor to move him to the prison hospital to start an IV.

When the supervisor arrived to escort Blakey to our medical wing, he mumbled something and shook his head. "Are you refusing medical care?" the supervisor asked. Blakey mumbled again and nodded, which was interpreted as a refusal. The supervisor left and notified medical staff that he was declining care. When the nurse returned to check on him again a couple hours later, she found Blakey dead in his cell. The suddenness of his death stunned everyone on my staff.

I was aware of Blakey's hunger strike during my regular rounds that week. He was responsive to my questions each time I walked by his cell, so I moved on. Blakey did not appear to be in any sort of distress that would require emergency care. Deputy wardens also made rounds every day, and they never noticed anything that would require immediate intervention before that final day.

Hunger strikes were nothing new to my staff. Occasionally, we would offer the inmate a hamburger from Hardee's, and that would end the standoff. (Blakey refused, despite our best efforts.) I do not recall anyone else dying from a hunger strike, but we had also sought emergency court orders to force-feed inmates when their health deteriorated. In Blakey's case, it was simply too late to request judicial intervention. His condition deteriorated so rapidly over twenty-four hours that medical personnel did not have time to react. Tellingly, Blakey's autopsy did not reveal any pathologic abnormalities that contributed to his sudden death. He was dehydrated and malnourished, but not much else. In the end, Charles Blakey killed himself by refusing to eat.

This was one of the saddest days of my career. I called the deputy commissioner and commissioner to request an external review. That review ultimately found fault with KSP's medical staff, but I disagreed with that conclusion. The nurse practitioner ordered that Blakey be relocated to the hospital the moment she observed his critical condition. My staff had done everything by the book, and it still wasn't enough.

There were only two times in my career that I shut the door to my office and wept. The first was Harold McQueen's execution; the second was Charles Blakey's death. I had witnessed my share of suicides, murders, and executions over the past thirty years. I was no stranger to death. Blakey's passing, however, affected me deeply. What had we done? What had become of our humanity? We let an inmate die lying on a slab of concrete, without so much as a blanket for comfort. He passed away lonely, cold, and hungry. Whether Blakey was partially to blame for the situation or not was irrelevant. His death could have—should have—been prevented. It was a moment that stays with me to this day.

TWENTY-SEVEN

THE DEATH OF KENTUCKY'S DEATH PENALTY

WHEN DEATH SENTENCES WERE HANDED DOWN AT THE TURN OF the twentieth century, they would generally be carried out very quickly. While the appeals process was nowhere near as drawn out at the time, a review of the historical record suggests that prison wardens wielded an unusual amount of influence over the execution process. A warden would review the case in question, talk to the condemned inmate, and occasionally talk to the judge. If the warden believed that a mistake had been made or that the inmate was possibly innocent, he would call the governor and ask for clemency.

In keeping with that tradition, I always spent time familiarizing myself with the backstory, the crime, and the victims of each death-row inmate under my watch. Unlike a few of my early predecessors, however, I never harbored any doubts about the guilt of the accused. I also never heard a single death-row inmate tell me he was innocent. If I'd ever had reason to believe that a man on death row had suffered an injustice, I certainly would have expressed my concern to the attorney general's office. Though it was well outside of the scope of my professional responsibility, I would have fought for somebody I believed to be innocent, even if doing so jeopardized my career.

Throughout my terms as warden, I took great care to monitor each death-row inmate for any changes in their mental condition. I made sure anyone facing execution was seen regularly by a prison psychologist. We could not execute a person who was in the throes of mental illness. Such an individual would have to be restored to sanity before the state could end his life, as crazy as that might sound.

Later in my second term as warden, the lethal injection process faced a perfect storm of setbacks that delayed hundreds of executions across the country—some indefinitely. First, executions were halted nationwide after the sole U.S. manufacturer of one of the drugs, Hospira, stopped producing sodium pentothal over objections that the drug was being used to carry out lethal injections. Hospira did this despite the fact that thiopental sodium was one of the safest and most effective anesthetics in the world. The company rationalized its decision, in part, by arguing that there were equally effective anesthetics available for medical procedures. They were right, of course. The only problem was that states could not use those drugs to carry out executions because they had not been adequately tested for that purpose.

Second, use of the three-drug cocktail had been litigated in almost every state that carried out lethal injections, and it had withstood every legal challenge up to that point. Switching drugs invariably meant years of litigation and additional delays.

Kentucky's Department of Corrections did not see the shortage of sodium pentothal coming. Just prior to Hospira's decision to halt production, I ordered a supply of the drug, which would be enough to carry out up to three executions. Unfortunately, like all drugs, sodium pentothal has a limited shelf life. The batch at KSP eventually expired. I made several unsuccessful attempts to obtain more before I finally located a compounding pharmacy in Georgia that was willing to make

it for the DOC. I ordered enough doses for five executions, and I notified my counterparts in several other states who were facing similar
shortages of sodium pentothal.

I received the drugs from the compounding pharmacy and notified
the state that KSP was now equipped to continue carrying out executions. Our general counsel and the attorney general's office gave it their
blessing and were prepared to legally defend its use.

Several weeks later, I answered a phone call from the Atlanta division of the Drug Enforcement Administration. The agent on the other
end of the line wanted to know if I had recently purchased a large
amount of sodium pentothal. When I placed the order, I had used a
DEA number that is issued to wardens who oversee executions. My
DEA number had apparently flagged the transaction in their system. I
swallowed hard, lit a cigarette, and replied, "Yes, I did." The agent probably had the information right in front of him. For a moment, I felt
like a drug dealer who had been caught red-handed, but then I quickly
remembered that our general counsel and the attorney general had
approved of me using the compounding pharmacy to place the order.

The DEA agent's voice interrupted my train of thought. "I'll have to
confiscate the drugs, Warden Parker."

"Not so fast," I told him. "I obtained these drugs legally, and I don't
have the authority to turn them over. I'll have to call the attorney
general's office." I paused a moment, waiting for a response. When
none came, I finally asked, "What's the problem?"

"You aren't the problem," the agent assured me. "The compounding
pharmacy imported some of the ingredients without DEA approval."

I almost groaned out loud. "That doesn't sound right to me. I'm
trying to figure out why a federal agency is interfering with state-sanc-
tioned capital punishment. This feels like a political maneuver." He
replied that it was not political, but I knew it was. For one thing, the
Catholic Conference in Kentucky was vehemently opposed to capital
punishment. Secondly, I knew the Department of Public Advocacy

would use any means possible to interfere with and halt capital punishment in Kentucky—even if it meant getting the feds involved.

I knew there was little use in fighting this, but I told the agent I would call him back. I immediately phoned one of our attorneys, Connie Malone, and explained the situation. She confirmed what I suspected, that we had no choice but to surrender our drug supply to the DEA.

I called the agent back and told him we were ready to turn over the drugs. He wanted me to bring them to him in Atlanta, which was a nonstarter. I politely explained that I didn't have the time to transport drugs hundreds of miles to his office, and I told him I was not about to ship them in the mail, either, now that they had been classified as "illegal."

"Fine," the agent replied. "I'll be there Monday morning." He wasn't happy.

I brought the drugs to my office and had my team prepare a detailed release form before the week was out. When the agent arrived the following Monday, he was hesitant to sign his name to anything. I made it clear, however, that signing that receipt was the only way he was going to walk out of KSP with the drugs. After some additional pushback, he signed the form and was on his way.

That afternoon I reached out to Connie Malone, who in turn notified Assistant Attorney General David Smith and the governor's office of the drug transfer. Only half-jokingly, I asked Malone who was responsible for bailing me out if the DEA arrested me. She chuckled and agreed with my assessment that someone had clearly tipped off the DEA about the drug purchase. We were pretty sure the attorneys in the Department of Public Advocacy were responsible, but there was nothing we could do about it.

From that point on, we were never able to obtain sodium pentothal. Lethal injections were paused nationwide before some states settled on an alternative, a benzodiazepine called Midazolam. The federal government and several states, including Texas, Georgia, and Missouri, began using a single drug called pentobarbital to carry out executions. Seven other states abandoned the death penalty altogether.

Prior to this nationwide shift in lethal injection procedures, at the beginning of my second term as warden in 2009, I was told to prepare for five executions. All five inmates had lost their appeals, and it was just a matter of time before the attorney general and the governor decided their fates.

We soon found out that inmate Gregory Wilson was first. Wilson was sentenced to death for kidnapping a woman named Deborah Pooley, then raping and strangling her in the backseat of a car while a female accomplice drove.

His execution date, September 16, 2010, was stayed by Franklin Circuit Judge Phillip Shepherd. I was notified the stay would likely be lifted, and the execution date would remain the same. Shepherd prohibited us from overtly preparing Wilson for execution, but I was also instructed by Justice Secretary J. Michael Brown to be ready to conduct the execution on the date selected by Governor Steve Beshear. This was insanity. How could my staff be prepared to carry out an execution but not prepare for the execution itself? I had no choice but to continue our preparations behind the scenes.

I discussed this with my supervisor, Deputy Commissioner Al Parke. His only advice was to attempt to maintain normal operations, but also be ready to execute at the last minute if Wilson's stay was lifted. I made it clear to Parke how unprecedented this was. Either we prepare properly or we don't. I couldn't ride the fence on this. Parke agreed and said, "Phil, just go ahead and get ready as best you can." His response was hardly reassuring, but it was all I had to work with.

Gov. Beshear had given me just twenty-one days to prepare for the execution on September 16. I moved Wilson to Death Watch five days prior to the execution date. Moving him may have violated the judge's order forbidding us from preparing the condemned for execution, but it was a risk I was willing to take. When I notified Wilson we were moving him, he didn't raise any objections. I assured him that he would be treated in a respectful and dignified manner if he behaved, and Wilson promised he would not cause any problems. When I checked on him after the move to Death Watch, Wilson thanked me for the way he had been treated by my staff.

I really didn't bother myself with the reason for the court-ordered stay. In fact, I didn't even have a copy; I was simply told that it would most likely be lifted at the eleventh hour. I notified Parke of everything we were doing to complete our preparation checklist, but I did not discuss our activities with Commissioner LaDonna Thompson. I assumed that Thompson, who was out of town attending a conference at the time, was being kept in the loop by her deputy commissioner.

When the execution date arrived, I locked down the KSP. The assistant attorneys general were present, and Parke arrived early that morning. The execution team reported to duty, and I had the execution drugs prepped in my office. The deadline was less than twelve hours away.

Once Parke was seated in my office, we decided to report our progress to Commissioner Thompson. At eight thirty a.m., I notified her by email that we had the institution on lockdown and were making final preparations. Within minutes, the phone rang. It was Thompson, and she was livid.

"What do you think you're doing?" she asked Deputy Commissioner Parke on speakerphone. "We have a court order preventing us from preparing for the execution."

"Phil was told by Secretary Brown to continue preparing behind the scenes," Parke replied, "because the execution stay would likely be lifted at the eleventh hour. We're at the point of no return. If we don't start the execution protocol now, we won't be ready for a possible seven p.m. deadline."

Thompson didn't want to hear it. She ordered us to cease and desist.

Staring at each other in disbelief, Park and I told her we would resume normal operations—but that meant the execution could not be scheduled later that day. "Fine," she responded and abruptly hung up.

I looked at Parke. "I thought she knew what I was doing."

"I did, too," he replied, "but apparently we didn't communicate."

I was dumbfounded. "Secretary Brown knew damn well this is what we were preparing, because he specifically asked me to do it." This was one of the strangest professional situations I'd ever encountered. How the hell was I supposed to be ready for an execution without taking the myriad steps necessary to prepare for it?

If that's what Thompson wanted, fine. I picked up the phone and told Deputy Warden Williams to turn the inmates out and resume normal operations. I also had him inform the execution team and the assistant attorneys general that we were not moving forward today, and they were free to leave. Wilson was returned to his cell in Six Cell House.

Secretary Brown and Commissioner Thompson had asked me to do the impossible, and their misstep could have endangered the security of the penitentiary. In retrospect, I don't think they ever fully understood this. If I had tried to lock down later in the day to execute an inmate without any forewarning, it could have created a situation where the inmates refused to lock down. We always gave them notice of this in the past, and the inmates were generally fine with it. But suddenly initiating an execution lockdown late in the day, without warning, could have triggered a riot. It would have been terribly unfair to Wilson to postpone his execution minutes ahead of time because the prison was descending into chaos around him. Wilson was preparing himself mentally and spiritually at this point, and he deserved an orderly and peaceful final few hours. He probably would have fought us every step of the way in the middle of a prison riot, and I would not have blamed him.

Parke met with Brown and Thompson a few days after the postponement, and he tried to convey these concerns to his superiors. It didn't go well, and he resigned in protest. I hated to see Al Parke's career end that way. I had tremendous respect for the man. He was my mentor and the best warden I had ever worked for. But Parke was also principled, and he wasn't about to let this go without telling the secretary and commissioner they'd placed the institution in a perilous situation that could have endangered lives.

A few months after Parke's departure, I decided that I was ready to move on for good. I needed a change. Deputy Commissioner Jim Erwin asked me to keep my plans quiet as he searched for a replacement. To my disappointment, I had to wait until my final day to notify my staff that I was leaving. It felt downright bizarre to close out my career without a chance to say goodbye to people I had worked with for decades. There was no retirement party. Not even a congratulatory phone call from the Central Office.

I welcomed the new warden, Randy White, and wished him all the success in the world. White is a good man, and I felt like I was leaving the old Castle in good hands. By all accounts he did an excellent job running KSP for almost five years.

TWENTY-EIGHT

THE WARDEN'S CURSE

It should come as little surprise that overseeing two executions was very hard on me. Much harder than I ever anticipated when I agreed to assume the responsibilities of running KSP. I often found myself reflecting back on my relationships and interactions with the condemned men under my watch. I never made friends with death-row inmates. I just interacted with them occasionally and worked hard to extend the same level of respect and compassion I would expect if the situation were reversed. That said, I do not believe that respect and professionalism adequately describe the dynamic between a warden and a condemned individual. There is something more elemental, more primitive to the relationship. A man on Death Watch is totally helpless. He is dependent on his keepers for every little thing, even more so than inmates in general population. The sense of pervasive dread that haunts a death-row inmate's daily existence quickly breaks down his defenses. Every minute and every second become precious.

I always suspected that individuals on death row viewed me as a sort of Grim Reaper. After all, I would be the one who oversaw their final moments on Earth. Cognizant of this dynamic and how it informed our interactions, I always tried to treat death-row inmates with the utmost consideration and respect. In turn, they always returned the gesture.

I was profoundly moved by McQueen's decision to share his last meal with me. He did so not because he thought I was hungry, but because it was one of the few things he had left to offer me. McQueen even tried to console me when he was only a few hours from death. There was no hate, no hostility, no bitterness. Only love and respect.

Harper trusted me with the most important thing in his life just moments before his execution. He gave me a message to carry to the woman he loved. Harper pleaded with me—the warden, the Grim Reaper overseeing his death—to carry out his final wish. The vulnerability of that moment still moves me.

Over time, I came to view this strange bond between inmate and executioner as the warden's curse. Every death-row warden faces the same harrowing burden. Fate thrusts two disparate souls together—one who wields all the power, and another on a path to extinction—to navigate the most tragic of human circumstances. I felt like a harbinger of doom at times, tasked with leading another person to certain death.

This warden's curse weighed heavily on me then, and it haunts me still. I often find myself revisiting the tragic moments that unfolded behind those prison walls. When this happens, I feel like I am seated alone in a dark theater, forced to watch the scariest scenes of a horror movie over and over again. The movie projector flickers to life at the most inconvenient times: in the middle of the night, while I am mowing the grass, during a trip to the grocery store. No matter how hard I try, I can never find the emergency exit to escape that dark and dreary theater of the mind.

I suffered from anxiety and depression for many years after my retirement. Following my first panic attack at KSP, I convinced myself that time and distance would heal my wounds. I was wrong. As time progressed, I began to self-medicate more and more with Jack Daniel's. The booze offered a temporary reprieve from my demons, but they always returned. Sometimes with a vengeance.

Eventually the mental torture of my experiences wore me down to the point I was ready to take my own life. Out of desperation, I went to a psychologist for counseling. He was unable to help. I called the National Suicide Hotline. No help. I turned to faith, but my symptoms persisted. I was very close to giving up. Then, mercifully, I found a doctor who was able to accurately diagnose my pain. Seated in his office, feeling hopeless, I wrote down my symptoms and described a few of my professional experiences. "Just take a minute to read this," I implored him as I handed him my notes.

The doctor read everything carefully. Then he looked over at me and said simply, "I understand."

"Could this be post-traumatic stress disorder?" I asked. "Maybe I need to be tested for it."

"I don't need to test you, Phil," he replied. "You have a severe case of PTSD. The good news is that it's treatable. We can work together to get you on a path to recovery."

I was relieved almost to the point of tears. Maybe, just maybe, there was a light at the end of the tunnel. As we sat and talked, the doctor wrote several prescriptions to target my anxiety and depression. I went home feeling more hopeful that afternoon than I had in a long, long time.

Sure enough, the medicine began to work. I started to feel better. I found myself smiling more frequently. I slept more soundly. I looked forward to waking up each day.

I began enjoying life again.

TWENTY-NINE

WHAT'S PAST IS PROLOGUE

Paul McCartney's melancholy lyrics about lost love in the Beatles' song "Yesterday" could very well describe the downward slope of a lifelong journey. Reading them now, I see hints of my own story in those timeless words.

As time passes, I've found myself revisiting my own yesterdays more and more. I've always had a complicated relationship with the past, and this book speaks to that tangled web of retrospection. I occasionally ask myself whether it was all worth it. Did I make a difference? Did my efforts really matter? God, I hope so. I recoil at the thought that my life's work was in vain.

As I navigated the lead role in a decades-long drama of danger, violence, and death, the possibility of emotional fallout never really occurred to me. At least not until it was too late. I took everything in stride—the challenges, the hazards, the stress. I felt gratified each time I rose to meet the obstacles. Rather than practicing self-care, I simply thought, *This doesn't bother me.* For the most part, I remained confident, competent, and relatively content. I had no idea that constant exposure to stress and trauma would slowly eat away at my health and well-being like a cancer, inflicting damage just as surely as staring into the sun will cause blindness. All my troubles seemed so far away—but now there's a shadow hanging over me.

As confident as I often felt, there were days when I questioned whether I was really making much of a difference. Success is hard to gauge in an objectively strange and hostile environment like a maximum security prison. One small moment of personal achievement can feel insignificant in the face of growing calamity. Humor and humanity are in constant conflict with profound tragedy and pain. Most of the time, little victories felt inconsequential in the overwrought world of prison operations.

As I slowly worked my way up the career ladder, fate thrust me into what at times felt like an endless series of traumatic events. Moments that affected me as profoundly as they did my career. Somehow, through a combination of hard work and sheer luck, I made the right choices and fought the right battles to survive with my sanity (more or less) intact. And I always tried my best to help those in need, on either side of the wall, along the way.

My colleagues and I witnessed things that no one should ever have to see. The stress of not knowing what would happen next was a daily reality for each of us. We survived incidents that would scare the toughest people on Earth.

Many of us coped with our stress in unhealthy ways. We smoked heavily throughout the 1970s, '80s, and '90s. We were sleep deprived. We drank to excess, and a number of us struggled with alcoholism (me included). By the time many of us reached retirement, our health was poor. I can name a number of colleagues who died from lung cancer. Most everyone I knew was taking blood pressure medication before they were forty years old, including me.

So the question remains: why did any of us want to pursue a career in corrections that promised low pay and high stress? I still can't answer that. Perhaps we came to work day after day just to see what happened next. I think that sense of morbid curiosity was part of my motivation —but I was also eager to face down and conquer the challenges that awaited us every single day.

Was it a rewarding career?

In some ways, I believe it was. At the same time, I'm not sure the emotional and physical price was worth it. No one that I know escaped the profoundly negative effects that this work had on our personal and professional lives. The heart attacks, cancer, suicides, and divorce rates were a very real consequence of our existence in a chaotic, dangerous world.

Would I do it all over again?

Yes, I would. I believe my work made a positive difference in the lives of prisoners and colleagues alike. Each day I served in the prison system, 95 percent of the inmates walked the yard in safety. They were cared for and protected. The vast majority of these individuals survived their time in prison and returned home to their family and friends. They did their time and went on with their lives.

William "Snake" Woolum is a vivid example of this redemptive process. Fate thrust the two of us into a confrontation that, by any reasonable measure, should have ended in violence and death. Woolum held that gun to Officer Jasper's head, and my fellow teammates and I were given a green light to kill him. But I believe that God had other ideas for both of us that day. Woolum found God as his life in prison went from bad to worse, and he embraced his newfound faith against all odds. My life was also a mess, despite a long and fairly distinguished career, and I turned to faith to find healing and peace. We were both suffering in our own way. Neither of us had much of a reason to hope or heal. But with God's grace, we survived.

If someone had told me forty years ago that I would someday develop respect for (let alone a friendship with) a man who threatened to kill my colleague, I would have laughed at the suggestion. Woolum was one of the most dangerous men I'd ever known. But he served his time, he became a better man, and he earned his freedom. Now I actually look forward to mail correspondence and the occasional phone conversation with Woolum. I couldn't be prouder of his journey.

Justice Bill Cunningham prosecuted Woolum decades ago for a prison murder, securing a sentence that essentially guaranteed Woolum would never be released back into society. As time went on, however, Cunningham and Woolum began to exchange correspondence with one another. Cunningham became impressed with Woolum's redemptive path behind bars. He recognized Woolum had amassed decades of clear conduct and was living a peaceful and productive life in prison, and Cunningham began advocating for his release behind the scenes. As I watched this process unfold, I also grew to believe that Woolum was ready for release. I began to support Cunningham's efforts to parole Woolum. I had never done this for any inmate before.

Finally, after forty-four years in prison, William Woolum was paroled in December 2021. He is embracing life on the outside, traveling and volunteering his time to help the less fortunate. He has the loving support of a good woman, and the unconditional love of his best friend, Tracy, a mixed-breed dog.

There are countless individuals like William Woolum across America. Former inmates whose stories of recovery and redemption strengthen our communities and enrich our collective lives.

Woolum's life should serve as a reminder that our criminal justice system—imperfect, unpredictable, and challenging though it may be— still has the capacity to affect positive change in the world.

In a small clearing behind Kentucky State Penitentiary, hidden from public view, there exists an old and neglected pauper's inmate cemetery. Therein lie the remains of forgotten souls, buried anonymously in unmarked and unkempt graves. On a simple marker in that lonely space, the following words appear:

"Neither the crushing boots of fate, nor the ruinous winds of wrong, can drive one soul from the loving eyes of God."

If God's purpose was to love them, my purpose was to take care of them.

I am grateful for that opportunity.

And I would do it all over again.

ACKNOWLEDGMENTS

Much of what occurs in the narrative of this book I witnessed firsthand or I was a participant if for no other reason than being present at work when the events occurred. Portions of this book are based on public accounts, private papers, old reports, scrapbooks, and incidents that were related to me by those involved. Much is based on my memories. Because memories can vary widely from person to person, even concerning recent events, I have made every effort to be historically accurate and truthful, but I must admit my memory may have waned in my later years. Nevertheless, it is my account of what I remember. A big thank-you to all those who helped me recall events for this book.

The reader should also understand that I have deliberately changed the names of some of the staff and inmates. Some of the things that happened would be terribly embarrassing to them if their identities were revealed. I have no intention of libeling or embarrassing any of the men or women I worked with in the prisons. Fictional names of some of the staff and inmates are the only way I could write or publish this in good conscience.

I wish to first acknowledge some of my friends and mentors who were veterans of the armed forces.

In the late 1970s, I was privileged to share an office with Robert Kerstetter, a retired World War II pilot and colonel.

I also worked with Sgt. Haskle Riddle. He never talked about his years in the army and the Vietnam War. It wasn't until I attended his military funeral that I learned he had been a POW in Vietnam.

I worked with Deputy Warden Bill Bain at Northpoint Training Center. He had flown dive bombers off an aircraft carrier during WWII, targeting the Japanese Navy.

Probably the most influential veteran was General Dan Cherry, who for a time had been the Secretary of the Kentucky Department of Justice. General Cherry had a long, highly decorated service flying an F4 in Vietnam, claiming a victory in one of the first combat dog fights over North Vietnam. He went on to command the Thunderbirds, an elite group of Air Force pilots who demonstrate the capabilities of sophisticated aircraft at public events.

Kentucky Supreme Court Justice Bill Cunningham was influential all throughout my career. Besides his long, distinguished career as lawyer and judge, Justice Cunningham was drafted in 1969 during the Vietnam War. He served until 1973 and was on the last planeload of combat troops to leave after the Paris Peace Accord. He served on the Joint Four Power Commission that negotiated ceasefire violations with the North Vietnamese and POW exchange after the Peace Accord.

Larry Napier was another military veteran who had a profound influence on my style and decisions. I hired Napier as a correctional officer at Northpoint Training Center and he quickly promoted to lieutenant. He had a twenty-one-year career in the Marine Corps and retired as a First Sergeant (E8). He served one tour in Vietnam where he was awarded two Purple Hearts. After his Vietnam combat experience, he was a drill instructor at the recruit depot in San Diego, California. Larry had outstanding leadership qualities that I admired. He was our E-Squad commander at Northpoint, and he later joined me in Ohio where he commanded our Corrections Emergency Response Team.

Dewey Sowders was in the military police in the army before beginning his career as a correctional officer. Sowders taught me a lot and inspired me to pursue a career in corrections.

A special thank-you to all the military veterans who befriended me or followed my lead. Thank you for your service.

My career was also influenced by other professionals. Mike Samburg was a career professional who encouraged me throughout my career.

Early on, there were many "old-school guards" who took me under their wing and helped me learn the ropes. Sr. Captain Billy Adams is one that stands out as a natural leader who set an example. Rodney Nicholas was a marine and an old-school guard who helped me learn the ropes.

Warden Al Parke set a professional example and was instrumental in helping me launch a career in corrections.

There are many others who helped me along the way. I can't begin to recognize everyone who was helpful and became friends.

This book wouldn't have been possible without the love and support of my wife Katie, who had the daunting task of interpreting my illegible handwriting and committing it to the magic of the modern computer. I could not have done this without her encouragement, patience, and constructive criticism.

I am grateful for many former and retired employees that I could call on to refresh my memory or fill in details that I had forgotten. Most notably, Byron Jasis was my go-to person when I needed a name or a phone number. Before his death, former Deputy Warden Bill Henderson could easily recall details and was happy to contribute to this book. He and I were like brothers during our time at the penitentiary. Others that I would call from time to time for information were

Barry Banister, Vicki Patton, Al Parke, Charlie Holt, Freddie Richardville, Suzanne Conley, Ernie Williams, Lt. Billy Adams, Troy Belt, Harry Whisman, Hobert Huddleston, Joel Dunlap, Dennis Yeager, Tommy Stewart, Rod Kincaid, and Linda Cooper.

A sincere thank-you to William "Snake" Woolum, who was paroled after forty-four years in prison and consented to an interview for this book.

My good friend Justice Bill Cunningham encouraged me throughout the journey of writing this book. I am eternally grateful to him.

Another notable contribution was the editing efforts of Perry T. Ryan, a retired attorney in the Kentucky Attorney General's office. He gave of his time selflessly, and we quickly became good friends.

I also wish to acknowledge my final editor and good friend Christian Greco for his assistance and support in putting this book together.

I realize it is not possible to recognize everyone who may have contributed in some way. Please accept my apologies for not mentioning each one individually.

Made in the USA
Middletown, DE
30 August 2024